THE
BABES
IN THE
WOODS
MURDERS

THE
BABES
IN THE
WOODS
MURDERS

The heartbreaking true story of
two families' fight for justice

PAUL CHESTON

JOHN BLAKE

Published by John Blake Publishing,
The Plaza,
535 Kings Road,
Chelsea Harbour,
London SW10 0SZ

www.johnblakebooks.com

www.facebook.com/johnblakebooks
twitter.com/jblakebooks

First published in paperback in 2019

ISBN: 978 1 78946 076 6
eBook ISBN: 978 1 78946 129 9

British Library Cataloguing-in-Publication Data:

A catalogue record for this book is available from the British Library.

Design by www.envydesign.co.uk

Printed and bound in Great Britain by Clays Ltd, Elcograf S.p.A.

3 5 7 9 10 8 6 4 2

John Blake Publishing is an imprint of Bonnier Books UK
www.bonnierbooks.co.uk

To Barrie and Sue, who have suffered more than any man or woman should, and Nigel, without whom there might have been no justice.

PAUL CHESTON was the courts correspondent of the London *Evening Standard* for twenty-three years. On his retirement in 2016, the Recorder of London described him in an Old Bailey valedictory ceremony as 'an exemplar of fair and accurate reporting'. In a Fleet Street career of thirty-four years, he also reported from Iran, Iraq, Bosnia, France, Germany, Ireland, Cyprus, Malta, Morocco and The Troubles in Northern Ireland. He continues to suffer from a lifelong devotion to Norwich City Football Club and a high golf handicap.

CONTENTS

PREFACE   ix

CHAPTER 1 – BEDLAM   1

CHAPTER 2 – THE FELLOWS AND THE
            HADAWAYS   9

CHAPTER 3 – ENTER RUSSELL BISHOP   23

CHAPTER 4 – THE SEARCH   35

CHAPTER 5 – THE HUNT   51

CHAPTER 6 – PRIME SUSPECT   67

CHAPTER 7 – AN "INEXORABLE" LINK   85

CHAPTER 8 – OMNISHAMBLES   101

CHAPTER 9 – THE FALL-OUT   113

CHAPTER 10 – THE FIGHT BACK   127

CHAPTER 11 – "NO ONE WANTED TO KNOW"   143

CHAPTER 12 – BACK TO LEWES   153

CHAPTER 13 – BUT STILL NO JUSTICE   171

CHAPTER 14 – DOUBLE JEOPARDY   189

CHAPTER 15 – BREAKTHROUGH   201

CHAPTER 16 – "HELLO, RUSSELL, WE'RE FROM
              SUSSEX POLICE"   213

CHAPTER 17 – SIR IVAN   225

CHAPTER 18 – HEART ATTACK   233

CHAPTER 19 – "OVERWHELMING,
              COMPELLING AND POWERFUL"   241

CHAPTER 20 – FACING BISHOP   249

CHAPTER 21 – TURNING POINT   263

CHAPTER 22 – "BELITTLE AND SHAME"   275

CHAPTER 23 – "HE WAS MY FIRST LOVE"   293

CHAPTER 24 – ENDGAME   303

CHAPTER 25 – PEACE   315

APPENDIX I – TIMELINE   325

APPENDIX II – THE FAMILIES   329

ACKNOWLEDGEMENTS   331

PREFACE

This is a story of two mums. One still lives in Brighton and the other moved away many years ago to Surrey.

They used to be friends. Their daughters were inseparable. Children, mothers and grandmothers were always in each 'other's homes laughing and chatting.

But then they suffered the cruellest blow a random God can bestow when their daughters were abducted, sexually abused and strangled.

They bore that suffering together and then it split them apart. Not just from each other but wife from husband and their relatives from their spouses.

For thirty years, the mums grieved separately and barely exchanged a word with each other. They were but two of the many, many unrecognised victims of Russell Bishop whose grief and suffering went unnoticed.

But then, after an unceasing thirty-year campaign, the chance of justice came along and suddenly in a courtroom in London the two mums could sit together and experience the same emotions they had shared all those years earlier, and little by little the old kinship was reawakened.

When their 'daughters' killer was finally convicted they realised that the bond they had always shared was far, far greater than anything that might have kept them apart.

This is their story.

But it is not just a book about two mums, 'it's a book about four brothers, too, one of whom was monstrously and falsely accused of killing his own daughter – first by word of mouth, whispers behind his back by strangers and neighbours, and then finally by a desperate killer intent on inflicting the maximum misery because he would spend the rest of his life behind bars.

The other three brothers make an unusual trio: the ex-conman, the giant and the former copper.

It's a story of how these brothers set out together to right the wrong of a bungled prosecution that let a double child killer loose to strike again.

It's also a story about a son who lost his sister and suffered in silence storing up all the turmoil in his mind, a father who never recovered from what happened to his daughter and an uncle who fought as hard as anyone for justice.

Sadly, all three passed away before Russell Bishop could finally be brought to justice.

As this is a story unashamedly written from the victims' viewpoint, I have found little room for insight into the approach of the police or the intricacies of the scientific evidence. Sorry, but those interested can look elsewhere.

Included is a guide to the members of the two families who can be easily confused. For instance, there are two Karens, three

Christines and two Mabels. For ease of identification, I have also referred throughout to the Fellows and the Hadaways as they were identified in court, even though Susan Fellows became Susan Eisman, and Michelle Hadaway reverted to her maiden name of Michelle Johnson.

But the biggest area of potential confusion lies in the Heffrons and the Fellows. Barrie Fellows is the half-brother of Nigel, Kevin and Ian Heffron. Same mother but different fathers, as they explain it. However, they are adamant that they have always been full brothers in their bond and love.

PAUL CHESTON,
2019

CHAPTER 1

BEDLAM

"Will the foreman please stand."

Breaking the silence, the court clerk's voice was stark yet sombre. Greying wig, coal-black gown, the white-sheet indictment in her left hand.

Heart thumping, the presiding juror rose, confirmed her four male and seven female colleagues were all in agreement and was told to answer the next question simply guilty or not guilty.

"Do you find the defendant Russell Bishop guilty or not guilty of the murder of Nicola Fellows?"

A visible pause for breath. "Not guilty."

Bedlam. Bishop's brothers were on their feet, yelling, his mother Sylvia was in tears, her husband Roy pale and shaking. Bishop himself had tears in his eyes as he buried his head in his hands. Suddenly, his brother Alec leaped over the tiny balustrade dividing the nineteenth-century dock from the public gallery in a desperate bid to hug his vindicated brother.

Four prison officers surrounding the defendant grabbed Alec by the arms and throat and threw him to the ground. Meanwhile, uniformed police officers raced in and plainclothes detectives spun round in the well of the court as angry faces in the public gallery surged forward to try to defend Alec.

Sylvia, who was shaking with emotion, screamed, "Let me get to my boy." Then, seeing her husband slumped on the wooden bench next to her, she shrieked, "*He's got a bad heart! If my husband has a heart attack, I'll kill you!*"

With the scuffles intensifying, the judge battled in vain to keep order and the second verdict of "Not guilty", in relation to the murder of Karen Hadaway, was lost in the mayhem. As the jury scurried out of court and the huge press contingent rushed out to the telephones, the defendant was discharged.

Through tears, Bishop turned to his family at the heart of the chaos and begged: "That's enough, lets have some respect – pack it in."

By now, three people had already left the upstairs gallery reserved for friends and families of the "Babes in the Wood", as the media had dubbed the murder victims. In October 1986, these two young girls – Nicola Fellows and Karen Hadaway – had been strangled, sexually abused and left hidden in dense undergrowth in the Brighton beauty spot of Wild Park, approximately eight miles from the scene of chaos now playing out almost a year later in Lewes Crown Court.

Karen's parents, Lee and Michelle, and Nicola's uncles, Nigel and Ian Heffron, had been the only members of the girls' respective families who had been able to face going to court to hear what they all suspected would be the inevitable verdicts of the disastrously run prosecution.

From their seats twenty feet directly above the jury box, the two grieving families had sat for three weeks and watched the Crown's case lurch from one crashing calamity to another.

With the jury set to retire to consider their verdicts on the final day, Nicola's parents, Barrie and Susan Fellows, could not bear the thought of watching Bishop go free. Barrie had been put up by ITN in a local hotel, the film crew there to capture his instant reaction to the outcome. Susan, meanwhile, waited at her brother's home for what they were convinced would be bad news.

Those who did make it to court now had to endure sickening scenes of triumphalism and watch the man they still thought was guilty, walk free.

Karen's parents, Lee and Michelle, walked downstairs and out onto Lewes High Street, where her father told reporters, with admirable restraint, "*Someone* must have killed my baby. Now it seems we'll never know."

Meanwhile, Nicola's uncles were met at the door to the public gallery by a police officer, who ushered the two men to an upstairs room in the court building. Police feared, understandably, that with anger and adrenaline running so high there might be clashes between the families of the victims and the defendant, all sharing the same Brighton neighbourhood.

"We just knew it was going to be 'not guilty' because of all the things that kept going wrong during the trial," said Nigel.

"Bishop's partner, Jennie Johnson, retracted her evidence and had to be treated as a hostile witness – and she was the prosecution's most important witness – the Pinto sweatshirt cock-up, all the forensic mix-ups in court – and we didn't even know then about the witnesses they could have called but didn't.

"But every time we asked the police what was happening they kept saying, 'Don''t worry, don't worry, don't worry, we have got good stuff coming up, wait for that," but the good stuff never materialised.

"Even in the judge's summing up there was nothing there for us to say, honestly, that Bishop was going to be found guilty. We had spent so much time on the case and we were losing it.

"When the jury came back [after just two hours and 10 minutes deliberations]... it was so quick. If they had been out longer, we could have had some hope that they could have been considering a guilty verdict. I thought they must be back to ask the judge a question not deliver the verdicts.

"When they said not guilty I just sat there in shock. However much you know it's going to happen you still sit there dumbstruck. You just can't believe it.

"There was bedlam down there and I'm watching all this going on and I can't believe it. It was like you see in the movies, the main character is there on the screen and everything behind him is just flying around. That's what it felt like, I was numb and I could not believe it. I knew it was going to happen but I could not believe what had just happened."

Upstairs in an attic-style room two floors above the court, the brothers could hear the commotion out in Lewes High Street, which was now packed with TV news crews and press photographers spilling onto the road and halting the traffic. Later that night, the victims' families would witness on TV bulletins one of the Bishop brothers bursting out onto the courthouse steps, thrusting his arms back in exhalation and bellowing a victory cry as if he had just scored the winning goal in the World Cup Final.

But for now, the two Heffron brothers and a couple of officers just looked at each other and tried to make small talk. "What happened here?" "What do you think went wrong?"

Nigel lit a cigarette, before noticing a long trestle table across the far side of the room stacked with piles and piles of blue folders marked SUSSEX POLICE.

"I said to the copper, 'Can I read that?' He said, 'No, you can't." Jokingly, to lighten the mood, I said, 'I would like to see it, you wouldn't miss it if I slipped it into my back pocket." He said: 'Nigel, you will never see that.'

"Well, that was like a red rag to me. I had just witnessed something that I had hoped never to see. Three weeks earlier, we had walked into that court expecting a guilty verdict. For the past fourteen months, we'd even through all the grieving, the funerals, the media, everything ...

"From that moment, I knew that my life had changed for ever with those words, 'Not guilty.' I was determined to get those documents and try and prove the case that we had just seen fail. Even my brother Ian, who is a police officer with the Essex force, told me I wouldn't be allowed to see the papers but I was determined."

The brothers left the court building quietly, slipped unnoticed past the hullabaloo that showed little sign of abating and met Barrie, who looked shell shocked, a broken man.

Said Nigel: "It was that meeting in that small room at Lewes Crown Court that started the ball rolling.

"My feeling was, if the police thought they had the right man, and that's what they said, that they were not looking for anyone else, then why didn't they get it right? We had to find out and hope to put it right.

"My life changed with the words not guilty, not least because my marriage was to break up because I could not let it go."

More than thirty years later, these families look back, if not fondly but with some satisfaction that their vow to get justice for the two little girls was finally achieved, if only after the most astonishing switchback ride of moments of elation mixed with dark, dark nights of despair.

During that time, hope had surged when the police ordered new reviews of the evidence, only for them to come up short. Barrie had to face a maliciously whipped-up whispering campaign that forced him out of his home town and even led to his arrest on allegations of child pornography involving his own daughter.

Then he had to sit and face all the same allegations repeated in open court in one of the most disgraceful defences ever conceived by a murderer trying to save his own skin.

Over the coming years, a combination of unending grief, trauma and an obsession for justice was to rip apart their marriages.

But Nigel did get his hands on the police evidence – and from a most unexpected source. His family, and others, did mount an extraordinarily successful campaign which helped the Home Secretary to reverse a centuries-old law that was to bring the killer to justice. And Russell Bishop was only to enjoy another three more years of freedom before he was back behind bars after striking again – just as he was swaggering around town proclaiming his innocence.

This time, he snatched, sexually abused, stripped and strangled a third little girl, leaving her for dead. Thankfully, she made a miraculous recovery and, thanks to a properly run prosecution, Bishop was jailed for life.

But even life sentences can come to an end and just as he expected to win parole and walk free for a second time, dramatic new and damning evidence was uncovered.

Bishop was forced to face a new Babes in the Wood jury, this time at the Old Bailey, where, in front of the Fellows and the Hadaway families, justice was finally served.

As Susan Fellows said, "Only now can the little girls rest at peace in their little angel bed."

CHAPTER 2

THE FELLOWS AND
THE HADAWAYS

It was the two little girls who brought the families together. Before they had found themselves as neighbours in Newick Road, Moulsecoomb, the Fellows and the Hadaways had known *of* each other rather than *known* each other.

All that changed when the girls found themselves a couple of doors apart and became best friends.

Nicola's mother, Susan Fellows, was born and brought up in Brighton – in Barcombe Road, which leads into Newick Road, to be precise.

"I couldn't wait to leave school. I didn't have a lot of schooling to be honest. I was in and out of hospital because of my eye disability. As a result I was always very shy, I was always with my mum and dad until I was about fourteen," she remembers.

"It happened when I was two and I stuck a pen in my left eye. I was doing rolly-pollys down the stairs in my nan's house and rolled into the living room, reached up to the dresser and this old-fashioned pen with its nib you dipped into ink came down and went straight into my eye, into the corner.

"My mum panicked, the pen came out but my mum waited for my dad to come home and he just said 'the hospital'. When we got there they just said there were two options: Either we keep the eye and she will probably end up blind in the other eye because of the poison in the ink, or we have it out.

"My dad was a lorry driver and he had to make a big decision. I had to have the eye removed to save the other one. It was a twelve-hour operation at the Royal Alexandra children's hospital and then I was in and out of the Sussex County Hospital eye department for three months.

"I also got whooping cough at that time and they had to redo all the stitches around the eye.

"I didn't want to go to school because people took the micky out of me. Children would not play with me because their parents told them not to in case of catching an infection! Absolutely ridiculous.

"That was at Moulsecoomb School. Then I went to a school in Hollingdean and I loved that school because the headmaster was so nice. He wanted me to have private lessons so I would catch up but my mum and dad didn't want me to do that. They didn't tell me why.

"At that time, I wanted to be a window dresser. I loved looking at the massive windows at Hanningtons. I would have loved to have done that. Then I wanted to go into the army but because of my disability that was not on.

"I have always wanted to be treated as a normal person, I don't think about the disability because I just want to be normal, even though I have only got fifty-per-cent vision, I can only see out of one eye. I can be chatting away with someone and if they move only a little they suddenly disappear. I say where have you gone, am I talking to myself?

"My dad said I would never get a boyfriend, but I did and had a few before I met Barrie. The first thing he said to me was, 'I know what's wrong with you but it doesn't matter to me, I still love you.' We got married two years later.

"I always wanted children, just the two, a boy and a girl and that's what happened. Before Nicky was taken away from me."

Susan is in her sixties now. Friendly to those she comes to trust and who have time to sit and chat, she is otherwise shy, slow to rouse. Even in the darkest hours, she was only driven once to lose control in anger and resentment and, as we will find out, with good cause

At 17, Susan met Barrie Fellows, who she thought was working as a bouncer at the Flamingo Club in Wardour Street.

"I was there with some friends. One of my friends was with Frank, Barrie's friend, and that's how we met. I was actually going out with someone else at the time. It's funny how things are," she recalled as her mind briefly wandered a long way away.

"At that time," she went on, "Barrie was living in London but within a couple of weeks he had moved to Brighton and lived in a flat in the Old Shoreham Road working in a factory in Burgess Hill.

"We were engaged for two years. We lived in Falmer with my mother, Mabel Streeter, whom everybody called Edna, then we took a flat in Hollingbury.

"We were married at Saint Mark's Church in Kemp Town on my twenty-first birthday on 19 September 1970 and Jonathan –

who always liked to be known as John – was born in December 1971 and went to the Carleton School in Patcham.

"Barrie was away when Jonathan was born – in fact, 'away', as in prison, for the first fifteen months of John's life.

"Two weeks before I was due to have him, Barrie went down. He broke into the flat we had just left, he still had the keys, and he went back and took a clock – so he did time for it."

Susan laughs about it now, nearly fifty years on, but there is no hiding her bitterness at having been left on her own to cope with the birth of their first child by her husband's selfishness.

And all for a clock in a break-in using keys that only he could have had. Not for the first time, Susan used laughter to make light of the tragedy and to mask the pain of the bad days in her marriage.

"Barrie went on to get another nine months for receiving stolen goods," Susan continued. He also has a third conviction for obtaining property by use of a forged instrument.

"It was in prison that he took a hell of a kicking, he actually was the wrong person to be attacked it was mistaken identity, and that's when his epilepsy took over.

"I remember when he came home he was bathing John when he had a fit for the first time. There was this crash upstairs and we went up and he was on the ground. The ambulance came and took him to hospital, he went for tests and that's when he was diagnosed with epilepsy."

Nigel believes the prison attack brought about a life-changing transformation.

"Barrie had acted like he was a hard man until then but then he became more of a... wimp," he said, delivering the telling last word after hesitation and with a measure of disdain but still compassion for his older brother.

"There was a time he threw a man through a chip-shop window. He acted as a minder for me, even though I didn't want him to. I hated him doing that so I took up judo to prove to Barrie that I could stand on my own two feet."

Nicola was born on 22 February 1977 and Susan was overjoyed: "I had always wanted one of each and that was it. I had always wanted a daughter and Nicky was absolutely beautiful."

But a bigger family required bigger accommodation, which was provided by Brighton Council, and the next move was a nightmare.

"When I had Nicky, they moved us to the worst street in Moulsecoomb – Birdham Road. It was very rough, everything was rough about it – the people, the houses, the gardens, the street lighting, absolutely everything. But we had to stay there until Nicky was two, when we moved to Swanbrough Drive on the Whitehawk estate with my mother and my nan.

"It was after that that we moved to Twenty-six Newick Road and the worst time of my life."

*

Karen's mother Michelle, also a Brighton girl, was more than seven years younger than Susan. She married Lee Hadaway in August 1974 when she was just seventeen. He was a sometime builder's labourer, sometime window cleaner, sometime removal man and eight years her senior.

They started by living with her grandparents in Ditchling Road, then moved to Lavender Street in Kemp Town before getting a council house in Birdham Road, Moulsecoomb, in 1976.

Their son Darren had been born in November 1974 and Karen came along soon after they arrived in Moulsecoomb. Lyndsey was born in January 1981, and towards the end of the following year they moved to 20 Newick Road.

The first blow to the family came when Darren fell out of a window of their home in Birdham Road, which led to such serious injuries he had to attend a special boarding school in Brighton.

"At that time, we were a close family. We showed the children love and they did the same to me. I brought them up, as best I could in our circumstance," said Michelle.

"In the mid-eighties, times were very different. We were such a close-knit community with all the children playing in the road. Karen and Lyndsey would go out and play with local children, not every day, but there were lots of children around.

"Lyndsey went to Coldean Infants School and Karen started at Moulsecoomb Junior School but moved to Coldean Junior because it would be easier to have them both in the same school.

"Nicola lived three doors down from us. She was one of Karen's friends and was known as Nicky.

"The threat of strangers was part and parcel of our teaching with Karen. She understood about the dangers. Karen would not go off with a stranger but only people she knew and trusted.

"Most of the time if she out she would tell me where she was. She was always in the vicinity and never too far away from me. If she went to the shops in Coldean Lane, she would come back and say, 'I'm back now.'

"She was a very sensible girl. She was cheeky she would

answer you back but all children did that it she would always do good in the end.

"Her behaviour was pretty good really but by the summer of 1986 she started being a bit cheeky to me and my husband asked her why she was behaving like this and she didn't really have an answer.

"She was a very clean girl, sometimes she would bath twice a day. She liked to keep her hair nice and clean, that was her daily routine."

Lee thought Nicola was the stronger of the two little friends, and Michelle told the police that Nicola was "a very friendly girl, very outgoing and would speak her mind to the point of embarrassing her mother".

She described Karen as "a very sensible girl who knew right from wrong but could be cheeky like all children".

Tellingly, they were both scared of the dark.

At the time of the murders, Michelle was seven months pregnant with Kimberley, who arrived in December 1986.

Michelle's mother, Maisie Johnson, worked with Susan Fellows at teacher-training college in Falmer. It was there that Susan first met Michelle, but only briefly because their age difference meant they had little in common, and it wasn't until later, when they became neighbour's in Newick Road, that all that would change.

Said Susan: "We used to see each other before then but not to talk much. When they moved into Newick Road we would talk more because the girls started talking and playing around. Karen used to come to the house to see Nicky, then they stopped being friends, then they were friends again. You know how little girls are? There were always ups and downs between the two."

As soon as she could walk and talk, Nicola was happy and helpful and never less than forthright.

Susan again: "She spoke her mind and she told us what she thought. If she didn't like something she would tell you. I always thought I would get into trouble over something she said.

"People might think Nicky was a little so and so, and she was, I won't stick up for her even though she was my baby. None of the other children in Moulsecoomb were goody two shoes either. She was like a tomboy, she would rather climb a tree than put a pretty little dress on a doll.

"But she was fun. There was the time my mum and Nicky had a silly argument and Nicky stood up and said, 'I'm going to leave then!' She went upstairs and in a little suitcase that she had she packed her teddy, that's all, and walked out the door.

"She went round the block and came back. And she was seven.

"But she would help anybody. People told me that she would knock on their door and come into their house and ask if there was anything they wanted at the shops.

"I told her not to do it any more because it could be seen as begging. I didn't want her knocking on doors because you didn't know who might be coming to the door."

Nicola went to Moulsecoomb middle school, in The Highway, a short walk from home, where reports of her are mixed.

On the one hand, her class teacher Donald Rees described Nicola as a happy, healthy child, friendly and non-disruptive.

On the other, the school's headmaster, Allen Roochove, painted a picture of a sullen, spiteful and friendless girl who once stole some trinkets from a classmate.

He said he took up the larceny with Barrie Fellows, who

returned a number of items and – according to a police statement made when the girls were missing and as yet undiscovered – threatened to cut off his daughter's fingers if this was to happen again.

"Nicola and Fellows came into my office. He placed a number of items on my desk and said he didn't know what had been taken but was returning these items," Roochove told the police in a statement that would later be used against Barrie in court.

"He took hold of Nicola by the right hand, held it down on my desk, looked into my face and said, 'If she does it again, she knows what I would do,' indicating cutting her finger off.

"He said the threat was enough and she would not do it again. I said he should not cut her fingers off and he said he would not.

"I formed the impression that Nicola was very nervous in the company of her father . She was terrified of her father."

This incident took place a month before the girls were murdered.

The Fellows family are horrified by the allegations and dispute the headmaster's account. Susan suggested the bad report may be down to her daughter's habit of speaking her mind.

Nigel Heffron is inclined to believe his brother's threat as an example of "Barrie putting his gob into gear before using his brain first".

Nigel went on: "The family has got a temper. Ian and I learned to control it, Barrie didn't. When it blew it blew.

"Barrie would refer to chopping fingers off as something he would do to all thieves. So if Barrie did say it, then it was just him putting spin on. He would never have hurt Nicky."

As Barrie had been already been convicted of burglary himself when he said this, presumably he was pleased his personal views about thieves were not actually law.

Roochove suspected Nicola lived in fear of her father. Barrie – and the Fellows family in general – deny that accusation vehemently, but her father did admit to losing his temper with her – including the time he had taken her to the headmaster over the stolen property, admitting he had been angry with her.

Susan also disagrees with the headmaster's theory and for good reason – Barrie beat her, not the kids.

"He was the father of the family, he dealt with everything and I just sat back but if he was too hard on the kids I would step in," she said.

"He used to slap the kids on the hand or the leg, but I would get it. He used to hit me before the separation, I did go through hell with him. I didn't end up in hospital but I was black and blue around the face.

"He threw a clock at me once; it went straight through the window and landed outside the house near Michelle." She said 'I didn't know time flies.'

"She made a joke of it but it wasn't one for me. John came in and said 'what you doing?' Barrie said 'nothing, get downstairs.'

"John was frightened of him, I was frightened of him but I don't think Nicky was. Barrie was never there for the children, he never took them out. I took them out."

Even Edna Streeter, who as Barrie's mother-in-law was hardly his greatest fan, denied he scared his daughter: "Barrie would not hurt Nicky; she had a great relationship with her mother and father and was not afraid of Barrie when he lost his temper," she told the police.

But there was another side to Barrie, too. He enjoyed taking part in the Christmas panto and helping to raise money for charity.

Susan remembered: "There was also a charity event to raise money for a blind boy. It was in Wild Park and Barrie would let people throw things at him, like eggs, wet sponges, shaving foam pies and all sorts of things, and many of them were not soft! But it was all to raise money. Barrie was good like that."

So, that was Barrie. No one would suggest that in the eighties he was any sort of a role model for his children. But he did his best – or what he thought was his best – for them and did indeed love them.

It's just that he so often acted as his own worst enemy. He is remembered for his former life as a self-styled hard man, his criminal record, his slovenly, beer-belly appearance, his hair-trigger temper and his unequalled ability to act rashly first and leave the thinking for a long time later.

*

Thirty years later and 200 miles away from Moulsecoomb, Barrie spreads himself out on a large recliner sofa in his home in Cheshire.

"I've grown up now, I'm sixty-nine," he says. Outside his eyeline, younger brother Nigel silently raises his eyebrows to the heavens.

"I've been to prison twice and I've beaten people up in Brighton. I was what I call 'naughty' evil [unlike the likes of Russell Bishop, who he calls '"evil" evil']."

As he chomps away on a spectacular cheese-and-pickle

baguette, I see a still-large man with the medical problems that come with being older and overweight, but also a man who has proved, finally, to be a good father.

There are still flashes of bravado and his temper is still salted with uninhibited swearing, but over the decades he has found happiness with a new wife, now sadly deceased, and children without losing touch with his first family or ceasing his fight for closure over his dead daughter.

Barrie was brought up in Fulham, in a house at the back of Hurlingham Park, before moving to a home off the Walworth Road and then a variety of locations around Brixton and Tulse Hill.

"I didn't give a monkey's for school and left when I was fifteen," he continued.

"I had a dream to be a chef. I had a job as laundry boy at the Savoy Hotel. I met Susan at the Flamingo, a club which played soul music and Tamla Motown."

He laughs raucously at the suggestion he was a bouncer at the club. "Anybody causing trouble I would throw out so you could call me a bouncer, if you like," he said.

"The two friends who brought us together were Jackie and Frank. It wasn't love at first bite, I promise you, it wasn't a great romance from the first moment.

"I said to her, 'Oi, you, don't you want to sit down here?'. She said, 'All right,' and the chat-up line was, 'Do you want to go for a walk?' You know what I was after!

"The following weekend, I said I'd come down to see her and I thumbed a lift down the A23, as it was then, and got lost, but I got there and met her mum and dad.

"I got a job as a chef at Ledbelly's, next to the Theatre Royal.

I moved to a flat in Portslade and then to the Old Shoreham Road and Sue and I got engaged.

"She was very conscious of her glass eye and I remember saying to her: 'Why are you looking away? I have already seen it. I'm not interested in that I'm interested in you.' And that broke down a barrier.

"Ever since that day, I loved her and I love her still because she is the mother of my children."

"We got married but the only member of my family to go was my brother Keith because I'd had fights with the rest of them.

"I lived with Sue and her parents but I was sent down when she was eight and a half months pregnant with John. She wasn't happy, her mother wasn't happy, I wasn't happy, nobody was happy.

"I was sent from Pentonville to Camp Hill on the Isle of Wight and it was here I got into a major, major fight. I was smacked and went straight into one of the urinals striking my head and I don't remember anything until waking up in sickbay, and they said, 'You've been fighting again.'

"Then I had a couple of fits in my cell which scared me and ever since then I have been epileptic. And every time I think about my little girl [Nicola] it brings it on.

"On release, I couldn't work again as a chef because of my health record and I became long term sick.

"I was present at Nicky's birth really to make up for not being there for John and I think I owed it to Susan and Nicky and John to keep out of trouble. But I didn't. I stole a barometer from a house. How stupid. I was still getting myself into trouble, hence the naughty-boy tag."

Barrie dissolves in tears at the memories, and Laura, his stepdaughter, comes over to the sofa give him a hug of comfort.

"Every fit I used to have, she was there. She used to sit with me and hold my hands because I wasn't properly in control.

"She was a sweetheart although she was off her bonce. She had a daring streak, children are invincible and Karen Hadaway was the same.

"They used to go to each other's houses. They were inseparable. Lyndsey used to tag along but they would send her home although Nicky used to treat Lyndsey like a little sister."

On the chopped-fingers comment, Barrie is adamant: "It's a saying, it's not an intended action, it was taken out of context," he said.

"Nicky had stolen and I was not happy about it. I did bang John around the ear-hole when he needed it at the time and I smacked Nicky's legs when she did something that was stupidly dangerous like run into a road but if she wanted something she only had to ask. She was not frightened of me.

"One of the last things I heard she had done was give a small boy some sweets after his sweets had fallen out of his hands outside a shop in Barcombe Road.

"It was a typical act of kindness and generosity and that's what she was. It was the last thing I heard she had done."

CHAPTER 3

ENTER RUSSELL BISHOP

I f Brighton and Hove is the cool-dude, breezy, sassy, bohemian borough with a royal history, then Moulsecoomb is its disturbing, secret brother locked away in the attic.

The Royal Pavilion, vibrant pier (the one left standing), wedding-cake frontage of the Grand Hotel, and even the I360 – the bagel on a pole skypod – are the pin-ups of the confident, prosperous, fun city Brighton likes to portray.

But on its north-eastern outskirts lies the grubby, sprawling estate used to house those people the council's tourist chiefs don't want spoiling visitors' views.

The Fellows and the Hadaways are two families with their own character and foibles, but the estate where they lived is also important, because Moulsecoomb, its culture, its way of life, its people and how it was portrayed in the media is a major player in this tragic story, too.

It was built in the 1920s by local-authority planners intent on replacing the grimy, back-to-back inner-city terracing with nice, new brick semis with inside toilets and small gardens and allotments bordering the airy greenness of Wild Park and Stamner.

As ever, the planners' dreams fell through, not least from a lack of money. Those 7,000 moving in – mostly locals but a significant number of South London overspillers – found few shops, no amenities and everything, including hospitals and even the dole office, a bus ride away.

This bred a lack of respect for the surroundings and a sense of isolationism; hence, the apocryphal stories of children brought up in Moulsecoomb who have never seen the sea.

In the Thatcher era of the eightiesmid-eighties, unemployment on the estate was high, crime was high, vandalism was high... and morale was low.

While the rest of Brighton and south east England prospered, a subculture grew here, described, at best, as a freelance entrepreneurship, even a spirit of Thatcherism enterprise, and, at worst, thieving, criminality and cheap gangsterism.

There were easy headlines about the Cinderella estate of broken bottles and broken families, and jokes about wiping your feet when leaving. In every street there always seemed to be someone trying to repair or salvage a very used car and, in some areas, by night there was an air of unease, if not out and out threat.

As a result of the Babes in the Wood case, much more money was spent by an embarrassed council and today it is much spruced up in comparison with the dog days of 1986. The estate is now housing association properties rather than council housing.

But even in the eighties, there was also a core of decency and responsibility, of families trying to bering up their children the right way, to have pride in their appearance, their homes and their jobs or search for employment. The Fellows and the Hadaways were two such families.

Shan Lancaster has lived in Brighton for more than forty years and written about the estate as a reporter for both the *Evening Argus* and the *Sun*. She has a fondness for Moulsecoomb of that era, and remembers thinking the worse thing about Moulsecoomb was learning how to spell it.

"There were some wonderful gardens up there, the original estate was designed so people could grow their own veg and have plenty of space for kids to play, and nothing grew in so many of them but rusty old cars and fridges and pushchairs and smelly rubbish bags," she told me.

"I do remember talking to an old boy about his chrysanths and he was saying he was giving up , there was so much vandalism, if anyone saw anything being lovingly cultivated it was a target. I'd had similar problems with an allotment plot and a nearby feral family so we bonded!

"There were two sorts of people in Moulsecoomb – families sent down from London and the old Brighton families displaced by the slum clearance and, later, the Churchill Square development.

"There were no mean streets in Moulsecoomb in those days. Certainly, nothing as bad as parts of Whitehawk and even Kemp Town."

Then she smiled. "There were a lot of old fashioned Sun readers," leaving no doubt that this was a term of esteem as well as endearment.

But there are others who take a different view: Terry Garoghan – dubbed the "Unofficial Mayor of Brighton" – is the parody songwriter who penned "Moulsecoomb – Govt Health Warning" to the tune of the Marcels' "Blue Moon", in which he complains about being left alone on the estate, without a Chieftain tank.

*

Leave Moulsecoomb, cross the busy A270 Lewes Road, head towards Brighton for about fifteen minutes on foot and, up and behind Moulsecoomb railway station, you'll find another estate at the bottom end of Hollingbury.

Built in a similar style, the estate in Hollingbury has much less of the depressed-ghetto profile of Moulsecoomb; and there, in a ground-floor flat of a tower block in Stephens Road, lived Russell Bishop. Five foot, five inches tall, ten and a half stone, fair hair, weak moustache, blue eyes… and a mile and a half away from Newick Road and the little girls.

Like many in that area in the eighties, he was a difficult man to pigeon hole. Sometime roofer, sometime car repairer/wheeler dealer, sometime crook, mostly unemployed, constantly scruffy.

At the time of the murders, Bishop had been living for two years with Jennie Johnson, the mother of his child who was later to bear him two more. Nowadays, they would be described as partners but then she was known as his common-law wife, although theirs was far from a straightforward relationship.

Bishop was a familiar sight around the area, tinkering with his ever-changing rota of used cars, helping neighbours with this and that, on the lookout for drugs or a car to steal and generally filling in time between picking up his benefits.

His unusual childhood had prepared him for this sort of lifestyle.

His mother, Sylvia, a well-respected dog trainer and Crufts winner, lived with husband Roy, a roofer, in Coldean Lane, on the opposite side of Wild Park, just over the Lewes Road from Newick Road.

Jim Hatley, a reporter on the Brighton *Evening Argus*, remembers Sylvia as "an obviously house-proud woman who came over as a hugely protective mother and worried about her son and what he could get himself into even though he was now a grown-up.

"You could tell she was not rich but the house was neat and tidy and anything but threadbare. It was way better than many over the road in the Moulsecoomb estate. Better than the flat I was living in at the time," he said, laughing.

She had written books on dogs and had hopes of becoming a TV personality – the new Barbara Woodhouse. While locals were wary of Bishop, with his petty thieving, tall tales and unsavoury private life, they respected his mother.

Russell was the youngest of her five grown-up sons and, she rather candidly admitted, was the only one she had planned.

As happens to many a youngest child, his mother spoiled him, imbuing him with the belief and arrogance that he could have, or take, whatever he wanted. Sylvia was a domineering woman but she doted on him beyond even the unconditional love of a mother.

While open to his personal failings – she would describe him as a "wally" and compulsive liar – she was blind to anything more sinister and hostile to any suggestion he was anything other than a lovable scamp.

In an interview with Hatley in 1987, Sylvia Bishop told of her son's upbringing: he had been born five months before

England won the World Cup in 1966, following four older brothers: Alec, David, Andrew and Michael.

Said Mrs Bishop: "I had lost another child and Russell was the only one of them I had planned. He was the child I had to fill the gap of the one who died.

"I love him to death, he's my baby. He wanted attention for years and we were too stupid to realise it."

In an aside that with hindsight is utterly chilling yet at the time intended entirely innocently, Mrs Bishop added, "He absolutely adores children."

The young Bishop went to Coldean School, close to the family home, but he suffered learning difficulties, which may have led to bullying, and developed behavioural problems. He was found to be slightly educationally subnormal and at fourteen was diagnosed dyslexic. Even in his twenties, he had never really mastered reading and writing.

His mother sent him off to a special Catholic school in Worcester but he didn't settle and soon returned to Sussex.

Then he was sent as a border to the council-run St Mary's School, in Horam, near Heathfield, but that didn't work either and, homesick, he would abscond and hitchhike home. Finally, his mother tried home tuition.

Whatever was tried there was no way Bishop could be described as academic. What he loved was playing football, fishing, smoking cannabis, when he could afford it, and he joined the citizens-band (CB) radio craze of the early eighties, which was how he met Jennie Johnson.

In the days long before mobile phones, CB radio was a way of having instant contact with your friends, as long as they also had the equipment. Bishop's fellow members gave him the call sign "Light Bulb" but he found it rather demeaning so changed it to "Silver Bullet". Jennie was "Panda Bear".

But most of all, he loved bigging himself up by lying in search of the status and respect he had never had at school. Some thought his exaggerations – his whoppers – were even part of his charm.

Geoffrey Caswell, a fishing pal and neighbour in Stephens Road, said that after the murders, Bishop told him he had hired a big-shot American lawyer to prove his innocence.

He also told Caswell that he had insured his dog, Misty, a splendid white, brown and black terrier cross, for £17,000 and would refer to it as a Border collie.

"He doesn't tell malicious lies, he tells innocent little lies," Caswell said then.

Acting big and talking big was part and parcel of chancing his arm in the disorganised underworld of Brighton. In 1983, Bishop was convicted of a minor driving offence. The following year, he was fined £200 for burglary while, in 1985, it was five burglaries, with five others taken into consideration and other motoring offences, all of which brought him a 150-hour Community Service order.

By 1986, Bishop and Johnson, both aged 20, had one child – one-year-old Victor – and she was heavily pregnant with a second child, Hayley, while a third, Stacey, was to arrive later. None of this was nowhere near enough to keep Bishop happy at home.

*

Back on Moulsecoomb, turn right out of Newick Road and immediately left and you will be in Barcombe Road, another typical collection of semis on the estate. Here with her parents lived Marion Stevenson, and Bishop fancied her.

In 1986, Stevenson was just 16 and what people would call "a right little madam", hanging out with all sorts of wrong people, including older men, such as convicted the paedophile Ernie Pullen, who also lived in Barcombe Road.

Pullen, 58, called himself a photographer but specialised in pornographic videos of young girls and, at this time, had not long been released from a prison sentence for having sex with an under-aged girl.

Stevenson had actually started her fling with Bishop when just 15, but then Moulsecoomb was the sort of place where men in their twenties did go out with schoolgirls under the legal age of consent.

By her own admission, at 16, she had found herself out of school, unemployed, having regular sex with a father who lived with a pregnant partner, smoked cannabis, drank heavily and watched pornographic films.

Stevenson and Bishop would have sex in his car and even in his flat when Johnson was out. The affair had started behind Johnson's back but she soon found out.

With Johnson on the warpath, the rows with Bishop were the stuff of local legend, often spilling onto the street, keeping the neighbours at first amused and then so angry and frustrated there were even plans for a petition to have them evicted.

Johnson's fiery temper made sure Bishop suffered when she caught him out but she was fiercely loyal, and ever optimistic that eventually they would marry and settle down together as a family.

It was the combustible and unpredictable nature of their

relationship which was to later confuse the police and prosecutors and save Bishop's skin.

Stevenson lived with her parents, Jim and Rosalind, and Bishop took every opportunity to see her in Moulsecoomb, often, Johnson suspected, when he had told her he was going fishing or when she was out working as a cleaner at American Express.

Johnson's parents lived in Heath Hill Avenue in Bevendean, a similar estate adjoining Moulsecoomb, so that when she visited them she would pass close to Newick Road and Barcombe Road and inevitably spotted Bishop and Stevenson together.

After one row with Johnson, Bishop took Stevenson and moved in with her into bed-and-breakfast accommodation for a few weeks, before complaining she couldn't cook and going back to the long-suffering mother of his child.

Another reason why Bishop hung around the Moulsecoomb estate was to see his friend Dougie Judd – and that was how he came to know Nicola Fellows and Karen Hadaway.

Bishop would tell the police later, "My relationship with Jennie was very, very difficult in 1986. We were cheating on each other."

He had two shoulder operations, in 1985 and 1986, that, he claimed, affected his ability to work.

"It was a struggle at times. We were not rich but we were not broke. I was offered labouring jobs which I took against doctor's advice and I should not have done it.

"It was through labouring that I met Marion Stevenson in the summer of 1986 and ended up having a relationship. When that job came to an end, I didn't see Marion again for quite some weeks.

"In between jobs, I spent most of my time on the beach fishing and one day she turned up, we started chatting and that's how it first started.

"I met Dougie Judd through her, we became good friends. I knew Barrie Fellows for some time through playing football in the park.

"I would not say we were good friends. I just knew him as Barrie. Once I knew Dougie, I would see Barrie much more." As always its right to be very cautious about anything Russell Bishop ever says.

Judd was two years older than Bishop and had met Barrie through CB radio.

His girlfriend in October 1986 was Jackie Gravett (later, Spencer). They had first started going out in February when she was 15 and by this time was 16, still at school and living with her mother, Valerie, her mother's boyfriend and Jackie's brother and sister in Ashurst Road, Moulsecoomb.

Dougie and Jackie had met through her friends Sarah and Cherell Nevard who lived in Newick Road. Dougie's younger brother Tim was going out with Sarah.

Dougie was a heavy smoker of cannabis and when he moved in with the Fellows he would continue the habit, smoking with Bishop and Stevenson in his room. Bishop occasionally stayed overnight.

He was rumoured to have had affairs with Stevenson and Jennie Johnson but denied it categorically.

Said Barrie: "Dougie came to stay at my house. I knew him through CB radio. I was called Basil Brush. He lived in Ringmer Road or Chailley Road in Moulsecoomb but his mum kicked him out – I don't know why, she was a bit eccentric."

Said Susan: "His girlfriend was Jackie Grabbett who went to Falmer High School. I knew his brother Steve and Teresa who lived at 138 Moulsecoomb Way.

"Bishop used to stop outside my house and talk to Dougie, when he was in, and the children. That was he first time I saw him, probably back in 1985. He and Dougie and Barrie would go to the park and play football every Sunday.

"It was just a kick about with friends. I would sit on the side and watch. Some girls would be in it, too, but it was too rough and I said I'm not doing that. It was called Murderball [after *Rollerball*, the ultra-violent US film from the 1970s]. It was a rough game and most of us girls kept out of it."

Barrie added: "I don't remember exactly when I first met Bishop, it must have been through Dougie.

"We played football. I remember Bishop was very swift. I was the goalie and he put a few passed me, but that's what younger men did! I was a bit older than him and not as swift as I used to be."

It was pretty cramped in 26 Newick Road, with mother, father, son, daughter sharing a room with Edna, and also a lodger, but they somehow managed.

Michelle said, "I only got to know Bishop at the beginning of the summer of 1986, once he started being with Marion."

Michelle's mother Maisie Johnson lived with the family and was friendly with Marion Stevenson's mother. "My mum felt sorry for Marion and she used to come round and my mum would make her a cup of tea. I knew Dougie Judd was a lodger at Sue and Barrie's and that he was a friend of Russell Bishop but I didn't give it another thought.

"I saw Karen in the company of Bishop and Marion. She

asked on a number of occasions to take Karen to Saunders Park, which was a playground with swings. There were two or three outings with Nicky and Karen, once they took them to the beach. Bishop had a car.

"I remember the car was parked outside Barrie Fellows's house and there was a disagreement between Bishop and Barrie about the sexual relationship with Marion. Jennie Johnson said the Fellows were condoning the fact Bishop was carrying on with Marion when she [Jennie] had a little boy.

"Barrie told Marion not to go round any more. I banned Marion from coming to my house too because her father had knocked on my door saying he had had a problem with Bishop and Marion seeing each other and she saying she wasn't going to see him any more but she did.

"Karen liked Marion and Bishop. She had no reason not to like them."

So, Bishop would see Stevenson and drop in on his friend Judd at Number 26, where he would run into Nicola and her friend Karen. He also shared an interest in sea fishing with Lee Hadaway.

When Stevenson's parents banned Bishop from their house, or when he considered it too dangerous to see her or to arrange a secret meeting, he would use Nicola and Karen as messengers.

But by this time, such was the fatal attraction Bishop had for the two little girls, there was nothing Michelle or Susan could have done to stop him.

CHAPTER 4

THE SEARCH

It was a school day, 9 October 1986. Margaret Thatcher was in Number 10 and yuppies were still making big money in the City, before Black Wednesday brought it all crashing down the following year.

In fashion, it was a time of big hair and big shoulder pads and if you had tuned in to Portslade-based Southern Sound you'd be hearing the likes of Janet Jackson and Madonna.

Inside Number 26 Newick Road, the alarm went and Nicola was up first at about 7.30 a.m. – long before Barrie and Dougie, who had work to do that day. She was 4 foot 4 inches tall, dark complexion, hazel eyes, short dark-brown hair. She dressed in a brown-and-cream skirt and pink V-neck top (Moulsecoomb Junior School did not have a school uniform).

Inside Number 20, meanwhile, Lyndsey had had a bad night with a cold, but Karen was up and ready to catch the bus to Coldean Junior School when her friend Michelle called to pick her up. At 4 foot 1 inch, Karen was slightly shorter than

Nicola and had straight light-brown shoulder-length hair, fair complexion and blue eyes. She was wearing a grey kilt-type skirt, blue T-shirt and green school sweater and had 73p in her pocket.

The mid-eighties was a less suspicious time for mothers. Young children walked to school and played unsupervised outside. It was more than half a decade before the Bulger case, when a toddler was abducted and killed by two schoolchildren, which introduced fear to the previously playful school and pre-school years.

Ironically, on this day, the *Argus* newspaper ran a front-page splash reporting a warning by police to schools about stranger danger after a man had tried three times to lure young girls into his car on their way home from school.

He was described as "twenty-five, blond or ginger, with a 'smart blue car', who told his intended victims that he had been sent by their mother to pick them up".

Of course, "stranger danger", as it was called, was not the threat to Nicola and Karen as Russell Bishop was well known to them.

By 8.15 a.m., both girls were on their way. Nicola was what her father called "dawdling" as she walked to her school in The Highway off Lewes Road.

Said Barrie: "The last time I saw her was when I was waiting at the bus stop to go to work in Hove and she was going to school. She was just doing what she does and I went, 'All right, sweetie? Love you,' and blew her a kiss. The next time I saw her, she was on a mortuary slab."

Barrie spent the day working with Dougie Judd on cleaning a swimming pool in Hove.

Lee Hadaway was helping Lee Judd (Dougie's brother) transport furniture in Cambridge and the Midlands but they headed off to the hamlet of Cambridge near Gloucester by mistake and had to spend the night in the lorry cab.

With the two men out of the way, the two mums busied themselves around the house then shared a cup of tea.

Said Michelle: "During the day, I visited Sue Fellows and stayed and had a cup of tea for about half an hour then went home. Later, I went back to Sue's and stayed until Nicky came in from school. I decided to leave as it was after three thirty and Karen would be coming home from school, too.

"I saw Tracey Cox, Bishop and Marion Stevenson come down the path. Tracey and Marion were both sixteen. I said to Sue, I wasn't going to leave while they were out there. They called at the door and asked for Dougie. Nicky slammed the door and shouted through the letterbox, 'Go away, you slag'. Lyndsey said, 'You must not say that.'

"Marion was wearing a green-velour suit top and skirt, Tracey had trousers and a top, Bishop wore a light-blue flecky jumper of thick material.

"The three left and Bishop went towards my house while the other two went towards Barcombe Road. I waited a couple of minutes then walked home. My mum was in but Bishop had not called.

"Karen came home at five past four and explained she was a bit late because she had missed the first bus. She was chatting that she was doing well at school, her class was doing assembly the next day and she wanted me to come. She also had a ticket for the school Friday night disco.

"She said she wanted to go to the shops in Coldean Lane and

spend her 10p she had got from her friend Clare [Shepherd]. She left the house about ten past four and came back from the shops around twenty minutes later so she was home about four thirty.

"I had a chat with her about changing out of her school uniform, which she would do every day. She was wearing a green long-sleeved top with Coldean School on it, a pleated grey skirt, under her top she wore a blue vest and knickers and socks and school shoes.

"But she just took off her white jacket and put it over the settee and sat talking to my mum. The jacket was like a cotton jacket with fleece but like a bomber jacket, it was only waist length.

"It was chicken pie for tea and I went into the kitchen. I shouted after her about changing out of her school uniform but she was off.

"It wasn't a problem – if it got dirty, I would wash it for the next day. I asked her where she was going and not to be long because I was putting the pie in the oven. She said, 'I'm only going over the road, I won't be long.'" Those were her last words to her mother.

Said Susan: "Nicky came home at three thirty. John got home as well. He had not gone to school that day because of a swollen knee from football training

"Michelle came over with Teresa Judd [Steve Judd's wife]. Lee and Steve were away driving a lorry and would not be home for a couple of days.

"Bishop turned up at the door with Marion Stevenson and Tracey Cox. They said they had come to see Dougie. Nicky didn't answer the door but shouted through the letter box, saying 'slag', which was directed at Stevenson. Nicky didn't like her. I didn't hear any response from Stevenson.

"Michelle and Teresa left and Nicky went out to play. I looked out and could see Nicky playing in [her friend] Lisa Bowles', garden. I saw Karen later talking to Nicky. It was around five p.m. I looked away then looked again and they [Nicky and Karen] were not there."

That was the last time Susan saw her daughter alive. "Nicky's last words to me were: 'I'm just going across the road, I won't be long.'

"Her last meal would have been a school dinner [although, unknown to her mother, Nicky and Karen were later to eat chips from the shop in Barcombe Road]. The dinner at home was ready but she didn't get to eat it.

"All her clothes were clean and new on that day. She had had an accident on the way home and she had changed her knickers when she had got home [and her socks and shoes]."

Michelle takes up the story: "I sat in the sitting room talking to my mum [Maisie] then I realised the time was about five p.m. Lyndsey was across the road playing with her friend Lisa Bowles in her garden and I decided to get her in for tea.

"Lyndsey said Nicky and Karen had run off down the road. I didn't take too much notice and I took Lyndsey in for her tea. At five twenty, after serving dinner, I thought that where ever they had gone they would come back play in the garden. I went to the Bowles house but Simon [Lisa's brother] had not seen Karen. I went to Sue's house but she had not seen Karen and she said that Nicky was out playing. Having told her what Lyndsey had said to me, I said I was going to look for Karen.

"I went back home and told Maisie to keep Lyndsey indoors

then I returned to Sue's and went up to Chailey Road then went back to Newick Road and Sue and I walked to the playground which has swings and things for kids. It was about five forty.

"I walked back to Chailey Road with Sue and saw Wayne Measor, who was fourteen, and his mum, Kathleen, who was a neighbour, and he said he had seen Karen playing at the bottom of Wild Park and talking to the park keeper.

"Sue was worried because Wayne had only mentioned Karen and not Nicky . We walked from Newick Road to Barcombe Road to the fish-and-chip shop then me and Sue crossed the Lewes Road and went towards Wild Park.

"We walked up the little pathway towards the pavilion calling out their names. There was a lot of mist that night so it was starting to get a bit dark. We went back passed the trees where Wayne had seen Karen and then back to Coldean Lane.

"We crossed back over Lewes Road to see if the girls had come home.

"Karen was frightened of the dark and she would never have stayed out by herself when it got dark, not at all. We stayed home for fifteen minutes and I called Clare Shepherd's mum as we're supposed to have gone to her house that night and Karen would never have missed that.

"Sue and I were panicking at this point. It was getting dark [sunset was 6.22 that night] and foggy.

"Sue and I went back out again and Sue went to see Janet Reid, who is the mother of Nicky's schoolfriend Kerrie and lives opposite Wild Park. This was now seven fifteen to seven thirty. Sue and I had been out looking for the best part of two hours.

"Marion Stevenson's mother came out and said Marion had

gone babysitting. I wondered whether she had taken the girls to where she was babysitting.

"The CB-radio people were becoming involved, too, and I went in the car of some friends from Chailey Road. I don't remember if Sue was with me, we went everywhere I could possibly think of, including the seafront.

"When we got back, the police were at my house and they told me to go indoors and leave it to them. But I was not having any of that and I carried on back and forward from my house all night. I didn't get any sleep. I was searching until after midnight.

"Lee was with Steve. I spoke to him a couple of times. You can imagine he was really worried but what could he do? He was miles and miles away."

Said Susan: "About five thirty, Michelle knocked on the door, asking if I knew where Karen was? I said, 'No.'

"She left and came back about six thirty. *Crossroads* was on the telly. She was worried that Karen had not come home, so me and Michelle went out looking for them. We went to Chailley Road, Moulsecoomb Way and Birdham Road. I didn't know where Barrie was. I was worried.

"Having gone out with Michelle I got back about seven twenty, and I told Barrie what had happened. I stayed at home not very long before going back out with Michelle to look, including Wild Park, until about nine p.m.

"We searched for hours. I knew in my heart that something had happened.

"I went up Coldean Lane, then went home because the police were there but I went out later in a car. Finally I stayed at home at about eleven thirty because that was what the police told me to do."

With the alarm raised the press arrived but at this stage it was just a local paper story.

Argus reporter Phil Mills remembers: "Michelle Hadaway was engulfed in worry and dread. She could not sit or stand in one place for more than a few seconds, constantly wandering outside to look both ways up and down the road for her daughter.

"There was hope that the girls had just gone on an adventure, and would turn up alive and well, and Michelle was hoping Karen would turn a corner and run into her arms."

She told the *Argus*: "I have searched Wild Park and Stamner Park. I have even been down to the seafront looking under every boat from the marina to the pier.

"Karen is a good girl. She is cheeky to me but has never run away before. She will never talk to strangers. She has been warned a thousand times that if anyone approaches her she should run."

Susan, in tears, added: "If anyone sees her please, please bring her home to me safe and well."

So where was Barrie while the mother's were frantic with worry? His movements and timings would be debated for the next 30 years.

What is not in doubt was that he and Dougie Judd had been working at a private home in Woodruff Avenue, Hove, and knocked off about 5 p.m. They walked through the park to George Street, where they caught a bus back to Moulsecoomb.

Barrie got off and visited Teresa Judd in Moulsecoomb Way, before returning home between 7 p.m. and 7.30 p.m., eating his dinner then going out to join the search for his missing daughter.

After hours of searching, the police were called at 8.30 p.m. It was that gap between bus stop and home that would cause the problems in the future.

*

Michelle and Susan had found virtually nobody who had seen the girls, so who *had* seen them?

At 4.40 p.m., Karen, Lyndsey and Nicola had definitely been playing in the street with other children.

Nicola and Karen had left Lyndsey behind and had headed off down Barcombe Road laughing and doing cartwheels, according to neighbour Sharon Bowles, who had been at the bus stop on her way to work at the American Express building in central Brighton.

Wayne Measor was right and the girls had been in Wild Park and had talked to the park keeper Roy Dadswell at around 5.15 p.m. as they played in the trees at the Coldean Lane end of the park.

Then, who should arrive but Russell Bishop. As the children played, he engaged Mr Dadswell in conversation about his shoulder operations before he headed off towards his home along Lewes Road.

Later, the girls left the trees and headed off towards the Moulsecoomb side of the Lewes Road.

Tracey Cox, who had visited the Fellows with Bishop and Stevenson that afternoon, saw the girls outside the shops at the bottom of Coldean Lane, she says, between 6.25 and 6.40 p.m. They asked her to go conker-collecting, but she declined.

"I told them it was time for them to go home and they said, 'All right,' and I walked off and left them there. They both shouted my name and then waved and said goodbye. That was the last I saw of them," she remembered.

"They were going to go home. It was dusk and there was a slight mist. I'll always remember them standing at the corner waving at me."

That may have been earlier than Cox recalls, because the girls were definitely seen around 6.30 p.m., eating chips outside the shops in Barcombe Road and crossing the Lewes Road back to the park, this time the viaduct end near the bus stop and, what was then, the police box and public toilets (now a tyre shop and car wash).

Where was Bishop? Witnesses, who knew him, said they saw him in that same area at exactly that same time.

One final witness may or may not be important. Beatrice Cooper lived in Park Close, which bordered Wild Park by Jacobs Ladder, a steep climb through the woods on the Coldean Lane side of the park.

Some time between 6.30 p.m. and 7 p.m., she was in her garden and, she said, heard a child crying as if it had been severely injured. It last two to three minutes and came from the area where the bodies were later to be discovered.

She thought nothing of it at the time, only coming forward later to the police. Had she heard the murders? Or was this a complete red herring?

One development that certainly was relevant and staggeringly important to the murder inquiry came in the early hours of the morning. A group of CB-radio fans were out searching when they came across a light blue sweatshirt with the logo Pinto on its front. It was lying on the grass near Moulsecoomb railway station.

At the time, everyone was looking for two children or their garments, so it was left on top of railings. More, much more, about the Pinto sweatshirt would emerge later.

*

As Thursday turned into Friday and, with none of the parents able to sleep, the police, who had continued the search through the night, intensified the activities from first light.

The police helicopter was sent up, tracker dogs called in and 140 officers were out on door-to-door inquiries in Moulsecoomb. An estimated 18,000 motorists were stopped and questioned on Lewes Road, causing a five-hour delay

Superintendent David Tomlinson told the *Argus*: "We are desperately concerned for the welfare of these children."

Nicola's headmaster, Allen Roochove, added, "The response from the school and community has been fantastic. Moulsecoomb has a terrible reputation which it doesn't deserve and it is at times like this, when something terrible has happened, that you see it in its true spirit."

Michelle picks up the narrative of the following morning.

"On the Friday morning, I went to Kathleen Measer first thing. We went to the tennis court area by Woburn Place and Jacobs Ladder. Kathleen could not get up the steps so I went up then came back down and sat on the bench to gather my thoughts, I was in a terrible state, just the two of us [this was about 12.45–1 p.m.].

"I saw Bishop and two other people walking along: Belle Badger, who lives across the road, and Marion Stevenson. I didn't speak to them but Kathleen did. We also spoke to a couple of joggers, dental students, who were also trying to help.

Kathleen was trying to get me to go home because she had to go to work that afternoon and she didn't really want to leave me there.

"I saw Dougie Judd and Bishop with a dog [Misty] walking towards me. It was just after two p.m. Russell said could he have a piece of Karen's clothing so his dog could get a scent to help the search. I thought of Karen's white jacket which was still on the back of the settee where she had left it.

"I told him to ask the policeman at the door of my house to let him have the white coat which I said would be all right. Bishop and the others walked off in the directions of my house and I was still on the bench when they came back. Bishop had a Sainsbury's carrier bag in which was Karen's white jacket.

"Kathleen and I started to make a move to leave. I said to her, 'If you are going to go back then I will go off and search again.' Then a car driver stopped and Dougie Judd spoke to him. I think they knew each other but I didn't know who the driver was. There was a conversation about going to 49 Acres to search and I said could I come with them. They said no but I persuaded them.

"We went up there close to Hollingbury golf course, north of Wild Park. The three men and the dog and me were in the car. Bishop and Dougie were having a discussion with the driver. We turned right to a picnic area, Dougie and I got out , we were there about fifteen minutes, calling their names in the picnic area. Then we went to 49 Acres.

"In total, I was with them about thirt-five minutes [this was up to about 3.05 p.m.]. Dougie and Bishop said they were going to walk back through the woods and they would see us by the police box in Lewes Road.

"I was just agitated because I wanted to keep searching. I asked the man to take me back to the park. I was exhausted and felt sick. When I got there I sat on the grass near the pavilion for some fresh air. A man walked past with his dog and asked if I was all right. I don't know what I said I was all confused I was petrified and I cried about my girl and both children.

"I started to walk and then I saw some sort of police action in the park. I walked back and said something to the man in the car. Then the police started coming, there was a helicopter in the air and when I saw the taping go up I knew something had happened.

"Bishop was standing by the entrance to the park. I saw Russell and I shouted at him. He was just standing there, he just looked at me and put his hand over his face. That moment is etched on my life for ever, I just collapsed. The police came over and I was taken home."

Michelle had learned the terrible truth from Bishop's reaction. She was expecting a baby in ten weeks' time.

The two girls had been found sexually assaulted and strangled in a tiny, den-like clearing in the woods above the pavilion on the Coldean Lane side of Wild Park.

Pathologist Dr Iain West later described the scene: "They both appeared to be fully clothed. Nicola was on her back at the opening of the clearing near an elder tree. Her left arm was by her side and her right arm across her chest. By her left hand lay Karen's green school jumper and her knickers. Karen was face down, at right angles to her friend at the far end of the clearing. Her right arm was across Nicola's body and her head rested on her right arm and Nicola's abdomen with her left arm at right angles to her body."

It turned out that Karen was not wearing knickers and Nicola had hers apparently put back on but inside out.

They had been discovered in the dense undergrowth by two local lads, Matthew Marchant and Kevin Rowland.

Hospital porter Rowland later told the *Argus*: "I only saw one of them at first. It just looked like a little girl lying down wearing a dress. Then I could see the other one.

"I called Matt over and we both sat down shocked and then started shouting for help."

At that time, Bishop, who had been around the park all day getting involved in the search as much as he could, was standing with local beat bobby PC Paul Smith.

They made an incongruous pair, the 6-foot-7-inches-tall bearded copper and the willowy 5-foot-five-inches Bishop, but that didn't stop his swaggering confidence. First, he asked the officer: "Do you think the kids are around here?" Smith replied that he didn't know. Bishop responded immediately with his own opinion "I reckon they've either gone north or if they're here they are finished."

Smith, somewhat taken aback, said, "Well, Brighton has some strange people in it." To which Bishop responds, "Yeah, anyway, I'm not searching any more. I mean, the Old Bill wouldn't believe it would they. If I found the girls and if they were done in, I'd get the blame, I'd get nicked."

With Smith puzzling over what he had just heard, the alarm was raised and the officer sent Bishop forward to the scene because he was younger and could run faster. Bishop scrambled up the bank and immediately tried to get to the bodies but Rowland stopped him.

Smith arrived moments later, crawled into the den and

radioed in the discovery at 4.21 p.m. "Charlie Oscar thirty-eight, over. I have found one of the girls. She looks dead. I am not going to touch her. We are north of the pavilion, up the hill its very steep. I want a senior officer here – *now*."

Smith checked that there were, in fact, two bodies then started clearing everyone away from the area before Superintendent David Tomlinson arrived to take charge of the scene.

Meanwhile, Barrie was standing with his brothers, Kevin and Nigel, by the Lewes Road police box when he heard the news on the police radio. At first, he thought that the girls had been discovered by the pavilion meant the Brighton Pavilion in the town centre and so they must have been found alive.

"I'll give her a bloody good smack," he announces with the bravado of relief.

"No, you won't, you'll give her a big hug," Kevin replied.

But when the truth was confirmed, Barrie shrieked a banshee wail and struck out wildly and aimlessly before being pinned to the ground by his brothers.

He later told the *Sunday People*: "It was the moment my world was torn apart.

"That's when I lost it big time. I swung without thinking at the nearest copper and went completely off my head.

"Everyone jumped on me, but I was like a madman. It took a lot of them to pin me down. It was like one of my worst epileptic fits. I was still sobbing and screaming and it took a while to calm down. When I did I told the police that under no circumstances were they to tell my wife Sue. That was my job. I went outside to look for her, but heard this terrible, high pitched scream of a wounded animal. It didn't sound human. That was Sue. I just knew.

"By the time I reached her, she was wailing and sobbing. I tried to comfort her but she was hysterical. Completely lost. I think that was the moment our marriage was lost, too. Nicky's murder cast a shadow over the family's life. Things were never the same again."

*

Susan was at home when she found out the bodies had been discovered. She said, "John came in and said they had been found. Sonia, our police liaison officer, said she would go and find out what had happened. She was gone for about half an hour. When she came back, I said, 'OK?' and she just said, 'No.'

"After that, I don't remember. I went into shock. A doctor gave me some medication, it was a very powerful sedative."

Miles and miles away on some motorway, Lee Hadaway heard about the discovery on the car radio as he headed back to Brighton.

That Friday night, the pubs were quiet in Moulsecoomb, there was no drunken singing or the usual petty vandalism, just a sullen silence, described by the *Argus* "as if the streets were in mourning".

Jodie Keating, a neighbour in Newick Road, told the *Argus*: "Friends have been coming to see them [the Fellows and Hadaways] but there's nothing that can be said to help now.

"Barrie came over but he was too upset to speak. He picked up my baby and that really seemed to get to him. He just held him."

CHAPTER 5

THE HUNT

The following morning, after another sleepless night, Barrie and Lee Hadaway had the grim task of formally identifying the bodies of their daughters at Brighton borough mortuary.

The Fellows walked across the road to the Hadaways before the men went to the morgue. The *Argus* reported that Susan "looked near to collapse and leaned sobbing against her husband".

The paper described how "the tough community of Moulsecoomb closed ranks amid bitter tears and vows of revenge.

"There were few children seen playing on the streets and behind the closed doors of the council houses the mood was a mixture of grief and anger."

While the search was on, friends and neighbours had made a steam of calls to the stricken mothers with words of comfort and hope. Once the news spread that there was now no hope, the stream stopped, people uncertain of what they could say and unwilling to intrude.

Even after the painful formalities had been completed, the coroner was still unable to release the bodies for burial because of police inquiries. The funeral would not be for another four months.

The night before, Dr West had carried out the post-mortems and found that Karen had been sexually assaulted before death, she had extensive bruises from her lower face to her thighs and had been throttled by one or both hands of her killer.

He concluded that she would have lost consciousness quickly but death would not have been instantaneous. But Nicola had suffered even more.

She been sexually assaulted before and after death and both vaginally and anally. She also had extensive bruising across her body but, in addition, such bruising to her left cheek which showed she had been punched in the face.

This suggested that the blow would have stunned her and might have enabled the killer to deal with Karen before returning to Nicola's stricken figure. However, there was no direct evidence in what order the girls were killed.

West concluded that the manual strangulation of Nicola would've taken longer to have killed her than her friend. He also found nothing to suggest that the girls had been killed elsewhere and then dragged to the den and remained neutral as to whether there had been one or two killers involved.

However, the pathologist was unable at this stage to give any accurate time of death (initially suggesting any time between 7 p.m. and 3 a.m.). As we will hear, that was to cause serious problems for the prosecution. Dr West faced widespread but misguided criticism that he had failed to take the body temperatures at the scene but today pathologists say that is an overestimated guide to time of death and blame TV detectives such as Morse, for this mistaken perception.

Once the girls had been found dead, the story leaped from being a local missing-children case to national-TV coverage and onto the front pages of all the national newspapers, tabloid and up-market broadsheet, alike.

It was not a great feat of imagination to dub the case the "Babes in the Wood" and reporters dashed down the M23 from Fleet Street (as it still was in those days) to cash in.

The mid-eighties saw a spike in rivalry between the Red Tops and to cheque-book journalism. At that time, the nation bought tabloid newspapers in their millions but, never, before or since, had the reputation of newspaper reporters and their alleged disregard for truth and fairness been lower.

With no immediate arrest imminent, the media concentrated on the "broken bottles and broken families" reputation of Moulsecoomb itself – the detritus of Brighton shovelled up and dumped on the outskirts of town, the crime and the vandalism, unemployment up to 30% – and much of it written by expense-account writers from the luxury of the Grand Hotel.

The apocryphal story of schoolgirls offering "chips for blow jobs" soon emerged in the red tops and even a respectable broadsheet reporter wrote, in what is known as a "colour piece", of the "mean streets of Moulsecoomb."

This apparent snobbery of well-dressed reporters besieging the estate angered local residents and created an oppressive, claustrophobic atmosphere behind the front doors. This, combined with the sense of grief and anger at the killer, helped to make an already toxic atmosphere worse.

One resident summed up the anger that was felt – a collective anger that was to turn against Barrie Fellows after the Bishop acquittal.

He told the *Argus*: "Nicola was a lovey affectionate girl who would come up to you and throw her arms around you to give you a cuddle. I cried my eyes out when I heard the news.

"Her parents thought the world of her. Both she and Karen were really beautiful kids.

"If I found out who did is I would carve him up without a second thought. I may go to prison for life but I would kill him and enjoy doing it."

Sensing the danger, the churches appeal for calm, Rev Michael Porteous calling on his congregation at the Holy Nativity Church to pray for the killer and "erase hatred from your hearts".

He had to admit, though, that "most of the people from that area are not churchgoers".

Soon after the girls had gone missing, Barrie's three brothers – Nigel, Ian and Kevin Heffron – had all been alerted and were on their way to help out.

Said Nigel: "The first I heard of the children going missing was when Kevin knocked on my door in South London.

"We went down to Brighton straight away. Passing under the viaduct on Lewes Road to the scene of police activity in Moulsecoomb was like passing through a curtain."

Ian, then an Essex policeman, was quickly told to stay at home. "At the time of the murders, I had been on Child Protection for five years and was dealing with a child rape.

I said, 'Shall I come to Brighton?' They said, 'No, we'll keep you posted.'"

Sensing the atmosphere, the brothers decided they had to get Susan out of Brighton.

Said Nigel: "The media were everywhere so the family decided to move Susan to give her some room to grieve."

Said Susan: "Two days later, I went to stay with Jill Heffron, Nigel's sister in New Addington. Jonathan went to stay with Nigel in Brixton. We drove up after we had put the flowers in the park.

"I didn't want to go, all my friends were there in Brighton, I had lived all my life in Brighton. It helped for a while but I could not shift what had happened out of my mind."

As is usual in a high-profile murder hunt, the police suggested to the parents they should give a press conference to keep media interest alive and, hopefully, provoke a reaction that might turn up something new.

On Monday, 13 October, two days after Barrie and Lee had identified the bodies, they and Michelle (Susan was in London) walked into one of the conference rooms in Brighton's John Street Police HQ to face fifty-odd pressmen, photographers TV-camera crews.

Despite the intimidating prospect, Michelle, flanked by the two men and police officers, characteristically took the lead.

In response to questions about who could have abducted her daughter, she said, "It was definitely someone she knew or they both knew. I would be very surprised if it was a stranger.

"Even if it was a stranger who spoke to her Karen would have run. She was that sort of girl.

"I know my daughter and she knew our standards. Perhaps I

was over-protective but she knew she wasn't to talk to strangers and we like to think that she never did."

Asked about the impact on her other children, she added, "Lyndsey has been told the truth and she cried but I don't think she really knows. She is just missing Karen at the moment because she hadn't seen her for a few days.

"Darren, who is at a boarding school for slow learners at the moment, came home at the weekend but asked to go back because it was all too upsetting.

"You do your best, you can't keep children locked up, you have to give them their freedom. It's just the society we live in."

Asked if somebody was protecting the killer, Michelle replied, "Why would anybody want to protect them? All the time they are protecting them, they are more likely to go out and do it to somebody else."

Barrie, described by the *Argus* as "looking tired, unshaven and smoking heavily", said the murderer was "an animal without a conscience".

He went on: "Imagine a child watching as her friend is killed. It's terrible. It should never have happened. You hear about these things from the newspapers but you never think it's going to happen to you."

Barrie was weary but his words packed a punch. "I want to get whoever did it," he said.

In a front-page leader, headlined WHO IS THE MONSTER?, the *Argus* warned, "There is a killer in our midst. A monster who may strike again, a monster who preys on defenceless, innocent children. Look around you."

This was uncharacteristic populism from the *Argus*. It may certainly have captured the zeitgeist of the moment but did little to temper the fear and lynch-mob mentality, which was to later turn against Barrie.

Meanwhile, he was doing little to help himself and his public reputation.

Straight from the press conference, he marched around to the *Argus* office, then in Robert Street, a few hundred yards away.

He was clutching the business card left by reporter Jim Hatley who had dropped it off at a neighbour's house at the weekend.

Striding into Reception, he demanded to speak to the reporter and insisted he should be allowed a free death notice in the paper's Classified section and had brought the wording with him – which he hadn't bothered to agree with the Hadaways.

Hatley remembers Barrie telling him: "The girl was the apple of my eye. The best day of my life would have been walking her down the aisle." Big nudge. "That's what you want to hear for the paper, isn't it."

The *Argus* editor had little option but to agree to Barrie's wishes and, in fact, introduced a new policy of offering free death notices to all murder victims from then on.

*

Three days later, at the exact time a week after they had gone missing, the police and BBC staged a reconstruction of the girls' last-known movements for the *Crimewatch* TV programme.

The girls were played by similar-looking local school-children – Nicola by Katrina Taylor, 9, from Bolney Avenue, Moulsecoomb – and Karen by Lianne Martin, 10, from Stamner.

Katrina had been a friend in the same class as Nicola, while Leanne went to Coldean Junior School and knew both girls.

The recording took two hours and led to five hours of traffic jams on the Lewes Road with tailbacks stretching to Grand Parade and the town centre as 300 police officers questioned every passing driver.

Barrie watched the filming with Nigel and Kevin but had to be led away in tears. "They looked so much like them. I couldn't take it. I just burst into tears and had to go home," he said.

Susan was in London when it was staged and briefly watched the broadcast.

"Katrina was the spitting image of Nicky. When she was at school, they thought she was Nicky, sometimes," she said.

"As I watched on TV, I didn't know what to think really. I knew what they were trying to do but it didn't really register. Some of these TV-reconstructions work, some don't. Nothing came from it."

In a further tragedy, in July 1996, Katrina, by then 19, was knifed six times and left to die in St Nicholas churchyard, just three miles from the *Crimewatch* reconstruction.

By now, a memorial to the Wild Park victims had sprung up by the hawthorne tree, which was the closest spot the police had allowed the families to the murder scene.

It started as an impromptu spot for flowers and photos of the girls, including a tribute, signed, NICOLA AND KAREN. NEVER FORGOTTEN. THE FAMILYS [sic], but it grew and grew and is now a fully-fledged memorial where the families gather every year on the anniversary for a sombre remembrance.

Susan's mother Edna told the *Argus*: "The family has not

stopped crying. Since it happened. Even now it's only just beginning to sink in.

"Barrie cannot stand being in the house surrounded by our baby's belongings. He finds he cannot stay indoors."

Barrie told the paper: "I may look and sound calm but I'm in bits. I'm likely to explode at any moment. I just hope it was someone I don't know. If it's someone I know, even a passing acquaintance I'll blow up.

"My daughter has given up her whole life. She could have lived until she was eighty and had her own family. She adored children.

"It's sinking in that she's been deprived of her own marriage, husband and children and I've been deprived of being a grandfather to them.

"I was going to walk that girl down the aisle on her wedding day. She had all her bridesmaids planned out and even had a little boyfriend at school called Alex. I found a note in her room that read, 'To Alex. Do you...' I'll never know what she was going to write."

The following Sunday, Barrie visited Kevin Rowland at his home in Ringmer Road, Moulsecoomb.

Rowland told *Argus* reporter Hatley: "He wanted to know how they were when we found them. When I told him they looked like they were asleep he seemed calmer. Then we both stood there and cried."

This wasn't quite correct, as Rowland later acknowledged he had not got close enough to see how they looked, but it was said out of kindness to spare the grieving fathers feelings. But cruelly this humane gesture was later used to attack Rowland's integrity in court and try in some way mitigate Bishop's own lies.

Rowland went on: "I suppose Matt and I both wish we hadn't found them but then somebody had to. You never think it's going to be you. Ninety-nine per cent of the time, it's the police.

"Neither of us will ever be able to forget it. I felt so terrible about it my doctor put me on tranquillisers. I see bodies every day at the hospital but this really shook me."

Others were not so charitable: the day after the TV reconstruction, former Eastbourne mayor and Tory councillor Una Gardner, known as "Goldie", caused outrage with an attack on the victims' parents.

She said during an East Sussex Education Committee meeting: "It was the responsibility of the parents. Why weren't they with the two children? As a mother, I would blame myself."

The *Argus* was not slow in seeking Barrie's predictably robust response.

"How the bloody hell could she say such a thing? She says I made my daughter go out and get murdered, that I forced her to go with that bloke and get strangled, is that it?

"I'm disgusted. I feel sorry for the lady if that's what she thinks. Ask this woman to come round and see me. I'll tell her a thing or two."

Gardner was disowned by her Tory colleagues but the comments stung – doubly so when spiteful and anonymous graffiti, mostly targeting Barrie, sprang up around Newick Road.

In fact, the parents were privately blaming themselves, however unfairly, because that is what grieving parents do.

But this ignorant criticism was nothing more than the kicking of someone already brought to their knees by grief.

Dave Barnard, chairman of the East Moulsecoomb Residents

Association, spoke for many not only in his sympathy for the parents but also of the wider issues of how the Gardner attack mirrored the way the estate had been treated for decades.

"Mrs Gardner has voiced the attitude that the county council has expressed by its deeds over the years," he said.

"She has voiced its lack of concern and thoughtlessness. For many years it has ignored the cries of the people of Moulsecoomb."

Within two days, Gardner had resigned as chairman (as they were called in those days) of the county council's further education subcommittee, claiming her words had been "misinterpreted", and she had not wished to add to the parents' sorrow.

Susan, now back in Brighton and in her first public comment for a week, said: "She doesn't even know me. Let her come here and see for herself. I'll tell her face to face what I think of her."

Barrie, clutching Nicola's favourite teddy, added, "We loved Nicky. Let Mrs Gardner come here and I'll tell her how much we loved her."

A week later, Gardner, who took her nickname from World War I veteran and land-speed champion Lt Col. Goldie Gardner, was back in print, apparently completely unrepentant.

"I feel rather like Prince Philip," she said.

"Looking back, what I said was politically unwise. It's all right to think these things. There are many people who think as I do. But the mistake I made was to say them out loud.

"This really is just a one-minute wonder. It will all be forgotten soon. I am sure Eastbourne is one hundred per cent behind me on this one."

The Gardner episode reinforced the feeling in Moulsecoomb that the murders were being treated as a class issue, us and them.

The residents were on the outside with the Conservative run county council and the Labour controllers of Brighton Council rushing to be seen to be ordering reports and freeing funds for Moulsecoomb solely to gain political advantage.

Those reports would end up gathering dust somewhere but when resources were provided, they were as welcome as they were long overdue.

But why did it take two dead children for the cash to be stumped up for one of the poorest areas of Brighton?

Reflecting many years later on that troubled time, Susan's eyes still flash and she has lost none of her righteous anger.

"What she said was terrible. I never sent my children shopping for me. She was out of order," she said.

"Nigel calls her a motormouth. How could she say that? She never knew my daughter and she didn't know me from Adam but I was getting the blame for everything. It's like saying I had deliberately let my daughter out to get what happened to her.

"There are some horrible people out there still even now, saying that Barrie had done it."

For Barrie, the stigma was far, far worse.

For more than thirty years, there were people who did not just accuse him of being indirectly responsible for the murders – he was actually thought to be the killer. And the problem was he did nothing to make people feel more sympathy for him.

Brighton was awash with stories and rumours of Barrie publicly bragging that his murdered daughter meant he would never have to buy a drink in the Hiker's Rest pub ever again.

There is even one of Barrie filling a supermarket basket full of beer and heading to the checkout to demand "Don't you know who I am?", expecting to have it for free. The manager was said to have been called and eventually agreed to write it off.

Three of the most experienced reporters in Brighton, who never thought for a second he could have been the killer, all saw how the suspicion, even hatred, built up.

Jim Hatley: "Barrie was hated on the estate. Long haired, beer belly hanging over his belt. He looked like a slob. What did it for many people was his refusal to join the hunt for the girls until he had finished his tea. That was a seriously wrong decision that set people asking what sort of a father would do that? A guilty one?"

Phil Mills: "Barrie was just not liked. He seemed to revel in a certain celebrity status. He honesty thought he was entitled. We all heard about the Hiker's Rest stories. Also he was supposed to have wanted free cab rides."

Shan Lancaster: "You could sense that everybody wanted it [the killer] to be Barrie Fellows."

Today, Barrie shrugs in a wry acknowledgement of his youthful stupidity, how people can't be stopped from thinking what they like and that the past is best forgotten.

"I know how it started but it never happened that way. I used to shop in the same shop, a deli, getting the same things like a ham I liked week after week. So, one time, I said, 'You know me, give me what I want.' Somebody must have overheard that and took it the wrong way, out of context, but I have always paid my way."

Susan is not so sure: "He used to go into supermarkets and say, 'This has happened and I'm the father.'

"I got that from my friends, not the papers, I was embarrassed. I have never begged for food or anything. I was well brought up.

"Barrie would deny it when I said, 'What's this about you got into shops and begging for food?'

"I used to do the shopping with my mum, not him. He did odd jobs."

Susan believes the Hiker's Rest story is more unlikely because Barrie was not allowed to drink when taking his epilepsy tablets.

"The only time he went into an off license was to get coke or crisps for the kids. He didn't drink," she said.

Barrie knows that's not quite true. "It [the rumours] was orchestrated by the Bishop family. I once took a pillowcase full of coke cans to the Hikers Rest to fucking do them. I was a drinker, I was a darts player so I was a drinker, the epilepsy never curtailed my drinking."

But far worse allegations about Barrie were made to the police in the days and weeks after the murders.

Typical of these was a woman called Daphne Skipper, who made a statement on 16 October.

As revealed in court, she told officers: "I would say Barrie Fellows is a very violent man... I know from what I have seen and been told he has beaten both his children.

"I would say that he is a dirty old man who put his hand up women's skirts in the pub and he had interfered with Nicola in the past and was dealt with and convicted."

Likewise, a woman named in court only as Mrs P, said in a police statement, "Over the last few weeks since the murders, I have heard several rumours in connection with Barrie Fellows that he had sexually assaulted Nicola."

All this is nothing more than a staggering mix of innuendo, hearsay, distortion and gross inaccuracy, not least the non-existent conviction for abusing Nicola.

It was typical of the febrile and entirely unjustified anti-Barrie atmosphere that existed on the estate.

But while Barrie was personally unpopular, the sympathy for the parents' loss was unabated.

An appeal fund sprung up spontaneously, initially for information leading to arrest, then later for the families and a memorial.

The money was raised by local businesses, but mostly Brighton residents and often by boxes in pubs. Two donations stand out. Builders pulled a truck around Brighton and raised £4,000 and £160 was sent in from inmates of Ford open prison.

In all, around £7,000 was raised, which went towards the cost of a memorial, a donation to a children's hospital and a small amount on expenses.

In a move that did nothing for Barrie's popularity, he told the *Argus* that the money would be spent on new clothes and floral tributes to the two girls but, in an unguarded moment he would regret, added that the family hoped for "a getaway from it all" holiday in the US.

This provoked a backlash from the Hadaways in a front-page splash in *Argus* the following day, which perhaps was the dawn of tension between the two families.

Under the headline, HADAWAYS REFUSE APPEAL FUND MONEY, chief reporter Jon Buss wrote that Michelle and Lee wanted all the money to go towards a memorial or playground.

Michelle said: "We don't want any of the money. We would like to see it go towards a community centre or somewhere he kids can play.

"You can't keep kids indoors. You can't even keep them in the garden, they need somewhere were they can go.

"They tried to give us some money but we said we didn't want it. People have been wonderful, absolutely wonderful, and we have no wish to offend them. But there is no way we want to benefit from our daughter's death.

"Sometimes I think it would be nice to get away for a holiday but it wouldn't be a holiday if Karen wasn't there."

The Hadaways also spoke of their plans to leave Brighton and be closer to relatives in Surrey.

"People in Moulsecoomb and in the whole of Brighton have just been so kind," she said.

"The police are doing everything that they can. But we know we can't stay here without Karen. The house isn't a home to us without her.

"People here go short of things because they are poor but the kids never go short of love. But without my Karen this house is an empty shell. We have got to try and start again for the sake of our two other children and the one on the way.

"Our grief is very great but it is private. Our children are our life but we want to thank people for the wonderful, wonderful cards and letters they have sent from all corners of the world."

Michelle and her family would set up home in Surrey. She never lived in Brighton again.

CHAPTER 6

PRIME SUSPECT

So while the Fellows and Hadaways were suffering, what had Russell Bishop been up to?

The first time the police knocked on his door had been at 2.30 a.m. on 10 October, the night the girls had disappeared.

Jennie Johnson answered and took officers to the bedroom at 17 Stephens Road, where her man was in bed.

At this stage, he was just a potential witness in the inquiry. He told them he had seen the girls playing in trees in Wild Park around 5.15 p.m. when he was talking to the park keeper.

Officers left after telling Bishop he would have to make a full statement later that day.

How Bishop must have loved that. Not only had the police arrived and not suspected what he had done, but they had made it clear he had a dramatic role in being one of the last to see them alive.

At 10 a.m., they returned to take that statement (Bishop was still in bed) and he told the officers about his visit to 26 Newick

Road to try to see Dougie Judd and his meeting with the park keeper two hours later. Afterwards he had crossed the Lewes Road to buy an *Argus* but found he didn't have enough money so had walked home. He didn't know what time he had got in and Johnson had been out at work.

That excited Bishop's sense of importance even more and he headed out to Wild Park hoping, no doubt, to give himself an even bigger role in the search and keep an eye on police activity.

After the bodies were discovered that afternoon, Bishop could not wait to talk about his new double role – first as one of the last to see the girls alive and now as one of the first to find them dead.

He told his fishing friend Geoffrey Caswell he had seen the bodies and they didn't seem badly injured. He appeared "grief stricken" and said he would never forget feeling for their pulse.

Later, he told another friend Michael Evans the opposite, that he wasn't bothered about the discovery but described exactly how they were lying across each other and that one had blood in the corner of her mouth. How did he know?

Police turned up again at Stephens Road at 7 p.m. and Johnson directed them to the Hiker's Rest, where they found Bishop and took him to Brighton police station for a second witness statement – and one that would take four hours to complete.

He repeated his story of the girls in the trees, the park keeper, the failed trip to the newsagent's and described his route home walking past Moulsecoomb library and the railway station. This was important because it took past the spot where the Pinto sweatshirt had been discovered although neither the police nor Bishop realised the significance of that yet.

He said he had got home when it was still light and stayed in alone that night doing his washing before Johnson came home. He said he had had no callers or anyone who had seen him there.

Asked about the discovery of the bodies, Bishop said he had been talking with PC Smith and heard a shout: "We've found them!" He raced over to the scene, saw the bodies huddled together and blood covered foam on Nicola's lips. He said he checked the pulse on each girl's neck and they were cold and stiff.

As he was driven home, Bishop told the officer driving, as he had PC Smith the previous day, that he feared he was the number one suspect. He was told that an alibi or someone who had see him that evening would help him "no end" to clear up any misunderstanding.

It was advice innocently offered, but Bishop took it very much to heart.

In fact, Bishop was already on a long list of suspects drawn up by the murder squad. Initial inquiries were clear that this was not a stranger abduction and that the girls had gone with someone they knew because there were no defence injuries on the bodies.

Obvious suspects would include Rowland and Marchant – only because they had found the bodies – and Barrie Fellows, because of his confused account of his journey home from work and his erratic behaviour before and since, and Bishop.

One possible suspect who was ruled out and released without charge was the convicted paedophile Ernie Pullen. Pullen had been convicted of creating and possessing child pornography and sentenced to two years' imprisonment. On 13 October, police raided his home in Barcombe Road and arrested him when they found cannabis but nothing linked him with the investigation.

Soon Bishop's obvious lies and inconsistencies, compared with the accounts of Rowland, Marchant and Smith, were to place him on a short list of one.

On 12 October, two days after the second statement and the alibi conversation, officers went to Bishop's parents' home in Coldean Lane, on an entirely different matter, asking to speak to Ted Dawes whom they believed was a relative.

Bishop was there and told them Dawes was his uncle, adding, "He is a bit of a wild man who lived in the woods out there [Stamner Woods]. Time means nothing to him, he comes and goes. He is my alibi! He will clear my name."

The officers, who at that point had no idea that Bishop was linked to the murdered girls, were bemused and went back to report what they had been told.

Three days after that, Bishop was brought in again to give a third witness statement. Asked why he had washed his clothes after getting home on the night the girls disappeared, he said, for the first time, that he had fallen in dog mess. After that he had a bath and sat in his dressing gown until Johnson came home with their son Victor between 8 and 8.30 p.m.

Turning to the bodies, Bishop, extraordinarily, changed his story again. This time he denied he had got into the den where they had been found and insisted he had not felt for a pulse.

Amazed, the officers showed him his previous statement – which he had signed as accurate – stating the exact opposite. Bishop claimed he had not realised that and it had been a mistake.

Asked how such a mistake could have happened, Bishop

turned turtle again and said he had felt for a pulse and claimed his previous denial was down to the fact that the policeman at the scene [Smith] had told him not to touch them.

Now clearly agitated, Bishop said, again, that he had not touched the bodies and that he had said that he had solely to make himself feel important. At the end of the interview, he again agreed that the statement produced was accurate.

Meanwhile, Bishop was loving the limelight and strutting around Moulsecoomb flush with self-importance.

Martyn Palmer was a reporter on *Today*, famous then for being Britain's first colour daily newspaper. He had worked on the *Argus* and knew Brighton well.

Speaking now, he remembered, "The week after the murders, probably 14 October, the police invited the big press contingent into its incident room to show how hard they were working on the inquiry. It was a PR job for Sussex Police but useful for them keeping us onside and the story strong in the papers.

"My colleague Russell Jenkins came out and rang me to say he had seen the name Russell Bishop on two pieces of paper. This was the first time we had heard of that name, so we set out to look for him in Moulsecoomb, knocking on doors. It didn't take long.

"At first, he refused to talk to us but, as days went by, police were privately telling us off the record, 'We really like him [as a suspect].'

"We had to get him to talk before he was nicked. Then we had a heads up he was going to be pulled in within the next twenty-four hours [for a further witness statement], so we had to act fast.

"Finally, he cracked and we met him at the home of Marion

Stevenson and her parents were present. The father said, 'We were wondering if there was any payment.'

"Of course we didn't have any money and we were under strict instructions not to offer him any, but we kept him talking."

At that time, *Today* was still owned by Eddie Shah and so was broke. Later, Shah sold the paper to Rupert Murdoch.

Palmer continued: "I remember Bishop was very monosyllabic, it was all about being stitched up by the police and he would not say much about his alibi.

"Photographer Steve Burton was pushing about getting a photo at the scene and eventually we drove up there with Bishop and Burton took pictures of him at the memorial next to the flowers placed there in memory of the girls. He was just looking sad and genuflecting.

"It produced a great front-page picture, but I remember being terrified that one of the families would see us, as they would justifiably be very angry. It was tough trying to do your job on that estate. Reporters were being spat at.

"But it was the first interview he ever did and from that moment I had no doubt whatsoever that he had killed those girls. Nobody professionally involved in that case had any doubt either."

Jenkins described Bishop as "an unbelievably selfish, unpleasant young man".

He added, "The cops seemed to be running out of ideas and to keep us interested they invited us in.

"I saw an in tray at a desk with an important looking copper and in it there was a paper describing Russell Bishop as a man of great in interest as a number of people had rung in saying that police should look at him.

"Martyn and I approached Bishop through Marion Stevenson. He was a man boy, he looked inadequate, a human slug. What was Stevenson, a pretty young girl, with such a man?

"He was taciturn except when denying he had anything to do with the murders.

"I had the feeling that Bishop wanted money but what he wanted more was being the centre of attention. He loved feeling that he was needed. He posed for pictures on the day of the TV reconstruction."

*

On 31 October, Bishop was officially moved from the status of witness to potential killer and arrested.

The breakthrough came when the police finally realising that they had the key to the whole inquiry, the item containing the treasure trove of evidence, which had been sitting in a storage room in John Street police station for the past three weeks.

That was the blue Pinto sweatshirt first discovered, as already described, on grass near Moulsecoomb railway station by the CB radio enthusiasts in the early hours of 10 October.

It was long-sleeved, round-necked and had a 40-inch chest measurement (Bishop was a 34). The logo was white writing on the blue background on the left of the chest and it had red staining on the chest and right cuff.

The searchers had left it on railings by the station after being told that night by the police that it wasn't what the girls had been wearing when they had disappeared.

At 3.30 p.m. on 11 October, it was picked up by Robert Garner, an Electricity Board engineer, who found it close to where it had been discarded. This was fifty minutes or so before the bodies were to be discovered.

Gander handed it in to the police at the Lewes Road police box, where the major incident post had been set up and PC Dave Edwards put it in brown paper bag and handed to Inspector Chris Verrion.

In the excitement of the bodies being found at the other end of Wild Park from the police box (and the movement of the major incident post to that location), the bag was almost forgotten but Verrion placed it in the back of his car and took it to John Street police station, where it was placed in an Exhibits store.

To be fair, at the time the police were looking for the clothing of two young girls. They were not so interested in a man's sweatshirt discarded a long way from the search area.

Initially, it was treated as a bit of lost property but, on 15 October, Scenes of Crime officer Eddie Redman noticed the red marks on the sleeve and carried out preliminary blood tests on the stains, which produced a slight positive reaction. In fact, later, more sophisticated tests found no blood.

Despite that initial result it was not until the end of the month that Redman realised the Pinto's potential importance in relation to Bishop and it was sent off to the forensic laboratory, where the microscopic links to Bishop and the dead girls were found by the scientific techniques available at that time.

However, those three weeks and the number of hands it had passed through and the potential for contamination considering its random storage and the fact it was not in a sealed bag but in one only folded over twice at the top, opened up a field day of possibilities for an able defence team to discredit these links in court.

At 8.20 a.m. on 31 October, the police knocked on Bishop's door again and took him to John Street for another interview. While he was away, DS Phil Swann and DC David Wilkinson returned to Stephens Road at 10.30 a.m. and showed Johnson the bag containing the Pinto. According to her signed statement, she confirmed Bishop had a top just like it with a logo beginning with a P and some red paint on one of its sleeves.

The officers' statements record her as saying, "Oh, I see you've brought Russell's sweatshirt back."

Armed with this apparently damning evidence, Swann and Wilkinson returned to the police station, where Bishop was being questioned by DC Barry Evans and PC Dave Edwards. Referring to his alleged alibi, he said that his uncle, Ted Dawes, had seen him on a bus at 5.45 p.m. but added that Dawes was now in America.

At 11.30 a.m., Bishop was arrested on suspicion of murder and responded, "No, no, it's not me, fuck off, leave it out." He was then interviewed for more than fifty hours over three days before being released on police bail.

These interviews were to produce yet new versions from Bishop of what he had been up to on the afternoon of the girls' disappearance.

Bishop claimed he had wanted to smoke some cannabis that he had bought off a dealer called Angie in Ringmer Road, on the Moulsecoomb estate. The dealer he referred to was Angie Cutter, who lived in Newick Road and she denied having seen him that day.

He then said that he had lied about trying to buy a paper (the newsagent had already told police that he knew Bishop and he had not been in his shop that day), that he had smoked the drugs in the public toilets near the police box on Lewes Road and then gone home.

Asked why he had not kept his agreed date with Marion Stevenson at 6 p.m. – she had given him an easily disproved false alibi by telling the police they were together thereby opening herself up to a charge of perverting the course of justice – Bishop replied that he had wanted to be alone.

He then claimed that he had lied about feeling for a pulse on the dead girls and that he had seen blood on Nicola's mouth. He said that had only got within eight feet of the bodies and had guessed about the blood.

The news that an arrest had been made was a relief to the families and the identity of the suspect was not a surprise.

Said Susan: "When he was arrested and was being questioned, the police came and told us, 'We've got him [meaning the killer].' I said to Barrie, 'If it's not him, who is it?'

"We knew it could not have been a stranger, it had to be somebody that the girls knew. I had never liked the look of him, he was very fishy, it was the way he was acting, going on with Jennie Johnson and Marion Stevenson and all. Nicky liked Jennie and didn't like Marion.

"It was his suspicious behaviour, I thought he was up to no good."

Nigel added: "We knew that Bishop knew that Stevenson was friends with Ernie Pullen and that he wanted to be more than friends with her."

On 21 November, three weeks after being bailed, Bishop decided he needed to speak to Barrie Fellows and headed off to 26 Newick Road to see him. Barrie, half astonished and half furious, allowed him to speak outside his front door.

Said Barrie: "At about 3 p.m., I was at home with Sue and Edna when Bishop called at my door. He was alone and he said to me, 'I have come to cleanse the air.' I said to him, 'You have got some fucking gall, haven't you? You are standing there and I'm going to call the police.'

"I went to Linda Green's house at Number 49 to tell the police he was at my house and I wanted to seek some advice.

"On the way back, I saw Bishop learning against a bush and he walked towards me and I said, 'I will hear you out.'

"He denied killing my daughter, and added, 'They came up my flat, they took all my clothing, all Jennie's clothing, carpets, Lino and washing machine. I have got a conference with the press and they will be paying me and I'm going to spend all the money on myself.'

"He then changed his story and said he would put the money into some charity for children. I said that if he wanted to do something useful why didn't he pay it into the relief fund?

"He said, 'I'm going to see Lee and Michelle.' I advised him not to because Lee might hit him.

"At some stage during the conversation, he said he had been 'cleared from the murders'. I said to him, 'What were you actually doing that Thursday evening? Did you see Nicky or Karen?' He replied something to the effect of, 'I saw them at half-past five and the park keeper was somewhere near and then I went to Angie's and bought some dope.'

"He went on to say to me, 'An insurance man and woman had called at my flat at six thirty that evening and saw me at home.' (This was the first sign of the false alibis that Bishop hoped would help his case 'no end'.)

"I asked how Jennie was because I was concerned about

her. He said she had been in hospital but not had the baby yet. He said he was not the only one that the police had had down the police station for fifty-one hours and there had been three others."

Susan remembers: "When he was released and came round to our house, Barrie pushed me into the kitchen and didn't want me near him and spoke to him outside."

"Later, Barrie told me, 'Bishop said to me, "I didn't top the kids." 'What a way to put it. He didn't ask how I felt. He was always cold, he never came across warm or caring. He was very selfish.'"

The day after his visit to Barrie, Bishop called the police to claim his house had been burgled. When the uniformed officers arrived Bishop, out of the blue, produced a blue sweatshirt from behind a cushion, and said, "I'm guarding this with my life, I don't want CID getting their hands on it. I'm sorry but this jumper proves my innocence. This is the jumper with the red paint on that the murder squad say they have. I can prove this is the one."

As they were leaving, he added, "Will you tell the murder squad that I can prove that I was at home at six thirty that night? I have some insurance men who will testify to that, so their witnesses couldn't have seen me at the Wild Park."

The Bishops had been making payments into two insurance policies at that time. The two men who collected the payments, Sidney Giles of the Reliance Mutual Assurance Company, and Andrew Longford of the Britannia Assurance Company, both denied ever visiting or seeing Bishop on that evening.

Three weeks later, on 3 December and with the results on

the Pinto safely back from the forensic lab, Bishop was formally charged with the double murder. He replied, "I'm not guilty."

Looking back, Barrie said was shaken when he heard the news. "When I heard Bishop had been taken in for questioning I thought it can't be him? why would it be him? He comes to the house all the time, I played football with him on Sundays, you don't think that of someone you know."

Said Michelle: "It didn't seem real. You never think that somebody you actually know would come along and do such a terrible thing."

Bishop made his first appearance at Hove Magistrates Court on the following day, when he was remanded into custody. Crowds waited outside in the rain as he was brought in and out of the building by a prison van.

At a later hearing, the prosecution stated its reasons for objecting to bail, which included the threat of possible interference by Bishop with witnesses. He responded from the dock, "There ain't no witnesses."

In Brixton Prison, Bishop feared his food was being spiked with broken glass by fellow prisoners, his concern fuelled by the well-known aversion by fellow inmates to "nonces". He lived off fresh fruit, nuts and chocolates brought in by family on visits.

*

On Boxing Day, while he was inside, Johnson gives birth to their second child, Hayley.

By this time, Bishop was being represented by Ralph Haeems, head of Sampson and Co., Solicitors, with offices in Peckham and Reigate, and known as one of the leading criminal defence solicitors in the country.

Haeems was a surprise choice as he was known as a South London operator rather than a local man. But however he came to represent Bishop he was the perfect pick.

He had an unconventional background for a lawyer with an engineering degree, had studied for a Masters in chemistry and was a one-time parrot-breeder.

He was small, dark-haired, which was sometimes worn in a strange quiff, had a slight stammer but was a hugely successful harrier of the Establishment and a Trojan worker.

He acted for the three Kray brothers, Ronnie, Reggie and Charlie, winning acquittals in the notorious Hideaway blackmail case and the murder of Frank Mitchell, the Mad Axeman. In two other notorious trials, he had acted successfully for George Ince in the Braintree barn murder and Terence Patch in connection with the £26 million Brink's Mat robbery.

Haeems also represented serial killer Dennis Nielsen and the transvestite gunman David Martin.

Argus reporter Jim Hatley went to see Ralph Haeems over the Christmas period at his London office and found he was "very flash, clearly well off and had a very impressive office".

Haeems's first priority was to deal with the Johnson statement on the Pinto. She was to retract it in an affidavit taken in his office. He then had to decide when to disclose this bombshell development to the unsuspecting prosecution.

His mastery of tactics was allied to a skilful manipulation of the local media by providing a stream of red herrings and appeals for mystery alleged witnesses who could prove Bishop's innocence if they could only be traced.

Among these was a woman called Christine, a man called Dave and a mysterious CB-related caller dubbed Whispering

Willie. They all made good headlines even though, of course, they all remained either untraced or irrelevant.

The final hurdle before trial was the committal hearing early in 1987 and it was an "old-fashioned one". Nowadays, the prosecution gives a brief outline of the case and the district judge (formerly called a stipendiary) would send it through on the nod.

In the eighties, there was an option of an "old-fashioned" committal, in which the Crown has to call all its evidence and allow its witnesses to be cross-examined before the magistrate makes a decision on whether there is a sufficient case for the defendant to answer.

Importantly, the defence doesn't have to reveal its hand by calling any witnesses itself but can have a dress rehearsal of how the prosecution witnesses will react under fire.

There was small number of people outside Hove Magistrates Court to jeer Bishop's arrival from prison and for a week Charles Conway, defending, forensically picked away at a succession of policemen and expert witnesses exposing gaping holes in the evidence.

However, the case was sent for trial. The decision was not unexpected. It would have taken a brave magistrate to have released the man accused of one of the most shocking murder of the eighties, regardless of the paucity of the case against him.

Bishop was told he would stand trial by jury and was led, head bowed in disappointment, back to the cells.

Within a few weeks, one man was mentally rubbing his hands with glee at his desk in the heart of the Temple, the bastion of London's legal establishment close to where Fleet Street ends and the Strand begins.

Ivan Lawrence, QC, MP (later to become Sir Ivan), had been briefed by Haeems to lead the defence and as he read the case papers and, in particular, Conway's masterful dissection of the prosecution witnesses, he knew he was "on a winner".

Meanwhile, the Fellows and the Hadaways had two daughters to bury.

*

It was a silent, misty February morning in 1987 when the white coffins bearing the two girls set off on their final journey from Moulsecoomb to St Andrews Church, Hillside, and, finally, the children's plot in the Bear Road Cemetery.

It had taken four months for the coroner to tie up the red tape surrounding the murder, conclude the needs of the police and release the bodies.

Four months for the two families to recover from their violent loss and then to relive the whole trauma for a second time.

The church was filled with around 250 mourners with 100 gathering around the graveside, yet surprisingly Susan's memory is that it wasn't full.

Nicola's coffin was carried by Barrie and his brothers and Lee was one of four pall bearers for his daughter.

There were flowers in the shape of a Care Bear, a My Little Pony for Nicola and Cabbage Patch doll for Karen. Her brother Darren held a flower-filled basket containing a teddy bear.

Father Marcus Ronchetti lit candles on the altar as symbols of light and life and said the girls, although "not by any stretch of the imagination angels", had still been "gifts from God".

"Their young innocent lives were not corrupted by the wicked thoughts of the world," he told the congregation.

They had been snatched away for reasons "beyond our belief", which he could not begin to explain.

Michelle was led away in tears halfway through the service by Lee, and she was comforted in the arms of her police liaison officer PC Wendy King.

Susan was unable to stand during the service and just sat in her pew weeping.

The final hymn was "All Things Bright and Beautiful", during which Susan broke down, wailing, "*Oh, my baby, oh, my baby.*"

At the end of the service, she clung to Barrie's arm.

She has few memories now, or few that she would like to share when she has spent thirty years trying to mask the pain.

"All I remember was wanting to be with Nicky in the grave. I pulled at Barrie but he wanted to talk to some friends," she says now.

Barrie's memories thirty-plus years on, are similarly brief and bitter.

"It was supposed to be a private ceremony at the graveside but it wasn't very private with the press hanging over the wall taking photos. That was not very nice. It was like a paparazzi parade, it could not be private at all," he said.

"I was in absolute pieces. It was all a bit of a blur. I was burying my young child, that's not nice at all. As a parent you expect your children to outlive you. You don't expect to have to bury them."

Outside the church, 130 wreaths and bouquets had been arranged in four rows on the grass. They included the name Karen spelled out in red carnations and Nicky in pink from the two sets of parents.

There were also tributes from Sussex Police, the inmates of Lewes Prison, the two schools the girls had attended and the shops where Nicola and Karen had been last seen.

Two single red roses lay by the separate graves, bearing the messages MY LOVE GO WITH YOU FOR EVER AND EVER and YOU HAVE ONLY GONE TO PLAY. GOD BLESS YOU.

On separate cards, Michelle and Lee had written, "Remembering a wonderful daughter. Now and forever in our hearts. You will always be loved and you will never be forgotten. Your loving mum and dad."

Susan and Barrie wrote, "For Nicky, our very precious daughter. Jesus has you in his care. We have you in our hearts. We will love and miss you always. Sleep well little one."

Their son Jonathan's note read, "To my darling sister. I love you and miss you very much. Be good with Jesus. Love from John."

Nigel remembers: "There were some flowers from the Bishop family. We had them removed."

Bishop had been arrested, charged and committed for trial at Lewes Crown Court in October 1987. For the families, there was only one thing left to do: wait for justice to be done.

CHAPTER 7

AN "INEXORABLE" LINK

A big trial in Lewes always stops the traffic. Reporters block the pavement outside the crown court and TV cameramen and photographers spill into the High Street angering drivers, while locals stop outside the newsagent's and the White Hart opposite to gawp at the spectacle.

The Portland-brick-built courthouse is an imposing sight beneath the castle in the heart of the town. Designed nearly thirty years before Queen Victoria came to the throne, it was originally intended to be the East Sussex county hall but its rich history of staging some of Britain's most notorious trials belies the size of this small county town.

They range from the conviction, in 1949 and, later, hanging, of John George Haigh, the Acid Bath Murderer, for six murders, although he confessed to nine, Roy Whiting who abducted and killed eight-year-old Sarah Payne from Littlehampton, Hastings, deputy headmaster Sion Jenkins who was convicted, but later retried and freed, of murdering his foster daughter, and Eastbourne schoolteacher Jeremy Forrest who fled to France with his fifteen-year-old pupil lover.

But none of these cases had or were to have the acres of media coverage spread over year after year that Russell Bishop's did.

On 11 November 1987, Michelle and Lee Hadaway, Barrie and Susan Fellows, and Nigel, Ian and Kevin Heffron made their way passed the press scrum, up the stone steps and through security to the corridors around Court One.

With so much pressure and raw emotion flowing around the trial, it's fair to say that the police and court staff were concerned about the potential for trouble between the Bishops – parents Roy and Sylvia and Russell's brothers Alec, David, Andrew and Michael – and the victims' families.

Rightly or wrongly, it was decided to segregate the two sides, with the Bishops in seating to the side of the dock and the victim's upstairs, in what looked more like a minstrels' gallery than a dress circle, on three sides of the court.

This is the reverse of the thinking at most courts, notably the Old Bailey, which prioritises the victim's families with the best seats in the well of the court closest to the action, while the defendants families have the seats further away.

But Court One at Lewes has a peculiar old-fashioned layout far from the security-conscious design of modern courthouses with their floor-to-ceiling reinforced glass.

Here, the dock is open and in the centre of the public gallery behind the counsel benches. The public can sit within feet of the defendant and even rest their arms on the tiny ornate tops of the dock sides.

Trouble has occurred in that courtroom because of the open design. Sion Jenkins, who had earlier been attacked outside the court, took private security guards into the dock with him for protection, and the father of Lyn Rogers aimed a haymaker over the dock rail at her killer Wayne Singleton as he was led to the cells after conviction.

In this case, the police were later taken by surprise when trouble erupted on verdict not from the Fellows or the Hadaways but from the Bishops alone.

That's not to say words were not exchanged by the victims' families in the concourse outside the court.

Said Nigel: "During the trial, I heard that some of the Bishops were calling some of my family dogs. I went straight over to them and said that if they didn't want a war between our two families they should watch their mouths.

"I said I have no problem with any of their family, only one member of it. Nothing more happened."

Taking their seats on the first morning of the trial, the Fellows and Hadaways found they were directly above the jury box with the judge, Mr Justice Schiemann, to their left and Russell Bishop in the dock to their right.

Fed by the blithely sunny approach of the police, the families were at this point optimistic about a guilty verdict. Down in the press box in the well of the court, Jim Hatley, of the *Argus*, however, knew better.

He had attended the committal hearing when the prosecution had outlined its case to magistrates and knew the paucity of the evidence.

Jim bet £10 with Tom Merrin of the *Daily Mirror* that Bishop would walk free. "That was a considerable amount out of my weekly pay, but that's how certain I was," he said.

"I thought it would be thrown out at the committal stage

and not even go before a jury. There was just no evidence. I was not convinced Bishop was innocent but I knew he was not going to get convicted."

The case was opened to the jury in the dry tones of prosecutor Brian Leary, QC, with a promise that the forensic evidence would prove an "inexorable link" between Russell Bishop and the murders.

It was a statement the Crown would never come close to fulfilling and one that, within a month, would haunt the police, the Forensic Science Service (FSS) and the Crown Prosecution Service (CPS).

Opinion in the robing rooms around the country is divided on Leary, who took the classic line to the Bar of public school, in his case King's College, Canterbury, and Oxford. There were those who admired his grit in helping to being down notorious crime rings in East and South London and, to be fair, he was once dubbed Gangbuster. There are others who refer to him only as Dreary Leary for his lack of advocacy skills.

In 1971, he had prosecuted the sensational Oz obscenity trial, in which magazine publishers were charged with "conspiracy to corrupt morals", and was described by Jonathan Dimbleby as "slim, dapper, sharp featured, his voice well trained in the arts of moral outrage and silky sarcasm".

In a stage re-enactment of the Oz case, Leary was played by the suave actor Julian Glover.

His opponent was the patrician, even Edwardian, figure of Ivan Lawrence, QC. Born in Brighton, Lawrence was a Conservative MP on the right wing of the party who held a Midlands seat from 1974 until defeat in the Blair landslide of 1997.

His Establishment bearing hid his rat-like cunning, much admired at the Bar, and vast experience of more than eighty-five murder trials by the time of his retirement, including that of the Kray twins and also that of serial killer Donald Nielsen, who had murdered fifteen young men in the early eighties.

Lawrence, who also happened to be the cousin of singer Alma Colgan, was supported by Conway, a dogged fighter who had shown at the committal his relish for down and dirty legal combat. They made a formidable pairing.

Leary outlined the events of thirteen months ago. How the two girls had returned home from school and gone to play. They had been seen swinging in some trees by a park keeper in Wild Park.

When they failed to come home, their mothers started to look, calling out their names in growing desperation as the light faded.

The police launched a massive search before the bodies were found at 4.15 p.m. the following day, lying in a little hollow in trees behind the pavilion.

Bishop had been talking to a nearby police officer and been actively involved in the search.

The jury was shown photos of the girls huddled together, defiled, their clothes torn away, dirt and debris around their faces but no sign of a struggle.

Said Leary: "Both girls went there not with a stranger but with somebody they knew and trusted.

"They were taken there and it was there that an attempt to sexually assault one was made. It's there that they died and where a further sexual assault was probably made."

Fatally, Leary pinpointed the time of the murders as being

between around 5.15 and 6.30 p.m. (doing so because witnesses had seen Bishop heading towards the exit of the park, towards his home, around 6.30 p.m., but that ignored evidence from other important witnesses, including the Crown's own pathologist).

The QC went on to explain how a blue Pinto sweatshirt had been found on what would have the route Bishop had taken from the murders to his home, although the defendant denied every owning the garment.

"The Crown suggests the sweatshirt can be connected with this man and can further be connected with the two girls," said Leary.

"Forensic scientists found fibres from the blue sweatshirt on the shirts worn by the two girls and a large number of tiny ivy hairs on all three garments."

Leary explained that such ivy had covered the hollow where the girls were found. He then stated that the Pinto was found to bear eighteen hairs that could have come from Bishop's head, fibres from the girls' sweatshirts and red-paint stains matching paint on cars Bishop had worked on.

Leary then turned to the hours of interviews Bishop had been subjected to at Brighton police station.

He said that Bishop had originally claimed that at the time the girls went missing, he had been trying to steal a car from Sussex University car park before heading home, stopping to talk to the park keeper and later bought some cannabis.

But in other statements, he said he had been to buy a newspaper at a shop in Barcombe Road, Moulsecoomb, but found he had no money.

At first, he told detectives he had seen the two girls lying in a clearing in undergrowth, had checked for a pulse and seen blood flecks on their lips.

But later, he withdrew that statement saying he had merely been bigging himself up. He said he had gone home, cooked a meal and washed his clothing because he had fallen in dog mess.

Said Leary: "Because of the inconsistencies we suggest his account of his movements is not to be believed.

"We suggest the descriptions of the girls' bodies and their faces contained details that could only have been known by someone who was much closer that the accused at the time their bodies were found."

After the first day's hearing, a woman juror fell ill and the judge decided to discharge the jury, swear in a new panel and start the trial again.

Finishing his opening speech for a second time, Leary called the first witness, Susan Fellows

Through her tears, she told how her daughter had come home from school and gone off to see her friend.

"Karen and Nicky came across the road towards my house but they didn't come in."

Leary: "Did you ever see Nicky again?"

Susan: "No."

She described how the two mothers had gone looking for the girls before returning home in darkness at 7.20 p.m. but had gone out looking again later.

Barrie Fellows was called and told the court he had been working in Hove with Judd on the afternoon his daughter disappeared. They had waited for a bus, dropped in on Judd's sister in Moulsecoomb Way and got home at 7 p.m.

He was told by his mother-in-law Edna that Nicola was

missing but said he was not too worried until 8 p.m. because she had gone missing before.

Leary: "Why didn't you go looking for the girls straight away?"

Barrie: "I don't know."

Leary: "Have you ever been a suspect?"

Barrie: "A lot of people were suspects and I suppose I was."

Lawrence rose slowly to his feet, cast his eye over some papers and leaned forward on his lectern – all old defence tricks to rack up the tension in court, prepare the jury for what he wants them to believe to be an important part of the case and increase the nerves in the witness.

"I want to be perfectly open with you," he eventually started. "There is no evidence of a positive kind you had any part in the death of this child. Do you understand that?"

Barrie: "Yes."

This was another old trick in setting out the fact that Barrie could not possibly have killed the girls – although the use of the word "positive" dangles before the jury the unstated chance there might be some other form of evidence – and then highlighting all Barrie's bad character traits to suggest he had as much right to be treated as the prime suspect as Bishop.

Lawrence then asked Barrie to confirm his own criminal record, including obtaining property by use of a forged instrument, burglary and receiving stolen goods, his own interest in videos and that he had watched porn videos.

All of which Barrie did, but he was then forced to deny Lawrence's next suggestions that he had shown porn to a ten-year-old boy and had deliberately broken his wife's grandmother's nose.

He also denied Lawrence's questions, insisting Nicola had

never been terrified of him, although he admitted losing his temper with her, including the time he had had to go with her to school when she had been accused of stealing.

It was a chastened and dejected figure who finally left the witness box. Barrie had entered it the grieving father of a murdered child and left it having been made to look by Bishop's lawyers to be a bad, uncaring man with a shady past.

Michele Hadaway was next to give evidence and told how she had warned her daughter to keep away from Bishop and Marion Stevenson believing Karen to be too young to mix with people of their age. She was also wary of the rows that erupted when Jennie Johnson would turn up at the Fellows house when Bishop and Stevenson were there.

On the fateful afternoon, she knew that her daughter had met up with Nicola and it was around teatime that she started looking for the girls with Susan Fellows.

A neighbour's son told them he had seen them at the entrance to Wild Park so the two mothers had set to work in the gloom, walking and calling out the girls' names.

Weeping, Michele recalled how Susan had thought she had heard a voice reply "Mum" but it was a false hope.

The following day, she resumed her search and saw Stevenson and Bishop who asked for an item of Karen's clothing so he could show it to his dog Misty who might be able to track the scent.

That afternoon she sat exhausted on a grass bank in the park when she realised that a sudden burst of police activity indicated something was up.

"Bishop was sitting on the ground. I asked him three times what was going on. The third time he just looked at me and put his hands over his face," she told the jury.

Questioned by Lawrence, Michelle said Karen had never complained about Bishop or Stevenson.

Shown the Pinto sweatshirt, Michelle said she had never seen it before.

*

Perhaps still shaken and shaking from his treatment in the witness box, Barrie stormed out of court when the trial resumed.

Lawrence had just held up a picture of Nicola's dead body in the undergrowth when her father leaped to his feet in the upstairs public gallery and in an angry voice broken by tears mumbled, "No, I can't stand it," and pushed his way out of court.

This was not the last time he was to find it impossible to watch the proceedings silently or contain his emotions. Grieving fathers should be cut some slack when confronted with harrowing pictures of their dead daughter but the other parents sitting alongside managed to control themselves.

Lawrence was showing the photo to Kevin Rowland, who was describing how he had discovered the bodies.

He said he had sent Matthew Marchant for help and when Bishop arrived the defendant had tried to push in for a better view but was told, "Don't go any closer." Rowland was adamant Bishop did not get any closer than fifteen feet from the girls.

Leary then examined Bishop's peculiar comments shortly before the bodies were found. PC Christopher Markham said Bishop had said to him, "I don't want to continue searching I don't want to find to find the girls if they have been messed up."

Continued the officer: "I was a little bit surprised by what he said. I was geared up to find the girls alive."

PC Paul Smith described the odd conversation he had with Bishop when the search was still at its height and the comment "If I found the girls and they were done in, I'd get the blame, I'd get nicked."

After the initial skirmishes, the prosecution came to the real battleground of the case – the Pinto sweatshirt and the forensic evidence it bore and what that did or did not prove.

Seeboard engineer Robert Gander told how he had come across the garment on the footpath near Moulsecoomb railway station and an electricity substation.

He thought it was stained with blood, that was the red paint, and it was sweaty and smelled but was otherwise dry.

He said he handed it in to a uniformed policeman, who "didn't seem very interested in it" and put it in a bag.

Inspector Christopher Verrion told the court he had taken the sweatshirt back to Brighton police station in a paper bag along with two anoraks also handed in. He said he had opened the bag once to take a brief look inside. "It was basically handed in as 'found property'."

Scenes of Crime officer Eddie Redman said he had inspected the Pinto but if he had realised its importance he would never have taken it out of its bag before sending it to the Aldermaston labs for forensic examination. "No one thought it was important at the time," he said.

On such seemingly small decisions hang monumental outcomes and Bishop's defence was set to take maximum advantage of the obvious opportunity to blame contamination.

But first, it was Jennie Johnson and what was to turn out to be a disastrous Friday afternoon prior to an even worse week for the Crown's case.

She had signed a statement the previous October that Bishop had owned a blue
sweatshirt with a brand name beginning with the letter "P" on the chest and red paint on the sleeve that she had had difficulty trying to remove.

The statement had been written in response to her answers to questions put by the two police officers who had gone to her home in Stephens Road after Bishop's arrest.

But what she was to say in the witness box was to horrify the Fellows and Hadaways and lead to one of the key figures in the Crown's case being designated a "hostile witness", that is, someone called by the prosecution but who turns out to be unsympathetic to its case and so would have to be, with the judge's permission, questioned more robustly. A humiliating position for Leary.

She claimed the Pinto was not Bishop's and she had never seen it before. She said the officers had bullied her into signing the document under duress and she would have put her name to anything just "to get shot" of them.

To Leary, she said she had signed it because the officers told her to and she had never realised what it was and that the contents were untrue.

"I just signed it where they wanted me to. The way they were treating me, you'd have done the same," she said.

"I was eight months pregnant [with their third child], I'd been up all night and they were like animals to me. They told me, 'If you say it's Russell Bishop's then you won't get accused of the murders. They were accusing me of being in on the murders."

To Lawrence, she told a slightly different version. She said that when they showed her the Pinto sweatshirt, she thought it was his blue jumper because of her bad eyesight.

She said she had signed the statement because she had been in a rage with Bishop. She knew it would have landed him in trouble but signed because the police had told her to.

She also said that one of the officers told her that Bishop was still carrying on with Stevenson despite the fact he had promised her never to see her again.

Johnson told how in the past she and Bishop had rowed over his affair and the police had had to be called. She had once locked him out of their home and he had kicked the door in.

She agreed with Lawrence's gentle suggestion that although she had been called as a prosecution witness she had not given the evidence they had been expecting.

The judge intervened to ask Johnson to clarify why she had ended up signing the statement. She replied: "I didn't do it to get him into trouble. I would have signed anything just to get shot of the policemen."

Clearly, Johnson was a woman capable of producing a variety of different responses and was hardly likely to want to see the father of her children put away for life, but this was a serious blow to the prosecution in the eyes of the jury and threw all the pressure on the forensic evidence to prove conclusively the link between the Pinto sweatshirt and Bishop. A burden it could not possibly bear.

It also felt like a devastating blow to the Fellows and Hadaways. They had feared that Johnson would never testify against her common-law husband and their fears were right.

Earlier, Johnson had said that Bishop had seemed perfectly normal on the night of the murders. She had arrived home from work at about 8.20 p.m. to find he had had a bath and was watching TV.

"He was a little bit creepy but that's just the way he is," she said to laughter around the court – another bad sign for the prosecution.

"He was trying to make up to me because we had had a tiff in the afternoon. He was just being nice to me."

He bore no scratches, no bruises, he was not agitated nor disturbed.

With the trial deep into its second week and the Crown's case in serious trouble, tension on all sides of the court was high and Bishop's defence team was intent on taking every opportunity to crank the pressure up.

With key witness Dr Anthony Peabody, a forensic scientist from the Home Office laboratories at Aldermaston, in the midst of his evidence, Lawrence saw the chance to mischievously tease Leary for the umpteenth time over an inconsequential point.

When Leary got the wrong date of some photos of the Pinto sweatshirt, he rose, looking directly at the jury, to say, "My learned friend really must be more accurate."

That was a spat too far for Mr Justice Schiemann, who, in a gentle but steely tone, reminded the pair, "This is a very serious trial. It's very nice to have games between the two of you, but don't."

If the judge thought his intervention would calm proceedings, he was mistaken.

Next to fire off was Bishop himself, in what, ironically, were to be the only words he uttered in public during the trial.

Leary had objected to a hypothetical question directed at

Peabody by Lawrence, who had asked whether the ivy hair found on the Pinto sweatshirt could have come from being kicked along the Moulsecoomb pathway where it was later found.

The judge ruled the question could not be put to the witness and suddenly Bishop was on his feet in the dock. "My lord, I am innocent of the charges and my defence has the right to question this bloke," he blurted out.

Bishop was calmed down and resumed his seat but Lawrence had achieved his objective in asking a hypothetical question, which he knew would almost certainly be ruled inadmissible, but still planted a seed in the minds of the jury.

Bishop's mother Sylvia was also feeling the tension. As Peabody continued his evidence, she stormed out of court, shouting "I can't take it any more. No, I'm sorry." Then turned towards the court and added, "Bastards." She later apologised

Peabody was the next to overreact in a seething exchange with Lawrence over dog hairs allegedly found on the Pinto sweatshirt.

The court heard that a scientist briefed by the defence had gone to Aldermaston to examine the exhibits and had found some dog hairs on the sweatshirt.

They did not match Bishop's dog, Misty, but Peabody said that following this discovery he too found three hairs on the Pinto but these ones did match Misty, even though his original report said he had found no animal hairs.

Peabody said that he had only examined the dog hairs later. Lawrence jumped on the apparent contradiction.

"It just so happened that examining them afterwards you happened to find three [hairs]," he fired at the scientist.

The judge, realising the potential gravity of the comment,

immediately wanted to know: "Are you suggesting this witness tampered with the evidence?"

Lawrence replied, languidly, "I make no suggestion, my lord... I do not make any conclusion from it. It is just coincidence."

There was silence until it was noticed that Peabody had started scribbling notes furiously. Asked what he was doing in the middle of a cross-examination, he replied, "I am reminding myself about the possibility of tampering with clothing. I must remind myself that this has been said."

It was an astonishing reaction. Lawrence was unlikely to be genuinely suggesting Peabody was corrupt but merely advancing the defence attack on the fault lines between the police and the scientific experts and potential carelessness or even incompetence that would call into question the accuracy of the evidence.

In fact, it was the judge who used the word "tampering" in questioning Peabody and the point about the dog hairs, Misty's or otherwise, ended without any firm conclusion.

Soon afterwards, those fault lines would be exposed in the final terminal blow to the prosecution case. And it was a blow the defence did not even have to land themselves, it was gifted to them.

CHAPTER 8

OMNISHAMBLES

In many trials there comes a moment when the game is up and, to borrow a 21st-century expression for a 20th-century scene, the prosecution case collapses into an "omnishambles".

At Lewes, Dr Anthony Peabody found what a lonely place a witness box can be in front of a packed courtroom with a defence counsel on the warpath, an increasingly exasperated judge and a prosecutor on the verge of despair.

After the hiatus over the word tampering, the evidence moved on to discuss three hairs and a fibre found by pathologist Dr Iain West on Nicola Fellows's private parts. The court heard they had been placed in an exhibits bag and sent to Peabody at Aldermaston.

And there the bag remained, the potentially crucial contents unexamined by Peabody or any other scientist for more than a year.

Russell Bishop had voluntarily supplied to police a sample of his hair so a comparison might have been possible with those found at the scene.

With Ivan Lawrence staring at the jury with the sort of wide-eyed incredulity perfected by actors as well as QCs, the judge stepped in.

"Why were they not examined? In principle it was a slip up," said Mr Justice Schiemann.

Peabody stared down at his paperwork. "With hindsight one might say yes," he replied.

In the well of the court, Brian Leary bit his lip, detectives stared at each other or put their head in their hands. Upstairs in the public gallery, the Fellows and the Hadaways knew they were done for.

Nigel Heffron even remembers the number of the plastic bag exhibit – IEW55 – to this day. "We knew it was all over from that moment," he said.

"It was such a cock-up, a muddle and Lawrence had an absolute field day proving the whole case was based on incompetence and contamination. From that moment we knew it would be a not guilty verdict."

The judge was not standing for this degree of ineptitude and ordered Peabody to leave the witness box, find the exhibit and examine it.

Five days later, Peabody returned to court but things did not go any better for him or the prosecution. The exhibit bag turned out to contain little more than dog hairs and anyway even if the hairs had turned out to be similar to Bishop's, scientific examination could still not prove they were his at all.

As the row raged, the judge admitted that the intricacies

of the evidence had become so complicated that even he had made a mistake in his notes.

In the end, all that the Crown could glean from Peabody's evidence on this part of the case – which Leary had promised the jury proved "inexorably" that Bishop was the killer – was that eleven green fibres and four pink fibres found on the Pinto sweatshirt were indistinguishable from the pink sweatshirt worn by Nicola and the green Coldean School jumper worn by Karen and that blue fibres found on both girls tops were identical to those on the Pinto.

But the girls' clothing had been mass-produced and been on sale for children of that age all over Brighton and beyond.

Peabody could not definitely say that the Pinto was worn by the killer, although it might have been, and he could not definitely say that Bishop had worn the Pinto, but he might have done.

As Lawrence pointed out, "buts" and "ifs" and "maybes" can never add up to "guilt beyond a reasonable doubt".

When the questioning turned from hairs and fibres to the ivy hairs on both the girls' clothing and the Pinto that matched the undergrowth where the bodies were found, the prosecution could make little headway either.

Peabody said he had never come across such hairs in any other murder case, but Lawrence pointed out that the similar ivy grew all over Wild Park and also in the area where the Pinto was found.

Even the countless hours of police work spent attempting to link the red paint stains on the Pinto to cars Bishop had been working on failed to produce the proof to save the case.

As he left court, Peabody was grabbed and pinned against

the wall by a police officer, furious at the way he had presented his evidence to the jury.

Whether that unsavoury incident was what led the scientist to take up the priesthood on his retirement is unknown, but it is worth remembering that Peabody was supported in what he had said in court by fellow scientists and, thirty years later, three senior Appeal Court judges were to conclude that Peabody should not be criticised.

With the trial running into the deep water of forensic-scientific detail, the focus finally turned back to the heart-rending reality of the trial – two little girls brutally murdered.

The pathologist, Dr West, told the jury how he had arrived at the murder scene that day as the light faded and the autumnal chill descended on Wild Park.

As West described what he found, Barrie Fellows could take no more and left the court in tears. He was not the only one to be so effected.

West went through his post-mortem. Karen had been strangled and marks and grazes indicated she had been dragged for a short distance across a dirty surface.

Bruising on her face indicated a hand had been placed across her mouth to stop her screaming but there were no defence injuries on her arms that would have suggest a struggle had taken place. Bruising to her neck indicated she probably lost consciousness very quickly.

At this point, two jurors were clearly in tears, too, and the judge stopped the trial briefly, saying, "It's hard to listen to this."

West added that Nicola had similar marks and injuries to Karen but a bloody face and a large bruise on her left cheek indicated a heavy blow to her face, probably from a fist.

A bruise to her right wrist showed she had probably been held with some force. She had also been sexually assaulted twice. It was chilling evidence.

The prosecution's case drew to a close with Bishop's statements to the police read to the jury. They showed how his story swung wildly from one account to another both before and after his arrest and how he claimed to have touched the bodies to feel for a pulse, then he didn't and then he did again? Sadly by now this had become not only the Crown's best evidence but virtually their only positive evidence.

*

Following a day off, the defence opened with Lawrence telling the jury that Bishop would not be giving evidence.

It's a measure of the confidence of the defence team that they saw no upside in putting the defendant in the witness box. Juries do expect to hear from the accused personally, especially in a murder trial, but Lawrence must have known that with the collapse of the forensic evidence they had very little more to do to convince the jury to return a not guilty verdict.

Subjecting Bishop, of uncertain temperament, to questioning in open court, particularly about his contradictory police statements would have handed the prosecution an advantage they had not earned. Besides, in those days, the defendant has a right to silence without the jury being allowed to draw an adverse conclusion. That law has since changed.

Instead, Lawrence chose to make a short opening speech to stamp all over the ashes of the Crown's case.

"It does not come within one thousand miles of proving this man committed those awful murders," he started.

It would be "inappropriate" for Bishop to have to tell his story again having made three statements to the police. Lawrence ignored the fact that the jurors may have been interested to hear which version of his activities on the day the girls disappeared Bishop would have put forward.

The QC went on to say that the prosecution had painted itself into a corner by insisting the murders must have been committed between 5.15 and 6.30 that evening when the defence had witnesses who would say they were still alive at 6.30.

"If the girls were alive at six thirty that evening then an already weak and feeble prosecution case is shot to pieces," he added.

"This is a horrible case but the next most serious horror would be if an innocent man who has already spent a year in custody was convicted of a crime he hadn't committed."

The defence witnesses concentrated on the timings issue. Brighton hairdresser Kevin Cathcart said he saw two title girls crossing the Lewes Road towards Wild Park at 6.40 p.m. They were holding each other's arms, "they were laughing, they were happy". He recognised them from photos published later in the *Argus* and when shown a picture in court he recognised Nicola.

Three other witnesses from the Moulsecoomb estate were allowed to give their evidence anonymously because of what they described as threats or fears of reprisals.

Hence, they were referred to as Miss Brown, Mrs White and Mrs Black after the colour of their tops, respectively. Mrs White, who said she had had "one or two problems" since speaking to the police, said she had seen the girls eating chips and waving to her at 6.22 p.m. Cross-examined by Leary, she admitted she had failed to tell Barrie Fellows that when he knocked on her door that night because "there was a lot of commotion going on".

Other witnesses agreed that the girls were eating chips around 6.30 p.m. and chips were found post-mortem in Nicola's stomach.

The last defence witness was Terence Ashdown, a car-accessory shop owner in the Lewes Road, who said he would have sold about thirty cans of the red spray paint similar to the stain found on the Pinto sweatshirt.

The defence case did not last long and Leary, in his closing speech, focused, understandably, on rhetoric rather than analysis of the evidence in his appeal to the jury.

"In Moulsecoomb, there is a great number of public-spirited people who are very fond of children," he said. "They spent a lot of time and trouble when it was heard that the two girls were missing.

"But it seems there are also some evil-minded people about. I'm speaking about the sort of people who deemed it appropriate to spray paint accusing Barrie Fellows of being a child molester and a child killer and saying, 'Fellows out!'

"To a family who have just lost one of their daughters one can imagine no more appalling thing to have done."

Lawrence held the aces in his hand and, in his closing speech, he wanted to play them mercilessly.

One of them was the claim that the police had ignored other possible suspects to throw all their attentions at Bishop. One of those suspects, he said, was Barrie Fellows.

His alibi was "at best weak", the QC suggested, and as a father he had sat down to eat his tea rather than go out looking for his daughter.

That was the final straw for Barrie, who stormed out of

court, shouting, "I've had enough." Having achieved the desired effect, Lawrence, of course, back-peddled. "I don't suggest for a moment that Barrie Fellows was the murderer and I'm sorry he left before he heard me say this. He can't be the murderer because of the times," he qualified, with the knowing smile of an experienced barrister who has seen his efforts go to plan.

Lawrence said his point was that there were just the same suspicious circumstances surrounding Barrie Fellows as there was around Russell Bishop.

The case against Bishop was "full of glaring holes" and the prosecution was "scraping the barrel". There was no evidence that Bishop had been seen alone with the girls that afternoon, let alone of killing them. There was no forensic evidence that the Pinto sweatshirt had been at the scene of the murder, nor that it was owned by Bishop, only that it *might* have been.

What about the police failures when it came to possible contamination? Lawrence counted off on his fingers the CB-radio enthusiasts who had originally found the Pinto then left it, Mr Gander who handed it in, and what he described as fifteen police officers and others who had handled it before it was "sanitised". He pointed out that it had even been examined on the same police-station table as the dead girls' clothing.

He told the jury that even the Scenes of Crime officer Eddie Redman had admitted in evidence that he might have accidentally contaminated the sweatshirt.

And to add to the confusion, Lawrence introduced a sighting of a ginger-haired man around the area. Nicola's mother had warned her to keep away from him, he said, and he hadn't been seen since!

Years later, Lawrence – by now Sir Ivan – received an email

from his old friend, Katy Kaul, QC, who is now a distinguished judge.

"You have been through so much," she wrote. "I can close my eyes and remember your speech in the Babes in the Wood [case]; it remains the best speech I have ever heard."

In his day-long summing up, the judge handed the jury a three-point document, which nowadays is called a "route to verdict" but was quite unusual in the eighties. It set out the three key questions to which jurors had to answer "Yes" in order to reach a "Guilty" verdict. If they were unsure on any point or answered "No" to any of the questions, they must automatically acquit, said the judge.

The three questions were: (1) Were the girls dead by 6.30 p.m., as alleged by the prosecution?; (2) Did Bishop wear the Pinto sweatshirt on the night the girls went missing?; and (3) Was the Pinto worn by the murderer?

He went through the evidence and summarised the prosecution and defence arguments on each point, which only served to highlight the weakness of the Crown's case.

On the timing issue, the judge singled out an exchange between Lawrence and the pathologist West about the witnesses who saw the girls eating chips at 6.30 p.m.

He told the jury that Lawrence had asked West: "'That would be consistent on your evidence of stomach contents showing a time of death one and a half hours later, so between eight p.m. and 12 midnight.'"

The judge said West replied: "No, within one and a half hours. I'm not saying any exact time but the likely time is seven to eight p.m."

There in its starkest terms was the disaster of the prosecution's tactical decision on timing. In terms of the judge's three questions to the jury, the case was over.

On the issue of fibres found on the girls' clothing the judge pointed out that their garments could be bought in Marks and Spencer or any High Street chain store.

"What evidence do we have in relation to the commonness of the fibres on the green sweatshirt, pink sweatshirt and blue sweatshirt?" he asked. "The answer to that question, you may think, is not very much. One does not blame anybody for this. Perhaps more research could have been done but it has not been."

The judge was entirely fair in his summing-up, correctly assessing the evidence pointed all one way and the Fellows and the Hadaways knew there could only be one verdict.

Argus reporter Phil Mills's thoughts were typical of the general mood. Throughout the trial, despite the paucity of evidence, he never doubted Bishop was guilty but always expected he would be cleared.

"There was just so much pointing in his direction, even though much of it was circumstantial, I was pretty certain they had the right man," he said.

*

The jury was sent out the following day and came back with their unanimous verdict around noon. The decision was so quick, Nigel was having a shave when all parties were summoned back to Court One.

Neither Susan nor Barrie were in court to hear it.

"I would have wanted to go to court for the verdict on the last day but Barrie said, 'Don't go because you might not want to hear the result,'" she said.

"So I was at the home of my older brother, Terry [eight years her senior] in Bevendean and I heard the outcome on the TV local news.

"I didn't really know what to expect. Barrie had not really kept me informed. I went to the beginning of the trial because I was the first witness but after that I didn't go very much."

Barrie couldn't face being there. "I was in a hotel with ITN. I admit it, I wanted the money to take Susan away from it all after all she had been through. Nigel and Ian were the only ones in court.

"Even before the verdict came through, the ITN reporter said to me I think it's going to be 'Not guilty' – what do you think about it? I was hoping the jury would get it wrong, but they didn't."

Once the bedlam that followed the verdict in court had died down, Bishop, clutching his prison possessions in two Asda shopping bags, left in a brown Mercedes, which was owned by his solicitor Ralph Haeems, his face buried in his hands.

He was off to reveal his thoughts exclusively to the *News of the World* [*NOTW*] for £7,500.

"I can't stop thinking about those poor girls and the fact that someone somewhere is walking the streets knowing they killed them," were his words, gullibly printed by the tabloid paper.

Outside court, Haeems said, "An innocent man has been locked up for over a year. He's been treated very badly. I just hope he is able to recover from it.

"I could never bring myself to believe that young Bishop could have done it and I was never happy with the way that the police conducted the case."

His brothers decamped to the White Hart, opposite the

courthouse, to quaff Moët & Chandon champagne at £21 a bottle.

His father Roy told reporters: "We knew all along that he was innocent. It's absolutely terrific. We just don't know what we are going to do when we get him home but obviously here will be a big celebration."

Alec Bishop, who had dived into the dock to embrace his brother on the verdict and was had been pinned to the ground by prison officers for his efforts, said, "He should never have been arrested in the first place. It's been a terrible time for my mother.

"I leaped into the dock because I wanted to hold him. It was a year of emotion coming out. A year of frustration just flooding out."

The beleaguered Sussex Police had a statement ready for the verdict they had more than half expected, which was duly delivered on the steps outside court by DCI Chris Page: "This case was thoroughly investigated by us at the time. No new information emerged during the trial and we have no plans to reopen the inquiry. But obviously any fresh information which was put to us would be carefully looked at."

A reporter asked: "Are you looking for anyone else?" The answer: "No."

In the chaos it went unnoticed that one juror sat in the front row in tears. In the courtroom, Mr Justice Schiemann thanked the eight women and four men for listening to this "long and difficult case" and excused them from further jury service for five years. He then rose, turned and left the chamber.

It was all over. Or so we thought.

CHAPTER 9

___

THE FALL-OUT

As the Bishop brothers supped champagne, *Mirror*man Tom Merrin reluctantly paid up the £10 bet to *Argus* reporter Jim Hatley and the police endured a firestorm of criticism, while the Fellows and Hadaways were left feeling lonely, forgotten and abandoned.

They had had to go through a harrowing trial, which amounted to a second grieving for their murdered daughters – three including the delayed funeral – and which had ended in a wildly celebrated triumph for the man they believed had killed their girls.

Ian Heffron felt it in more ways than one. "The worst thing about being a serving police officer was having to face my family after the acquittal and say that the police cocked it up. That was a huge weight on my shoulders."

The one thing the trial had achieved was finally crystallising in Barrie's mind the identity of his daughter's killer.

"When he was first pulled in, I had an open mind about

whether he had done it. Even when he was charged I wasn't sure and you couldn't go asking the police these things," he said.

"Sue had more contact with Bishop than me as I wasn't at home all the time and I would go ages without talking to him.

"But after the trial, I knew. I believed what the police had said and when they came out afterwards and said they were not looking for anybody else, in my opinion it had to be him and it was their opinion it had to be him as well.

"It was Bishop's first statement that convinced me, and it is always the first statement that's nearest the truth, when he said he had seen the blood fleck on Nicky's mouth, that was the truth."

But instead of being behind bars, Russell Bishop was being lauded. Somehow he had become the victim while the real victims were left to get on with their lives with the double killer, whoever he was at that stage, still at large.

The *Argus* ran a front-page lead, written by the paper's editor Terry Page, which was cleverly worded and summed up the sense of anger in Brighton, and Moulsecoomb in particular.

Headlined: "THE CHILLING QUESTION THAT NO ONE CAN ANSWER", it started, "Who killed the Babes in the Wood? A jury has decided it was not Russell Bishop. So who is the monster who strangled the nine-year-old playmates?"

Reviewing the uncontested evidence from the trial, it concluded, "It's a fair bet he lived close to them. He may even walk the same streets where Nicola and Karen and their chums played." The fact the police were not reopening case "leaves us with the chilling thought that the killer is still out there, somewhere..."

In Brighton, Barrie and Susan were facing the brunt of

having to deal with the backlash, but in Walton-on-Thames, Michelle and Lee also felt angry, upset, frustrated and isolated with no support or any explanation from the police as to why the trial had failed.

A shocking incident just a few days after the trial verdict symbolised just how the Fellows and Hadaways were no longer treated as tragic victims but as inconveniences who should be shunned, ignored and even threatened with arrest.

Angered by the lack of answers to the questions why the trial had been an utter shambles, Nigel, Susan and Michelle went to the Crown Prosecution Service (CPS) HQ in London to try to see Sir Allan Green, the Director of Public Prosecutions (DPP).

They arrived at Reception and asked politely to see the DPP. When they were rejected out of hand and bluntly told to go away, they refused to leave until they had seen him.

Having sat down to wait, the police suddenly arrived, told them to leave or face arrest and bundled them out of the building and onto the pavement outside. What a way to treat the families of two murdered little girls who had been failed and betrayed by the justice system.

Said Nigel: "I would have been happy if they had arrested us and put us in court. How would that have looked as a way of treating grieving mothers? We left."

But not before he let everyone in earshot know exactly how they felt about the way they had been treated, yelling, "You have declared war on my family. You'll regret that."

So, as 1987 passed into 1988 and onto 1989, who did people in Brighton blame for the murders? The police were refusing to reopen the case and virtually every individual officers believed they had got the right man but had failed to nail him.

The press, both national and local, also believed that privately – not publicly for obvious libel reasons and the *Argus* in particular maintained professional and neutral reporting as far as Bishop was concerned.

But the rest of Brighton, those out of the justice loop and perhaps less cynical, was split. A significant number believed Bishop must be innocent because a year-long investigation and a four-week trial had spectacularly failed to find any convincing evidence against him.

So, if it wasn't Russell Bishop, who had killed the little girls? Sadly, this is where the dark side of Moulsecoomb, what Brian Leary, QC, referred to as the "evil minded", came to the fore.

Far, far too many people appeared to not only want Barrie Fellows to be the killer but were actively willing it.

North Moulsecoomb Residents Association (NMRA) chairman Colin Bradford joined the police in appealing for calm and warned about old scores being settled.

"Whichever way the verdict went, there was bound to be problems. There are a lot of rumours and threats flying around," he said.

The *Argus* rang an unflattering profile on Barrie, stating, "Russell Bishop was the man on trial but often it was Barrie Fellows who snatched the attention."

It pointed out that at one time he had been a suspect in the killing of his own daughter, it repeated his criminal record, it trotted out the unspecified allegations about "promoting and showing porn videos" and stated he had a reputation as a hard man.

It repeated his evidence at the trial that although he had lost his temper on occasions with Nicola, she had always responded "respectfully", and that his mother-in-law (wrong person – it was his wife's grandmother's) had broken her nose but only in an accident and most definitely not as a result of him punching her.

The article accused Barrie of trading on the public's sympathy after the murders and playing to the gallery during the trial. It concluded that in Barrie's eyes the story seemed to be all about Barrie.

This piece may have accurately reflected the mood in Moulsecoomb. A backlash of bitterness and anger at the failure of the trial to pin the blame on Bishop and to cast around blindly to find someone else to blame. It was as if they felt the verdict had made them look foolish for previously believing Russell Bishop was guilty, and they wanted revenge on who they now blamed for that – somehow that person was Barrie Fellows.

*

The anger and feverish search for a scapegoat was fuelled by the *News of the World*, then the highest-selling newspaper in Europe. The Sunday after the trial, the paper published the fruits of their £7,500 investment in Bishop and all that came with him.

Apart from the usual tear-stained drivel about his innocence and suffering until he could clear his name in court, the real damage to the Fellows family was caused by Marion Stevenson.

She claimed that she had visited a house on the estate and seen the owner watching a video of one of his friends having sex with Nicola. Despite the lack of identities, anyone in the area would have immediately identified the two men as Barrie and Dougie Judd.

Her claim was a shocking and truly sensational one that the *NOTW* reporters lapped up, even though, they later admitted, they could not back up.

Stevenson also claimed that before the trial the police had bugged Bishop's home in Stephens Road and had tried to get her, aged 16, to have sex with him there and get him to confess to the murders. She insisted that Bishop had actually found the bug in an electric socket – a claim he has never made.

The Monday after the story appeared, Nigel, Ian and Kevin headed off to confront the *NOTW* and its lawyers about the video and found they were all too ready to back down.

Said Nigel: "We wanted a retraction printed on the front page. But Barrie had rung the *NOTW* first and they offered him ten grand to go away. He cocked it up so they printed the retraction but it was inside the paper and out of the way and not on the front page as we had wanted."

In revenge, the *NOTW* then printed a story claiming Barrie had tried to blackmail them, demanding £4,000 to stop him reporting them to the Press Council.

The retraction was so small and seemingly insignificant that, decades later, when the police tried to find a copy of it, they were stymied and had to make do with a report in the *Argus* that the *NOTW* had indeed disowned its story.

As the newspaper had calculated, retraction or no retraction, Stevenson's allegations were out there and being read by millions across the country, including a large number in Moulsecoomb.

The Fellows were furious. Said Susan: "Marion Stevenson claimed she had been in our house and seen Barrie watching Nicola in a porn film. It was diabolical, so obviously a pack of lies from top to bottom.

"Even the little things she said were obvious lies, like she said she had watched it standing behind my sofa. Well my sofa is against the wall so how could she have got behind it?

"Barrie wasn't watching any film, he was playing *Pac-man*, a child's toy on the TV.

"I threatened Marion Stevenson with a pair of scissors. Maisie [Michelle Hadaway's mother] said she had been on a bus and Stevenson was running down Nicky, saying she was in pornos.

"I'm a quiet person but it all built up inside me and I went round to see her. She denied it, and I said I would stab her. I'm a shy person normally but I wasn't shy that day, the anger got into me.

"John was also supposed to have hit her with a stick in the street. He was put up before the Juvenile Court. John said he had hit her because of what she had said about his sister. I said, 'Don't do it again, John,' and he said, 'I will if she carries on.'"

The *NOTW* splash epitomised the open season on Moulsecoomb declared by Fleet Street, with its lurid tales of "paedo porn rings" on the estate.

But what was worse was that Stevenson detailed all her allegations, particularly about Barrie, in a police statement.

In February 1988, less than two months after the acquittal, Marion Stevenson was interviewed by Detective Superintendent Roger Dice. Attached to the police Disciplinary and Complaints department, Dice isn't a detective who investigates criminals but one who seeks out corrupt policemen.

He was concerned by her claims that she had told the police about the alleged video and they had done nothing about it, as well as the alleged bugging and inducement to the teenager to have sex with a murder suspect.

His findings – the Dice Report, as it was known when revealed nearly thirty years later at the Old Bailey – showed that when questioned she not only repeated her *NOTW* claims but embellished them.

Sitting with Bishop's solicitor, Ralph Haeems, and her father, Jim, Stevenson told Dice that about two to three months before the murders she had gone with Bishop to the Fellows home to see Judd and sat with him in his room drinking and smoking cannabis.

"I went to get a glass of water," she said in her statement, which was not revealed publicly at the time.

"I went towards the kitchen and to get to it I had to enter through the lounge from the hallway. As I entered the lounge I saw Barrie Fellows sitting on the settee, the TV was on and Barrie was playing a video tape.

"I looked at the screen and saw a film of Nicola on a bed with Dougie Judd. I immediately identified both people as first Dougie got on top of Nicola who was facing the camera. In a few seconds, Dougie turned over and Nicola got on top of him.

"Both parties had no clothes on their top but both had a blanket covering their lower halves. From their actions they appeared to be having sex. I was horrified and ran out of the room. I don't know if Barrie knew I was there.

"Dougie was just leaving his room to go upstairs, presumably to the toilet, and I said to him, 'I just saw Nicola on a video on a bed with some bloke.' I didn't say I had recognised him. He said, 'Don''t worry about it.' I didn't tell Russell. I have never said anything to him about it.

"I have only mentioned this to DS Philip Swan [we will hear

more about him later] and WDC Wendy King. Swan appeared to take no notice, while saying, 'All right, I will look at it.' He was only interested in getting Russell."

Dice questioned her and found she changed elements of her story and he was unable to get any sort of answer from her about why she had failed to tell Bishop or Haeems about what she had seen.

Complaints officers have a reputation of being feared and hated by all policemen and not just the ones they are investigating, because of their fierce independence and rigorous grilling of their fellow officers.

But even from that stance, Dice had no doubts Stevenson was lying and pinpointed twelve separate reasons why, as he put it in his report, she was, literally, incredible. They were:

(1) With Moulsecoomb "being what it is", i.e. awash with gossip and vile rumours, why had nobody ever heard of the existence of this video before? Especially as so many people were prepared to think the worst of Barrie Fellows?

(2) Why is she the only person to have seen it?

(3) If she had seen it, she would have told Bishop as soon as the girls were murdered to support his claims of being innocent.

(4) Stevenson made eight statements to the police [in all she made nine] in October and November 1986 and never mentioned it once.

(5) Even when she was arrested on suspicion of complicity with Bishop after giving him a false alibi, she never mentioned it.

(6) She saw nine police officers, other than Swan, and never mentioned it.

(7) All officers on the murder inquiry were briefed every day to report anything they had been told. Dice said he fully supported Swan's commitment to the inquiry and he would have pestered senior officers incessantly had he had such a tip about Barrie.

(8) She never told Ralph Haeems about it.

(9) She admitted she didn't know anyone with a camera who could record such a video.

(10) She has a record of lying to officers on the murder inquiry.

(11) Nicola's hymen was found to be intact by the pathologist who conducted the post-mortem, suggesting she could not have had full sex in the video, or anywhere else.

(12) Stevenson admitted she had been plied with a lot of champagne by the press when she spoke to the *NOTW* and that she didn't know exactly what she had been saying to them.

When the merits of the alleged video claims were argued at the Old Bailey in 2018, there were further utterly compelling reasons why Stevenson was lying or mistaken but they cannot be made public for legal reasons.

Swan and King denied Stevenson had told them anything about a video and Swan also denied ordering her to have sex with Bishop. Barrie was made aware that her *NOTW* claims had blown up into a complaint to the police and he denied having any video recording device.

A few days later, a man purporting to be Barrie's brother Ian Heffron, an Essex police officer, rang Sussex Police and told them that the family had cut off contact with Barrie "in view of his cash-register mind", adding, "Barrie told you lies about not having a video recorder at the time of the Stevenson allegations. He had one that fell off the back of a lorry. He didn't. Trust me. He has obviously lied to you."

Did Ian make that call? He says it was not him and blames a hoaxster with ill-will towards the family.

Whether the call was from Ian or not, the caller did not make clear whether the video recorder he was referring to was a camcorder (an eighties device to make live-action film) or a video-cassette recorder that could record programmes off the television.

Nevertheless, for the clear reasons given by Dice (see above), Stevenson's complaint was binned by the police. But it would not be the end of this horrendous claim... not by any means.

*

During the weeks and months post-trial, the families were at a low ebb.

Understandably wanting to move out of the home that contained so many memories of their dead daughter, the Fellows were set to move into another house towards the southern end of Moulsecoomb.

But before they could make the move, someone found out and daubed the outside of the property with the message FELLOWS OUT, YOU'RE A MURDERER AND CHILD MOLESTER AND CHILD KILLER and hung a noose on the garden gate.

What is worse than losing your child to murder than being

accused, tacitly or otherwise, of being the killer? As with innocent mothers accused over the cot death of their baby, it is a devastating slur, one that not only prevents grieving but doubles the trauma.

"It was after the verdict that the shit hit the fan," said Barrie, reflecting both tearfully and angrily.

"We tried to move house to a new place but that was attacked with graffiti. It upset us so much, I said to Nigel, 'Get me out of here before I fucking kill somebody.'"

It was a seriously traumatic moment for Susan: "The graffiti attacks had started before the trial but it escalated afterwards. I don't know how they knew where we had moved to a new house the other side of Moulsecoomb school but they found it and attacked it.

"I was walking around like a zombie, I didn't know what to do and what not to do. I was still thinking that Nicky would come down the road again. I still get flashbacks of Nicky walking across the road towards the park. Was that wrong and did I do wrong? I still blame myself. She loved *EastEnders* [which was on TV that night], that's the only thing she would come indoors for. It was like a big black cloud over me. I wanted to scream.

"On the bus, I would hear people say, 'I knew he [Bishop] didn't do it, I went to school with him, but I know who did do it', meaning Barrie. I wanted to say something but I kept shtum, what could I say to them? At that time, my police-liaison officers were really good to me, Sonia and Brian. I could talk to them even though I could not come to terms with it."

In January 1988, Barrie made a statement to the police, complaining about the trial and appealing for the case to be reopened. He might as well have stood on Ditchling Beacon and whistled into the wind for all the good it did him.

"There are numerous questions my wife and I want answered," he said. He listed a number of mistakes the police had made during the murder investigation and wanted an response.

He said that Dougie Judd "could not account" for his alibi and demanded, "Why was this not followed up?"

He finished: "I am currently collecting signatures on a petition requesting the reopening of the Wild Park murder. As of today, I have 625 signatures."

It was no good, Nigel decided it was time to act. "It was not just a whispering campaign as the house got daubed. We had to get Susan and Barrie out of Brighton so I had a word with someone I knew in Lambeth housing and he arranged an exchange on a unit swap basis for a three unit accommodation to be made available."

Barrie's head was already swimming with a thousand thoughts of his dead daughter without having to deal with being called a pervert publicly.

"You try and imagine your heart being ripped out and being put back wrong and it's not functioning and the tightness and the overpowering sorrow and in your mind you are thinking: 'Why did it happen that day? Why did I go to work. Why did I clean the swimming pool? Why the fuck me? This happens to other people,'" he said.

"Our name is notorious as the Babes in the Wood murders, everybody thinks they know me and what I've been through but nobody knows me apart from my close knit family and nobody really knows what I've been through.

"Susan was mortified that I had been accused but who better

to know me than my wife? My door was always open, anybody could have come in, any Tom, Dick or Harry, and seen what was inside and could see there was no collection of kiddy porn or whatever. The door was never locked, it's called trust.

"Being accused like that was shit. I have never got over it, I'm still trying to come to terms with it. None of them apologised, not one person approached me to say they had got it wrong."

So it that was that, in late 1988, Susan and Barrie packed up and headed to the Brixton area to try to start a new life. But she always kept a box of Nicola's dolls and teddies close by her.

CHAPTER 10

THE FIGHT BACK

With the family in disarray, wrecked first by the murders, then by the shocking miscarriage of justice and now by the accusations against Barrie, there was only one thing for it – the Fellows had to fight back.

It was the three Heffron brothers – Nigel, the one-time chancer, Ian the ex-policeman, and Kevin, the giant – who took it on themselves to piece together the mess left from the shambles of the prosecution.

They were half-brothers to Barrie – the same mother, but different father – but always called themselves brothers and had been brought up in the same way even though they had each chosen a completely different direction for their lives.

Said Nigel: "I had been a conman, buying stuff and selling it, trainers, TVs, video cameras anything, conning people, I was part of the black economy, like *Only Fools and Horses*, like Del Boy but he was the master.

"I was making my living out of that in South London, and I

got to know some of the hardest-nosed families around. When the murders happened and the trial went wrong it allowed me to turn the skills I had learned to our advantage, I was able to con my way into places for my niece.

"I didn't move to Brighton until the early nineties. Up until then, I drove backwards and forwards from South London.

"That put a hell of a lot of strain on my marriage. My first marriage to Christine ended and I married my second wife, also Christine, who is the niece of Sue Fellows, who understood."

Nigel never returned to his old life and has worked for the Royal Voluntary Service at the Royal Sussex Hospital for many years.

Kevin was an enormous man, which came in handy if things got hairy on their inquiries in Moulsecoomb. Ted Hynds, a reporter who became a long-standing friend, remembered: "He was a scary sight. I was glad he was on our side."

Nigel and Kevin were very close. Kevin lived in Dulwich and hated school. As a boy he was always truanting until a sympathetic youth court magistrate offered him a deal – hold down a steady job and skip schooling, but if you can't hack it, you will go back behind the school desk.

It was a good deal for Kevin. He left school at fifteen and never looked back. He started at a stationers/printers, worked hard and found he loved it.

Sadly, he was to contract stomach cancer and died before Bishop faced justice.

Ian was always interested in the law. He started as a Special Constable in London and also had jobs at the Ministry of Defence, Borough Market and elsewhere to raise money for a mortgage. He stopped that when his application to join Essex Police was accepted.

"Ian and me went in two different sides of the track. Ian always told me that if I came to Essex and broke the law, he would nick me and I knew he would," said Nigel.

"Barrie was our brother, not half-brother. We were brought up as a family. You hurt one of us you hurt all of us, that was what our mother told us, but us three we went our different ways."

The first thing the brothers had to do was to get their hands on the police evidence, including the material that had not been used in the trial, which they had been tantalisingly shown in the upstairs room at Lewes Crown Court after the verdict. If the police weren't going to give them access then who would?

The surprising answer was Russell Bishop's legal team.

After appearing on LBC radio to attack the police handling of the case, Nigel contacted Ralph Haeems and managed to get the solicitor to agree to see him.

What he did not expect to find at the solicitors Peckham office was Russell Bishop and his mother Sylvia, keen to join forces with the Fellows and Hadaway families to hunt for who, to her mind, was 'the real killer'.

Bishop also claimed the police were bugging him, the fantasy which Marion Stevenson had told the *News of the World* and repeated to Detective Superintendent Roger Dice. It was the first time Nigel had met Bishop face to face.

At a further meeting, Nigel persuaded Haeems to allow him to take a copy of all the evidence, including previously unused police documents. It was an astonishing coup which Nigel believes had been authorised by Mrs Bishop. He immediately called in his brothers.

Nigel said, "Haeems gave us all the unused evidence as long as we read it and gave it back. The first thing we did was get it photocopied three times for me, Kev and Ian.

"Kev worked for a printing company and arranged to get photocopying paper, and we needed loads of it because there was four box loads of papers – some 3,000 statements plus photos, and then he arranged access to a building site office at night and over a weekend. It took two days. We were just drinking coffee and photocopying."

Ian is full of admiration for the way Nigel secured access to the papers.

"I went with Nigel and Kevin to see Haeems at his office in South London," he said. "I had a sense from the way he was talking that he was worried about Bishop. I said: 'I'm a police officer, and what you are doing here is extraordinary. Why are you doing this?'"

He said, "I believe there has been a travesty of justice. I didn't like the way Bishop's brothers celebrated on the steps outside court." It had clearly got to him. He would not be drawn on whether he thought that Bishop might have gotten away with it.

"We were shown into his conference room and there was piles of boxes of the bundles of undisclosed material sent to him from the CPS.

"I started reading through them and it became apparent that this would be a monster exercise. I asked him if we could have a copy.

"We read through them and picked up on five statements where three people had identified Bishop as being the owner of the Pinto sweatshirt. There was a lady who lived three or four doors from Bishop's flat and could look up at the street. She had seen him walking past, possibly during the ad break in *Crossroads*, which she was watching on TV. He was wearing a sleeveless body warmer with nothing underneath it.

"The police doubted her but it doesn't matter – she could have been brought to court and been asked about this man wearing a body warmer with nothing underneath on a cold October evening.

"We challenged the CPS about this. Why didn't they call these witnesses? But they were dead against us. Jennie Johnson had been caught lying and they could have used these statements but the prosecution had put its whole weight behind Johnson and they had no plan B when she denied it.

"The CPS insisted it had done nothing wrong but it is not answerable to anyone. We asked about an inquiry and they completely exonerated themselves."

In all, the brothers counted seven witnesses in the mountain of evidence who had made statements about Bishop and the Pinto sweatshirt. The families have never received any explanation about why they were never called to give evidence.

The brothers teamed up with Ted Hynds, and another hugely experienced investigative reporter Ray Levine, and together they tracked down exactly where the Pinto sweatshirt had come from – Jennie Johnson's father.

Said Nigel: "Police said it had been mass produced so could not trace its history. But Kevin found out that it had been a pirated rip off.

"A blue, medium-sized sweatshirt with Pinto printed on the front had been sold through magazine fliers. One had been sent to the Bevendean address of Jenny Johnson's parents."

Confronted by Levine, and tape-recorded, Fred Johnson admitted he had bought the sweatshirt as a present for Bishop. It was to be the cornerstone of the newspaper's dramatic front-page spread two years later that publicly named Bishop as the Babes in the Wood killer for the first time.

The existence of the seven witnesses and the new Pinto evidence was an astonishing breakthrough that raised the spirits of the families that there was a chance for justice after all.

Meanwhile, Nigel called in a favour from a most unlikely source. Sir Thomas Holmes Sellors was one of Britain's most distinguished cardiothoracic surgeons. He was also Nigel's godfather.

He was a quiet, generous man, with a reputation of never losing his temper even under the intense pressure of the operation theatre, and was in known to colleagues, friends and family alike as Uncle Tom.

Sir Thomas passed on the name of a reliable psychiatrist at Charing Cross Hospital and Nigel sent him a copy of Bishop's police statements for the expert's assessment.

According to Nigel, his opinion was that Bishop showed all the signs of a serial and violent paedophile who was certain to reoffend.

Armed with this shocking evaluation the brothers decided they had to act to warn Brighton of the danger in their midst and the only way they could do that was through a poster campaign.

They recruited a friend, to help them put up dozens of fliers naming Bishop as a threat. In order to avoid prosecution, they were careful not to damage any tree, lamppost or building the posters were attached to.

The police were not happy and the brothers were warned but they felt this controversial step was the only way they could get the warning – which was to prove tragically accurate – out to local people.

Sadly, and perhaps inevitably, the warning was to go unheeded, with Bishop used the campaign as another way of persuading residents that he was a persecuted victim who deserved respect and sympathy.

In fact, in those days life for Russell Bishop was sweet.

With the four-figure cheque from the *News of the World* in his pocket, he was basking in the warmth of positive PR.

All differences forgotten, Jennie Johnson was even talking of marriage. She told the *Argus*: "We want to get married, even though we are already classed as a married couple. He knew that however long it took, I would wait for him."

She said she had taken baby Hayley, born on Boxing Day 1986, to see him in prison before the trial and he had cried at her beauty.

Even Marion Stevenson announced she would be leaving them to their domestic bliss. "I don't want to talk about him anymore," she said, adding that she was convinced Bishop was innocent and "the killer is out there, I know he is."

Her suggestion that she would step aside was to prove as accurate as her evidence, for Stevenson was to play a central role in boosting Bishop's defence and bring misery to the Fellows for decades to come.

Sylvia Bishop said she had spent the past year living on tranquillisers and chain smoking and insisted her son was guilty of nothing more than harmless fantasies that had got him into trouble.

"We know what a wally he is really and we can see why the police made him a suspect from the start," she told the *Argus*.

Referring to his ability to describe exactly how the dead girls had looked, she added: "If Russell had heard an accident outside the house, he would be able to describe what happened even if he had not seen it. He does it for attention and he did the same in this case.

"That's what landed him in trouble and he has been paying for it ever since."

Admitting her son stole from cars, she insisted, "I know when he has done something wrong. I could tell from the start that he did not kill the girls."

After her son's arrest she said that she and husband Roy had "suffered terribly" but since then the public's response had changed.

"We never had one hate letter or call. We had scores of letters from people who were totally convinced Russell was innocent and the phone never stopped ringing. He is a popular lad around the estate and he's lived here all his life."

In fact, Bishop was to tell a different story three years later when, in a bid for the jury's sympathy, he sobbed in the witness box and claimed everybody thought he was the double killer even though he had been cleared.

But Mrs Bishop's words made a telling point, shared by many in Moulsecoomb, that Bishop was actually a hero – not least for beating the police – while the real victims, the Fellows and Hadaways, were made to feel guilty.

It was this attitude that was compromising the families' campaign to keep the murdered girls in the spotlight and force Sussex Police to reopen the inquiry.

Bishop saw his chance to hijack the campaign and use it as a vehicle to boost his own popularity. Increasingly, the Fellows and Hadaways were losing the battle to be the figureheads of the campaign and were being sidelined from their proper position as its driving force.

It got so bad that at a public meeting called in Moulsecoomb the Bishops were treated with honour and Barrie Fellows wasn't even invited.

Bishop was riding high but, suddenly, in February 1989, he claimed his home had been firebombed.

When firemen arrived in Stephens Road at midnight, Bishop was standing outside fully clothed with Johnson and their children.

How the fire started and who was responsible remains unproven but it had two consequences – Bishop and his family were re-housed in bigger and better accommodation in nearby Preston Barracks and Barrie Fellows and two of his brothers Nigel and Kevin were all arrested on suspicion of arson with intent to endanger life.

If that is what Bishop had intended, he could not have been happier. What's more, the arrests did little for the reputation of Sussex Police. At the time of the alleged attack the suspects were meeting the Attorney General Sir Patrick Mayhew at the Houses of Parliament!

Ian, who was with Essex Police at the time, takes up the story.

"I got called in that morning by my governor, who said, 'They want you to go to HQ [in Chelmsford] at 8 a.m. I don't know why, they wouldn't tell me.'

"I had already had calls from Kevin and Nigel's wives to say that they had been arrested and I rang Sue and she said Barrie had been arrested, too.

"My first thought was that we were going to be accused of stealing the undisclosed evidence given to us by Ralph Haeems, so I took all the copies in boxes and hid them behind rubbish bins on the A12.

"At HQ, there was a Detective Sergeant and a Detective Constable from Sussex Police, I don't remember their names. I said, 'Am I under arrest?' They said, 'No, you are not under arrest, Ian,' which made me immediately suspicious because they were using my Christian name and trying to be nice.

"I said, 'You have arrested my brothers.' They refused to say why or tell me any of the evidence they had against them but they did say, 'Tell us about your brothers.'" I said, 'You must be joking. But I can tell you about Russell Bishop and what a piece of shit he is.'

"I asked my governor, a superintendent, for the rest of the day off and he agreed but they said that under no circumstances was I to go to Sussex Police HQ. I showed them my warrant card and said I could go where I wanted to. I was still angry, I told them my brothers were innocent and I drove immediately to Brighton.

"I was then a naughty boy: I went to Sussex Fire Brigade HQ and showed my warrant card and asked to speak to the man dealing with the Bishop fire and he gave me a summery of the official report.

"Basically, he said it [the fire] was a 'crock of shit'. He said, 'There are things troubling us and we told your colleagues that. Firstly, Bishop and his three children were all fully clothed when we arrived at the scene at 3 a.m. They had woken up with the house on fire but had stopped to get dressed!

"'Secondly, the trajectory of where the firebomb bottle had

landed did not match Bishop's claim that it had come through the window. The landing spot was wrong and it landed on the carpet as if it had been dropped vertically. The fan or splash of the flammable liquid did not spread in a way it should have done had it been thrown from outside the house.'"

Ian went on: "I thought it was clear that this arson did not happen. I contacted the police officer dealing with it but he would not speak to me so I left a message. I said, 'Don't you think Barrie Fellows has gone through enough?' I was fully expecting to be arrested myself.

"At 11.30 p.m., they [his brothers] were released. No further action was taken against them, of course."

Barrie can afford to laugh now about the arrest but he was furious at the way they had all been accused.

In a rather childish prank a few days earlier, he and Kevin had laid a wreath at Bishop's door, as a reminder.

"We were all arrested separately in dawn raids and I said, 'Are you kidding? I would never endanger the lives of children,'" said Barrie.

"I was taken to a cell. I was absolutely livid. I was sweating and my heart was pounding. I said, 'Yes, I went to his house and put a wreath outside his door but I didn't set fire to it, he did that himself, he wanted the rest of the world to feel sorry for him.'

"When they let me go, Nigel said why did you do that [meaning the wreath]? But I was just pissed off by this fucking stupid allegation. We all had the same alibi we had been with the Attorney General in Parliament until late at night. It was ridiculously stupid to say that we had done it."

However stupid and unlikely, the arrests were terrifying for Susan.

"The police were at my door [they were then living in South London] in the early hours of the morning – *Bang, bang, bang*," she said.

"I heard the disturbance and went downstairs and opened the door, and they said, 'Where's Barrie Fellows.' I said, he's in bed I'll get him downstairs. They said they had come to take him away. I said I had to go to work. I was working at the time at Brixton College, helping escort the students onto buses. I was frightened."

Nigel took a more relaxed view.

"I was arrested at my home on the Tulse Hill estate. There were two from Sussex Police with two from the Met who I knew personally because they had previously used my back window for surveillance on a drug dealer opposite," he said.

"The Met officers said, 'Sorry, Nigel, about this,' and they came in and made me and them a cup of tea. The Sussex Police searched my flat but they never asked where I had been when the firebomb was meant to have been thrown at Bishop's house.

"We drove down to Brighton and when we got to the John Street station and, guess what...? There was the media. They had been tipped off.

"I knew that because we had been asking questions and campaigning, the police would come for us. I had even gone to my GP to have myself declared claustrophobic. I'm not but I had it put in my doctor's notes, so they couldn't put me in a cell.

"They had to stick me in a room and leave the door open and it had a TV, so I watched *Good Morning* or *Breakfast Time* or something.

"Eventually, they got round to interviewing me and asked

me where I was at the time of the alleged attack. I told them.
We were with the Attorney General, Sir Patrick Mayhew. We
had a meeting at the House of Commons, which didn't finish
until very late because he had to wait until the main Commons
business was over."

*

Six months later, 8,000 leaflets were distributed around
Moulsecoomb and Bevendean, calling for support for a protest
march to the John Street police station in Brighton and petition
for the murder inquiry to be reopened.

Local Labour councillor, Gordon Wingate said, "We as a
community owe it to the memory's these two little girls to bring
this evil man to justice."

The three-mile march, starting at Wild Park, took place on a
sunny Saturday afternoon and, to be truthful, it wasn't a grand
turnout. The *Argus* described it as a "small, sad procession".

But it wasn't the numbers that stuck in the craw of the two
families and their relatives and friends, but more the sight of
Bishop, joined by Jenny Johnson and Sylvia, at the heart of it,
handing out leaflets.

Susan Fellows described how even standing close to Bishop
"made my flesh creep".

Barrie even wanted to pull out rather than be near the man
he was convinced had murdered his daughter.

He said, "I refused to go on the march in the beginning
because Bishop was going to be there. Why would I want to
walk with a murderer? It was my brothers who said that I had
to do it but I said, 'No, he is an arsehole.'

"I hated Bishop but my brothers convinced me to go on the

march. I didn't want to do it, but I went for my daughter, for Nicky and Karen."

Bishop was pictured rattling a bucket around, jumping on and off buses, to get people to give money. He even gave an interview, dressed in a hi-viz jacket, to the BBC, saying, "My name is not cleared until somebody else is brought to justice – the real person."

It ended in angry scenes when the marchers realised that Chief Constance Roger Birch was not at the station and they had to hand the 5,000-signature petition to the head of Brighton Police, Chief Superintendent David Tomlinson.

Some of the marchers vowed to hold sit-ins and continue the demo until their demands were met.

In the end, Tomlinson invited the families in and Birch later agreed to meet them the following week.

But it was inside the John Street station on that Saturday afternoon where perhaps the final nail was hammered into the splintering relationship between the Fellows and the Hadaways.

Said Susan: "After the march we were shown into a room at the police station. It was the first time I ever really spoke out and I asked the police, 'If Bishop didn't do it, who did?' And Michelle Hadaway said, 'Why, Barrie of course,' and that's when the meeting had to stop. I didn't talk to Michelle much after that.

"People said they had proof it was Barrie who did the murders because when he came home that evening and we were looking for the girls he had sat down and eaten his dinner. But that's not proof. It's ridiculous."

As the decade drew to a close things looked bleak for the

Fellows and Hadaways and their fight for justice. And it was going to get worse.

CHAPTER 11

"NO ONE WANTED TO KNOW"

The trauma of violent loss can be so devastating that it can often force grieving parents to turn on the one they loved the most.

The parents of high-profile murder victims James Bulger, Stephen Lawrence and Sara Payne all ended their marriages and the Fellows and Hadaways were no different.

But first, reluctantly, the Fellows had decided to follow in the footsteps of the Hadaways and turn their back on Brighton by moving to a new home in South London.

Their home had been attacked, Barrie was being treated as a pariah and with their daughter dead the killer was striding around the neighbourhood like some sort of hero.

Michelle knew exactly what that felt like. She told the BBC: "The jury had found him not guilty and it's got to be the worst decision ever as far as we were concerned. When you don't get justice you feel everybody is laughing at you. You feel everybody thinks those little girls' lives were not worth it.

"After the trial it was as if nobody wanted to know."

Lee and Michelle Hadaway had already started a new life 50 miles away from the memories of Moulsecoomb. At the new home in Walton-on-Thames, Michelle was to build a little garden for her daughter full of pictures, cards, toys, teddies and two white weeping angles.

But sadly, distance between theme and their searing nightmare could not save their marriage.

They divorced in 1992 and Lee moved back to Brighton, but homeless and on tranquillisers he died in 1998.

Michelle said Lee had never got over the shock of identifying the body of his daughter. "He was away working at the time and he heard his daughter had been murdered on the radio," she said.

"On Saturday, 11 October, he had to go to Brighton mortuary to identify his daughter. She was our first born and the apple of his eye.

"He went into that mortuary the man I loved and adored and would do anything for and he came out a complete stranger.

"I could never get him back. My children have never had the dad he was, although his love for them never waned. He could never get over what Bishop had done to his little girl. It destroyed him."

Lyndsey told the BBC in 2018: "Lee always felt guilty. He felt he should have been there to protect her [Karen]. If we find justice he won't be here. My mother is not getting any younger."

Dave Dawson, a neighbour, friend and work colleague, told the *Argus*: "Lee became a broken man, he never got any closure before he died. I don't think he ever got over it, it's horrible that he didn't get to see the verdict."

The Fellows marriage followed similar lines and, although both lived through the trauma and also remarried – Barrie to Karen Pacitti and Sue to Peter Eisman – both also found happiness ripped away from them in the end.

Said Barrie: "About 18 months to two years after the murders, we moved to Brixton. John didn't want to move and Sue didn't want to move. I said to her that she would make new friends in London but she was a Brighton girl and she wanted to be near Nicky.

"We were starting to grow apart. I was leading a separate life. I used to leave her indoors and go up the bingo but she didn't want to come."

Susan agreed: "Barrie and I kept arguing about there being no justice for our daughter. We were leading separate lives under the one roof we blamed each other for what happened. Nobody can survive that pressure."

Looking back on that pressure, Barrie remembers: "Sue went into hospital over her gallstones and I was having an affair with Karen. Why did I do it? Was I looking for reassurance? Was I looking for a blessing? I fell in love with Karen and it lifted me out of the doldrums my life was in. It was not good for me and it wasn't good for Sue and in the end I think it was a case of being cruel to be kind.

"I don't regret it one bit because I made something of myself after I left her [Susan]. John was not happy and he came to where I was living with Karen and he threatened me. I understand that.

"It's all about the ripples that spread out when you thrown a pebble into a mill pond, except it's not ripples in the way it impacts on so many other people's lives, it's a tsunami."

Unsurprisingly, Susan remembers it slightly differently: "Barrie says I wasn't there for him and he wasn't there for me.

"But it was not like that. He was seeing someone else. A woman with five kids when he had one of his own [Jonathan], who was fifteen. After a while, I could just not handle it any more and wanted to come home to Brighton, I wanted to go back because my daughter was there. I didn't want to leave her behind for ever.

"So I came back in 1991/2 and stayed with Christine, now Nigel's wife. After six months I decided to get a divorce. I wanted it to be on the grounds of adultery, Barrie wanted it to be irreconcilable differences but I would not have it. "

In the days, weeks, months and years following the murders, Barrie, in the midst of his own personal crisis, had failed to realise there was another victim in the family – Jonathan.

Looking back to 1986, Susan said now: "John had not had to look after Nicky because in those days he was always out with the boys and he didn't want his little sister coming along.

"The trouble was that the last time he saw Nicky they had had a row and he had had a go at her for being selfish. That weighed on his mind all the time and it never left him, ever.

"When he was interviewed by the police for the first time it took him two hours before he was prepared to talk about the day she disappeared.

"As the years went by he was not a good boy but he got better. He had a job with Dynorod for a number of years and enjoyed it but then drink took over.

"Then he changed again and he was in rehab for four or five years for depression and alcohol problems.

"Barrie didn't know how to to talk to John about it. John

would talk to Nigel. Nigel told him he would answer any question truthfully, but told him to think carefully because he might not want to know the answer. Nigel was his second dad. He came to see Nigel as his second father.

"I had lost my daughter and I wasn't there for John. Nigel and Kevin were there for him but it's not the same as having your mum and dad there, but we had our problems to deal with."

Barrie dates the lack of trust between father and son even further back to the time he was in prison. The gap between them grew even wider after the murder and during the fall out following the not guilty verdict.

"John was upset and I never really bonded with him because I had been away," he said.

"John didn't like school either, probably my influence, he was quite delinquent but he was 13 and I wasn't fucking there for him."

He went on: "On or around the day she disappeared John had had a row with his sister Nicky. After she was murdered, he was riddled with guilt that he was not able to look after her as a big brother should. This had a huge impact throughout his life and he never truly recovered from her death."

Jonathan was to die aged 46 on 8 September, 2018 just over a month before the trial that was to bring his sister's killer finally to justice.

He had never wanted to be in the limelight and shied away from the cameras. In his final months he had been coming round to the idea that while nobody had listened to him before perhaps now was the time to speak out for the first time. Whether he would or whether he would not have done that, he never got that chance.

*

However, back in the 1990s there was a silver lining for Barrie and Susan because even though their divorce was inevitable, both were soon to find a better life with new partners.

For Susan it came from a chance encounter similar to her first meeting with Barrie.

"I came back to Brighton but went back to London for a short while, before returning, and it was then that my friend Jean fitted me up with a blind date with a German-Polish guy called Peter Eisman," she remembers.

"We went dancing in Crystal Palace and then he took me home, and we met the next day – which was his birthday, 13 March 1993 – and he said we should make a go of it.

"That was the weekend and on the Monday I went to the solicitors to swear the affidavits for the divorce.

"We met in March, got engaged in September and married in February 1994 between his daughter's birthday and what would have been Nicky's birthday.

"You could talk to Peter and he would talk back, he was a lovely man. When we met he said he had always wanted to meet a mother of the Babes in the Wood girls and now he had met me he wanted to stay with me. I said, 'Why?' And he said he wanted to hear my story."

Said Nigel: "He was a diamond geezer. When we met him Kevin shook his hand and said 'I forgive you.' Peter looked a bit surprised and Kevin said, 'One of your relatives bombed my dad's chip shop.' Of course our dad didn't have a chip shop and Peter was Polish German not German, but he loved it.

"Sadly he died in 2016. Susan rang me up in a terribly

distressed state. Peter had collapsed in the passageway. When we got there we couldn't get in as the ambulance staff were working on him and he died there."

With the divorce finalised, Barrie married Karen in St Matthew's, Brixton, in 1994.

"We had met when I was at a orphanage. I had wanted to bring along this kid so he could get to know people and make friends and that's where it happened.

"We were living on the Tulse Hill estate, which was a shit hole and the first thing I promised was that we would get out of there," he said.

"Amber had been born in January and the wedding and the christening took place on the same day. John was best man and Sue was there. Karen had five children aged from three to thirteen and we were to have eight in all.

"I was fed up with things in London but we had loved Blackpool when we had been there on holiday so we moved to try and get as close to it as we could.

"This house became available as an exchange. Two nurses wanted to move down to London and we came to Ellesmere Port in 1995. We moved in and have never looked back since.

"Karen died on 14 June 2017. She had had a bad back but had refused to take blood tests. When she finally agreed to do it they discovered she had terminal cancer. It was the second most horrible thing to happen to me.

"Karen made me the man I am today. If it wasn't for that woman, I would not be where I am today. I was a bit of a tearaway when I was a kid and she stoped that.

"I have worked at Morrisons for 12 years, the longest job I have ever had. She was the finest woman you would ever meet.

She has had to put up with me for a few years when it could not have been nice for her."

But that was in the future. Back in 1990, events were taking an extraordinary turn.

On 2 February, Sussex Police issued a statement once again ruling out any reopening of the Babes in the Wood murder inquiry and rejecting any idea that relevant new evidence had been unearthed.

Bishop was sent a personal letter by the police to say there would not be any new arrests.

Two days later on a Sunday afternoon a little girl on the Whitehawk estate strapped on her roller skates and set off for a local shop with a £1 coin from her father. On the way, she noticed a man working on a red car in the street.

A few hours later and fourteen miles away, David and Susan Clifton were sipping a cup of coffee on Devil's Dyke, the beauty spot just north of Brighton when they saw an "apparition" of a naked girl staggering towards them from the undergrowth.

She had clearly been sexually attacked and Mrs Clifton quickly wrapped her cardigan around the shivering waif and the couple took her off to the Devil's Dyke golf clubhouse to raise the alarm.

Seven hours after that, DI Malcolm Bacon and a colleague arrived on Russell Bishop's doorstep in Preston Barracks to arrest him. The police had a list of known and suspected paedophiles living in the area, but realistically it was always going to be him.

Bishop had struck again on the third anniversary of the funerals of Nicola Fellows and Karen Hadaway.

Said Nigel: "The night the child was attacked I got a phone

call from Kevin who said that he had heard that Bishop had been arrested. I rang Sylvia Bishop and made her think I was a journalist. She said she was saying nothing and that's when I knew it was true.

"DI Bacon rang me and asked me to make sure my family said nothing and did nothing that might put the trial in trouble. I said I couldn't do that but that if he made sure that we were treated as the victims in this trial as well as the last one and had full access, I would see what we could do. Eventually, we had a deal."

Barrie recalls, "I was in Brighton with Sue when the little girl was attacked because it was the anniversary of Nicky's burial and we wanted to put flowers on the grave in the cemetery. I had actually seen one of the Bishop brothers earlier that day and I gave him a filthy look.

" I got back to Victoria station and I rang Kev. He said there's a little girl missing and I said straight away 'that's Bishop' I knew one-hundred-per-cent certain.

"Why was he so stupid? Well it's not being stupid because he is a predatory paedophile. We should not have been surprised that he would strike again. He thought he was invincible because he had got away with it, with double murder, and he left her for dead. How could somebody be so evil?"

Susan added, "Kevin told Barrie that Bishop had been accused of the attack on the little girl. I said I had known after the trial it would happen again in the next two years."

It was not just the Fellows and Hadaways who, nearly thirty years later, knew exactly where they were when they heard that Russell Bishop had been arrested and was soon to be charged with the Devil's Dyke attack.

Like many people in Brighton, the first thought of *Evening Argus* crime reporter Phil Mills was: "It can't be Russell Bishop; he wouldn't be that stupid."

The day after the attack, the *Argus* newsroom was buzzing with the rumour that Bishop was being held.

Said Mills: "It was like that scene in the All The President's Men film, I was phoning round every police source I knew asking them if it was true. It was almost like, 'I'll count to 10 and if you haven't hung up I'll know it is true.' But not quite."

In the end, Mills got "three quasi confirmations" and the *Argus* ran the story on the front page under his by-line.

The following day, he received a phone call in the office from a woman asking for him by name.

"She was crying. She said that she had just heard on the radio that Bishop had been arrested and asked me, 'Is it true?' I said, 'Yes, it is.' Through her tears, she said she had been on the jury of the Babes in the Wood trial and she said that they had known he was guilty but there had been no evidence to find him guilty.

"I said, 'You did absolutely the right thing, you did your duty and you have nothing to be ashamed of.'

"The implication in her mind was that they had failed and thereby had let that poor girl, as she described her, be attacked."

CHAPTER 12

BACK TO LEWES

So, it was on 14 November, 1990, just three years and three days since the opening of the first trial, that Russell Bishop retraced his steps up the stairs from the cells and back into the dock of number one court at Lewes Crown Court.

He had been on remand since February and as he gazed around the familiar surroundings he nodded to his parents and brothers sitting on the same wooden benches on three sides of the dock.

Upstairs in the gallery sat, as before, Barrie and Susan Fellows, Nigel, Kevin and Ian Heffron, and Lee and Michelle Hadaway, now no longer victims in this case but members of the public, although treated by police, court staff and press as just as central to the plot.

Yet, this very similarity with the events of 1987 was the elephant in the room as the trial opened.

Seemingly everyone in Sussex knew the notoriety attached to the name of Russell Bishop, but dare not mention it within the four walls of the courtroom for fear of prejudicing the case and possibly allowing him to walk free.

Mr Justice Nolan made it unmistakeable plain that any hint about the Babes in the Wood would be an extremely serious contempt of court, could stop the trial and he would send the culprit to the cells.

Chris Fowler, the editor of the *Evening Argus*, had given his two trial reporters, Phil Mills and Paul Bracchi the strictest warning that, while he wanted wall to wall coverage of the case to meet the public appetite, nothing, absolutely nothing, must go wrong.

It was as if everyone in court was walking on eggshells, holding their breath, unable to articulate out loud what they were all thinking.

Yet, no one at that time could know that Bishop's legal team was planning to use Bishop's notoriety as a weapon in their bid to secure a second not guilty verdict.

Notwithstanding the eggshells underfoot, the trial from day one had a totally different feel to the Babes in the Wood hearings, and not just because of the strength of the Crown's case.

In place of nervousness there was an air of serenity and confidence that this time a guilty verdict was not just a hope but a certainty.

Much of this was down to the reassuring figure of prosecutor Ann Curnow, QC. Formidable seems almost an inadequate word for this powerful advocate who combined an iron grip on detail with total aversion to incompetence and excuses.

Deep-voiced thanks to a cigarette habit, she could dominate a courtroom like Margaret Thatcher dominated her Cabinet, but was never strident. She was imposing in argument but could never be described as a Christine Hamilton-type battleaxe .

Above all, she was not to be mucked around. Some months earlier I had seen her prosecute a case at Southwark Crown Court against half-a-dozen defendants, each with their own QC and junior barrister, all sat in row after row of counsel benches.

Moments before the judge entered court on day one, as defence lawyers muttered among themselves, no doubt plotting traps and ambushes for the lone prosecutor, Curnow turned and with a glare that could have melted ice, announced, "And I don't want any tricks." There was utter silence, no one moved. Then the judge came in and the trial proceeded without dropping a stitch all the way to guilty verdicts.

A pioneer for women advocates in the male-dominated Bar, she was married to the highly respected Judge Neil Denison, and her son, Simon Denison, is now also a leading criminal QC. Dark-haired, sharp-eyed and, at fifty-five years of age, at the top of her game, Curnow embodied the new confidence in R v. Bishop.

Opposite her was a very different customer in Ronald Thwaites, QC, brought in to lead the estimable Charles Conway as his junior. Similarly dark haired and with blazing eyes yet a beguiling grin, Thwaites was a maverick who could be touched with courtroom gold. I once saw him in a libel case give a closing speech entirely off the cuff, which had the jury rocking with laughter and which single-handedly won the case.

In a criminal trial, that spontaneity can be dangerous but Thwaites loved the brimstone of battle and seeking out and exploiting every tiny detail possible to win a case against the odds. In fact, he liked being the outsider representing the underdog and revelled in a reputation of defending the seemingly undefendable.

Much of that can be traced to his upbringing. Far from public school and Oxbridge, Thwaites took the extremely rare route to the Bar, via a secondary tech school in Stockton-on-Tees and a law degree from Kingston College of Technology.

As Curnow opened the case to the jury, Bishop, in striped grey shirt and grey trousers, started writing notes, a far busier and more confident figure than the first trial.

The QC told how the seven-year-old victim wearing a red and pink anorak, ski pants, a new Marks and Spencer acrylic jumper and white roller skates, had disappeared on that Sunday afternoon when she had popped to the shops for sweets.

A red Cortina had been seen in the road where she disappeared. She had been thrown in the boot of a car and driven for twenty-five minutes to Devil's Dyke where she had been stripped, sexually abused, strangled and left for dead.

Amazingly, she had come to and, sick, bleeding and dizzy, staggered off to be spotted by the Cliftons, who had raised the alarm. Earlier, two others, Richard and Pamela Symons, walking their dog, had noticed a red Cortina, with a "W" registration and a FOR SALE £750 ONO sign in the back window, parked across a track. The windows were steamed up and they had a feeling there was a courting couple inside.

The police swamped the area and found the roller-boots in a tree near South Down Way and her jumper and anorak half buried in the roots of an upturned tree. Later, a taxi driver found a discarded tracksuit bottoms in nearby Mill Road, which in due course was to yield a mine of forensic evidence.

Outside Bishop's front door in Preston Barracks was parked his red W-reg Cortina with an identical FOR SALE sign in the back window. He told the police he had spent the afternoon at his brother Alec's home fixing a satellite dish but had got a puncture so stopped there to change the wheel. Alec Bishop lived around 100 metres from where the girl disappeared.

He said he then went to his parents' home in Coldean Lane to wash his car. Russell Bishop was duly arrested.

Three days later came what the prosecutor called "the icing on the cake". The girl picked Bishop out of an identity parade.

Said Curnow: "The evidence conclusively proves that Russell Bishop was the man in the red car who took her [the victim] away."

Up in the public gallery, the Fellows and Hadaway had heard another prosecutor proudly announce that the evidence "inexorably" proved Bishop had murdered their daughters.

Not only they but everyone who had known Nicky and Karen at that point must have wished the girls could have had the astonishing luck of the young child who survived Bishop's hands around her throat.

But any ominous flashbacks to the forensic and evidential disaster of the Pinto sweatshirt was swept aside when Curnow detailed the strength of the scientists' findings.

DNA found on the blue tracksuit bottoms found by the cabbie in Mill Road matched Bishop's semen to the extent that the chances of it not being his was one in eighty million white males.

The chances that saliva also found on the tracksuit had not come from the girl was one in 5.7 million.

DNA on the girl's vest also matched Bishop's semen, with

odds of one in 19,000, and blood and saliva matched the girl in terms of one in 50,000.

Fragments of paintwork found on the victim's clothes and roller-boots matched the boot of Bishop's red Cortina. The boot had been vacuumed by the time it was seized by the police but fibres were found that matched the girl's brand new jumper.

The boot also contained a hammer, spray can and spanner just as the girl had described to police. Tyre tracks at the scene of the attack on Devil's Dyke matched Bishop's car.

That was the summery of the Crown's case, but would it be as strong when submitted to cross-examination in the witness box, or would it collapse like the last trial?

*

Day two proved again that this was a very different trial. The court was cleared of the public and the girl, now aged eight, entered the witness box protected by a screen shielding her from Bishop's sight.

I have covered dozens of trials – including the James Bulger murder and the Rosemary West House of Horrors trial –– and have listened to child victims, who, having survived attempted murder and sex abuse, have had to give evidence. Never have I seen such a composed and compelling child witness as this little girl.

The judge started by asking her if the robes and wigs around the court worried her. "No, that's OK," she replied confidently. He gently probed her life at school, and whether she knew the difference between right and wrong and truth and lies before declaring she was of sufficient intelligence to give evidence.

The girl told the jury how when she had got to the sweet

shop that afternoon it was closed but she had noticed a man fixing a red car and she crossed the road to avoid it.

"He jumped out and caught me. He grabbed me from behind, round my waist and pulled me into the boot of his car and closed it," she said.

Through a chink of light in the boot and the car's rear lights she was able to make out a collection of tools and a can of WD-40. She was on her knees being thrown around hitting her head as the car cornered. But she managed to pick up a hammer and strike the lid ten times.

"I started banging with a hammer and he said to shut up. I took off my roller-boots because if he had opened the boot I could have got away quicker."

The car stopped. "He took me out of the boot and strangled me." She passed out and regained consciousness naked in the gorse bushes.

"I felt sick and scared. I couldn't walk a lot. I was dizzy and kept falling over. There were bramble bushes that hurt me. There was a gap and I had to push the brambles out of the way and they hurt my hands and legs

"I tried to run but I kept falling over. But I saw a car and they were some nice people who helped me. He [the abductor] thought I was dead but I wasn't . He never strangled me long enough. I was in a deep sleep."

As Curnow pointed out, what a resourceful and resilient little girl she had been, bright enough to take her roller-boots off for a potential getaway, hammer on the inside of the boot, which was to produce important forensic evidence, and not only remember so much detail but deliver it faultlessly in the intimidating surroundings of a courtroom.

Thwaites was left with a thankless task after such a stunning performance. Might she have been mistaken in picking out the suspect form the ID parade? he had asked. She wasn't having that.

Then came the first inkling of the defence plan. "Did you know the name of the man who attacked you," asked Thwaites.

"People at school told me but I kept forgetting," she replied.

Thwaites also tried the same question on the girl's father: "Does the name Russell Bishop mean anything to you?"

He replied, "I think, possibly, yes, because I'm a local person and would have known about other things that have happened." A clever response in being truthful but stopping short of giving the game away.

The following day, Thwaites let the cat out of the bag and brought up the whole issue of the Babes in the Wood acquittal when cross examining police surgeon Dr Martin Knott.

There was a stunned silence in court that what, until then, should not be said had just been said. From then on Thwaites did not let a witness pass through the box without hammering away at what he saw as a conspiracy to "get" Bishop after the failure of the first trial.

In this conspiracy, through conscious participation, or otherwise, the barrister placed most of Sussex CID, a large number of forensic scientists and, by implication, any number of civilian bystanders.

It was a tactic that produced some results, but by its very repetition Thwaites ran the risk in front of the jury of over egging the pudding. In truth he had very little else to fight with.

Detective Sergeant Andy Young was one of the first officers to face the Thwaites barrage. His evidence upset

Sylvia Bishop so much she started shouting and stormed out of court in tears.

Young told the jury that Bishop had brandished a poker when told he was about to be arrested and Jennie Johnson had whacked him and struck DI Bacon around the head yelling hysterically about a police "stitch-up".

Young added that Mrs Bishop arrived and told her son, "Don't let them look at nothing. Keep your gob shut," before phoning solicitor Ralph Haeems.

Thwaites rose to his feet to cross-examine. After Bishop had been acquitted in 1987, had not the police said they were *not* looking for anybody else?" he asked. "In other words: We had the right man but he got away with it."

Young had also headed the inquiry into the firebombing of Bishop's home in 1989. Thwaites said firemen had told Bishop his family might have been killed if the bomb had gone through the bedroom window and not the lounge. Without waiting for a response the QC asked Young if he, the DS, had asked Bishop if he himself had started the blaze to embarrass the police.

"In all cases, we look at every possible reason for the offence," the officer replied, adding that three people had been arrested – but there had been insufficient evidence to charge any of them.

Young also denied that a police officer had been arrested but said one had been spoken to. Later, he clarified the position and, in a reference to Ian Heffron, said that a half-brother of the father of one of the Wild Park murder victims had been interviewed. "This man was a serving officer in Essex Police," he said.

Young then had to fend off suggestions from Thwaites that everyone in Sussex Police knew Bishop hated the police, especially as he was suing them for wrongful arrest, and that police had mounted regular surveillance of him.

But Young's ordeal was nothing compared with the unrelenting blitzkrieg Thwaites aimed at Bacon, amounting to nine hours in the witness box and him being recalled three times.

The focus of his attack was the second prong of the Bishop defence – that police officers, biased against Bishop because of the first trial, possibly deliberately, and possibly through incompetence, contaminated and invented the evidence used against him.

Bacon was asked if "evil minded" officers had tampered with the evidence, such as banging the Cortina's boot lid to fit the girl's account and create paint chards that were then planted on her clothing.

Thwaites accused Bacon of telling Bishop, "You got away with the last case, but you won t get away with this one." The QC then added, "You told him that when he got convicted you are coming back to get statements from him on the other matter – implying that you believed he was guilty of a crime of which he was acquitted."

With Bacon denying all the allegations thrown at him, Thwaites made detailed claims of alleged police failings, including placing the victim's clothing in unsealed bags when her family were asked to identify them, making no record of the roller-boots being taken to Brighton police station, and the logging-in book of evidence being incomplete.

When Thwaites accused another officer of failing to do his job properly "apart from sharpening pencils", the jury looked as if they might be getting tired of the QC's scattergun attack.

But he was making some progress. Detective Chief Inspector Tim O'Connor admitted he had heard police and civilians say that they thought Bishop had been wrongly acquitted in 1987. But he pointed out that neither he nor Bacon had worked on the Babes in the Wood inquiry and the two cases had been kept entirely separate.

When the evidence moved to the scientists, Thwaites renewed his attack, and Dr Michael Dabbs admitted that he, too, had heard people question the acquittals. But he repeated O'Connor's line that the samples and evidence sent to the Aldermaston labs from both inquiries were kept apart.
He emphasised that because of the controversy of the first trial, everything for the second trial had to be done with hyper-professionalism and "above board".

Nevertheless, Thwaites was still granted more scope for his allegations when forensic scientist David Northcott admitted he had accepted a file on blood tests of Bishop from the previous case that should have been destroyed on the acquittal.

Up in the public gallery, the Fellows and Hadaways were worried that history was repeating itself. Fortunately this admission and Thwaites's allegations were nowhere near as serious or far reaching as the Pinto sweatshirt blunders that had sunk the first case.

But Curnow had seen enough and was ready fight fire with fire. When Detective Sergeant Brian Smead told the court how Bishop had tried to change the colour of his hair prior to the ID parade by wetting it down and brushing it back, Thwaites returned to the attack.

Curnow interrupted to tell the jury that it seemed the defence case was that every police officer was guilty of "impropriety".

Thwaites insisted he had not been challenging Smead's integrity.

In a theatrical tone, Curnow announced, "Let the record show that this witness's integrity is not in question. As far as I know, everyone else's is." It was a telling moment not lost on the jury that if there had been a conspiracy there must have been an awful lot of people in it.

*

On 4 December, Bishop entered the witness box to answer questions for the first time in public.

The first question Thwaites asked was: "Did you abduct the girl, strangle her half to death, strip her naked and sexually assault her, as the prosecution alleges?"

Bishop answered, "No, sir, I did not."

He went on to deny all the forensic links to the girl and the tracksuit bottoms, which he said he had never owned. How did his DNA get on them? Simple. He had sex with Jennie Johnson the night before and placed two used condoms in a bin by the bedside. When the police raided his home they took his semen.

The rest was all down to the police stitching him up, he insisted when they came to arrest him, DI Bacon had said, "Come on, Russ, we have got you bang to rights this time, own up."

Even the police sitting in court smiled at that claim, which sounded more like dialogue from some 1950s black-and-white Ealing comedy of the.

His car's tyre tracks at Devil's Dyke? DI Bacon must have driven the car up there to plant them, said Bishop.

Thwaites showed the court a leaflet from the Fellows

poster campaign, headed: RUSSELL BISHOP THIS MAN IS A CHILD KILLER.

Turning to the Babes in the Wood case, Thwaites asked, "Did you commit those murders?"

Bishop: "No, sir."

Thwaites: "Can you help the jury understand why the police and scientists may have thought you guilty?"

Bishop: "With leaflets like that what can you expect."

There were tears in his eyes. An usher passed him a paper hankie.

The layout of the court places the press box next to and underneath the witness box. I could look up into Bishop's face just a few feet away with a view as close as the judge's and far closer than counsel or any member of the pubic gallery.

I have seen many murderers, rapists and clever fraudsters fake tears in the witness box over the years, but Bishop's seemed genuine. Was it possible that he genuinely believed he had not killed the little girls?

Was that how he survived so many hours of police interrogation, had the brass neck to campaign for the real killer to be found and convince so many people that he must be innocent?

Is his genuine belief that he didn't kill them because he has simply has no memory of it? Has he blacked out any memory because it was so horrific? If he has no memory of doing it then obviously, in his mind, he could not have done it.

Interestingly, the Fellows and Hadaways sitting in the gallery upstairs believe he was faking. They may be far closer to the truth than I was.

But perhaps Mr Justice Nolan, from his seat equally close to the witness, saw the same thing as me and, perhaps, that is why, when he came to sentence Bishop, that he was to speak the way he did.

That moment was still ten days away. Back in the room, Bishop recovered his composure and claimed that since acquittal he had been stopped by the police a dozen times. "Just harassment for getting off murder."

Earlier, Thwaites had made a short opening speech that was a masterpiece in brevity focusing the jury's mind on the two-pronged defence case, which was otherwise bereft of evidence.

He said the police and Forensic Science Service had "strained every fibre in their bodies to bring home his [Bishop's] head" – the trophy they had missed in 1987.

"Russell Bishop's name has become synonymous with the bogeyman as a man to strike fear and dread," he said.

The fact Bishop wanted the jury to hear about the previous murder charges made this "a truly exceptional case".

He said nobody could know why the first trial jury had come to their verdict but there was little doubt there had been a shortage of "believable, credible, cogent, compelling and persuasive evidence" because the police had been "hopeless".

Now the police and Forensic Science Service were prejudiced from the hangover of the failure of the previous prosecution.

Responding to Curnow's jibe, he denied he had been "police bashing" or had attacked the integrity of any police officer, "but I have attacked the madness and shambles of their handling of exhibits to demonstrate that if any policeman or scenes of crime investigator or scientist wanted to interfere with the exhibit, he or she had the opportunity to do so because there were no effective checks or safeguards to stop them."

As to the ordinary people of Brighton, the firebomb showed that there were some who thought Bishop should be "consumed by the flames".

Jennie Johnson enjoyed herself telling the jury how she had attacked "quite a few policemen" and used a poker as a weapon when they had arrived to arrest Bishop.

Sylvia Bishop confirmed Johnson had "thrown Bacon down the stairs, jumped on him and gave him a good hiding. Russell tried to pull her off and calm her down".

In her closing speech, Curnow said all the evidence pointed "inescapably" to Bishop, whom she described as "arrogant and perhaps simple minded."

She stressed that the police procedures had throughout been normal and ordinary. "Would you have expected anything less or is it just exactly what you would have hoped the police would do?"

The prosecutor dismissed the defence as nothing more than a smoke screen and mud slinging.

Thwaites repeated the intensity of his opening speech but had to admit that the girl had picked Bishop out of an ID parade. He suggested she may have been influenced by seeing the defendant's face on one of the leaflets in the poster campaign.

"The whole of the organisation of the Sussex constabulary must have been poisoned by Bishop fever," he said and claimed an independent outside force should have been called in to investigate the attack instead.

In his summing up, the judge reminded the jury of the dog walkers who saw a W-reg red Cortina with the FOR SALE £750 OR ONO sign in the back window. Unless there was a remarkable coincidence, "you may conclude the defendant's car was on the Dyke", he told them.

He described the girl as "an exceptionally intelligent, self-possessed and brave child describing an experience that would have left most children and adults paralysed with fear".

But he warned them she had only been seven at the time and was remembering events from ten months ago, so they should treat her evidence with caution.

Finally, he underlined that the Babes in the Wood case had to be ignored. It had concluded with not guilty verdicts and "that's the end of the matter".

When the verdict came, the Fellows and the Hadaways, who had attended virtually every day of the trial, were in their familiar seats.

The six man, six woman jury took four hours and twenty-two minutes – roughly twice as long as the Babes jury, in itself another indictment of the prosecution's 1987 case – to find Bishop guilty.

There was some minor cheering, applause and firm but muted sounds of approval but nothing like the pandemonium that had broken out in the first trial.

Wasn't Susan to take the chance to scream her years of anguish and hatred at Bishop? Instead she sat as if frozen to her seat.

"It wasn't for us that we were there, and neither was it for Nicky. It was on that other little girls behalf, too. I cannot forget that it almost took another child's life to bring him to justice," she said.

Nigel Heffron remembers: "The Judge looked up and mouthed 'thank you' towards us. We had been fighting to have

Bishop put away and we showed that our family just wanted to show respect for justice and the court process."

Sitting next to him was Barrie: "At the start of the trial, I had said to DI Bacon, 'Have out got him?' He said, 'We have got him.' I said, 'About time, too.'

"On the verdict, I looked down from the public gallery at him in the dock and thought he had done it, no way he had not done it. I don't give a shit about him as a person. He deserves all he gets. When is it going to be our turn? I wanted my day in court with him, which was to be long time away."

Bishop heard the verdict with his head down. Mr Justice Nolan, who had specialised at the Bar in tax law but had years of experience presiding over criminal trials, told him to stand.

Imposing a life sentence, the judge told him, "You have pleaded not guilty and insisted on your innocence in the face of overwhelming evidence against you."

Then, in a significant phrase, he pinpointed the essence of the threat Bishop posed to young children everywhere.

"I believe you are a very dangerous man, perhaps more dangerous than you realise."

He went on: "Your crimes are made all the more appalling by the fact at you are a father of three young children and come from a happy family background."

Bishop, wearing a dark-patterned shirt, wept as he was led back down the stairs to the cells by four security guards, as a woman shouted, "You're dead, Bishop!"

The judge then called forward DI Bacon, who had arrested Bishop, to praise him and his fellow officers in open court for their speed, thoroughness and integrity.

Watched by Thwaites and Curnow, the judge told DCI

O'Connor, who had headed the inquiry, "To you and the other officers, in particular DI Bacon and DC John Rouse [the Exhibits officer], who have bourne the brunt of very severe criticism and attacks, I offer you the commendation of the Bench and the gratitude, I am sure, of the public, for solving this crime."

Bacon later described the remorseless attack in the witness box as "the most aggressive cross-examination in my eighteen-year career" but he had the consolation that "the truth has now come out".

As Bishop was driven off to start his sentence, his father said there would be no appeal. Neither Sylvia Bishop nor Jennie Johnson were in court.

Michelle Hadaway strode off down Lewes High Street muttering to a TV reporter: "That was no less than he deserves but it doesn't stop there, I want justice for my little girl."

CHAPTER 13

BUT STILL NO JUSTICE

S o that was it then. If Russell Bishop attacked the little girl on Devil's Dyke, he must have killed the Babes in the Wood. Well it doesn't work like that.

There is no doubt there was barely a soul in Brighton who did not think now that Bishop was the murderer. Even if the actual abduction differed slightly from the way Nicola and Karen had been lured into the wood, all three victims had been stripped, strangled and sexually assaulted, then left for dead. Bishop had even tossed aside his own clothes bearing the incriminating evidence showing an identical MO.

Brighton simply did not believe, and didn't want to believe, that a second psychopathic paedophile could exist in their midst.

What did the people who had daubed CHILD MURDERER over Barrie Fellows's house feel now? Certainly no shame – he has never received an apology from anyone who had suspected him, let alone wrecked his home.

One comfort came on the weekend after the verdict when the *Sunday People*'s front-page headline screamed, YES, HE DID IT underneath BABES IN THE WOOD SENSATION ... THE PROOF. Beneath a picture of Bishop was a smaller one of Jennie Johnson and the strap line: AND SHE LIED AND LIED TO SAVE HIM.

Below, that readers were told, "At least today, Russell Bishop is shown for what he truly is, the lying, callous killer of two young children for whom he has shown no remorse."

Over two pages inside were the results of the hard work put in, with the help of the Heffron brothers, by investigative reporters Ted Hynds and Ray Levine.

They told how they had followed the trail of the Pinto sweatshirt right to the front door of Johnson's father Fred's house. He admitted on tape that he had bought it and passed it on to Johnson for Bishop.

They also found two other witnesses – Bishop's "best pal" Andrew Cater and Johnson's "close friend" Claire Tester – who both said they had seen Bishop wearing the Pinto.

What's more, the paper revealed that a defence forensic report of the key exhibits commissioned by Bishop's solicitor Ralph Haeems had backed the prosecution case.

The report stated, "We're totally convinced that Dr Peabody's results and conclusions relating to fibre exchange... are irrefutably correct." It went on: "This logically proves ... Bishop knows who owned or used the Pinto."

As the paper pointed out Haeems had had the report – which was part of the mountain of evidence he had disclosed to the brothers after the Bishop trial – while Ivan Lawrence was demolishing the prosecution's forensic case in court.

Other newspapers published the damning evidence gathered by the police that had been ruled inadmissible by the trial judge.

Ten days before the Devil's Dyke attack, an eight-year-old girl had reported she had been followed by a car in Hollingbury. She said it was a red Cortina and she scribbled down the registration number as "TJN 6?3". Five of the numbers and letters matched one man's car. It could only be Bishop.

Just two days before the attack, another small girl, blonde and with a pony tail just like the victim reported a similar experience.

There also emerged stories of Bishop turning up at Brighton Magistrates Court before the attack to sit in the public gallery to watch cases. What was behind that? It's unlikely he had developed a sudden interest in the law. Some suspect he was hoping to catch a similar case to his own and pick up tips either to defend himself in future or evade the police.

If that was the case he had dim-wittedly picked the wrong place. The Crown Court is where trials of such serious charges take place, the magistrate court would only hear minor cases or short committals and remands of the serious charges.

But, however satisfying that publicity was, the Devil's Dyke verdict still didn't amount to justice for Nicola and Karen or closure for their parents. Besides, the judge set the minimum term Bishop should serve at sixteen years, later reduced later to fourteen years, making him eligible for parole in 2004.

That did not mean that he would automatically be released on that date because he would have to convince a parole board that he was no longer a danger to the public. Least they forgot the board would have a copy of Mr Justice Nolan's strongly worded comments in which he spelled out exactly how dangerous he thought Bishop remained. But, even in 1990, 2004 did not look very far away.

Meanwhile, the parents of the Devil's Dyke victim wrote an open letter of thanks to the media and spoke optimistically of their daughter's recovery.

They thanked the "couple who found our little one, those at the golf club, the Red Cross Society who sent a vehicle to Devil's Dyke during the ambulance strike, the nurses and doctors at the hospital, the police at Brighton and Lewes, whose counselling and consoling made things easier to bear, the people of Lewes court for putting her at her ease, her teachers and classmates for being steadfast. There are many more but to all we say, thank you."

She had gone back to school after the attack and had settled back into normal routines. Child psychiatrists were said to be keeping an eye on her and, by the end of 1990, were reporting no problems.

Alas, it was not to last, with such terrifying violence and a near-death experience at so young an age leading to repercussions much later on. She had had plans to join the police but over the coming years she went so badly off the rails such hopes became unachievable.

To be fair, the Bishop family did not hide and fronted up to the trial verdict while staying loyal to Russell, clinging on to the belief that he was innocent.

One of his brothers, Mick Bishop, 25, a roof-tiler from Hollingbury, spoke to the *Argus*: "I think sex offenders deserve everything they get. They should be hanged, castrated, the lot, it's as simple as that. If he [Russell] admitted it to me I would disown him, I would have nothing to do with him. I would not shield him and neither would the rest of the family. But I just cannot see that he would do anything like that."

When his brother was first arrested, "my first thought was that he had been fitted up. He denied it every time I visited him.

"As far as I am concerned, he is my brother and I am convinced he is innocent. People are entitled to their opinion. If it was somebody I didn't know then I might think differently.

"As far as I am concerned, he would not hurt a fly. I am still convinced he has not done it. He is a real family man and he has never laid a finger on his three kids. He just loves his kids too much. There is no reason in the world why he would have done it."

Bishop went on to talk about his brother's relationship with Jennie Johnson. "She is a very strong woman. She has three kids to look after. She seems to be bottling up a lot. She was expecting him home for Christmas. There was not a shadow of doubt in her mind."

Did she regret not persuading Bishop to marry her in his years of freedom between acquittal and re-arrest? It seems at this stage that she could not bring herself to admit that he had betrayed her by his murderous lust for young girls, just as he had betrayed her love with Marion Stevenson.

The Bishop family had to endure more than just the shame of the trial. Three days after the verdict, his parent's Sylvia and Roy's home in Coldean Lane and his brother Alec's house in Whitehawk were firebombed.

At 10.10 p.m., a petrol bomb was thrown into the parents' garden and smashed on the patio and five minutes later a milk bottle full of petrol exploded near the brother's van outside his house.

DCI O'Connor confirmed, "someone could have been burned to death".

Nigel Heffron described the attacks as "pointless and stupid".

After the firebombing, Sylvia Bishop wrote an open letter "to the people of Sussex" appealing for an end to what she described as being "crucified" and insisting, "We don't want any hassle."

She said, "Six children could have died in the attack. In this instance it was five of my dogs that took the brunt of it, thank God, with no permanent harm.

"Russell has been pilloried from all sides, making him out to be some form of monster, certainly someone we have not known for twenty-five years.

"People are entitled to their opinions. [Some letters] are wide and varied, painful and even sick, but most, thank God, are warm and friendly and obviously sent with deep feelings.

"As a family, we are sticking by Russell. If at any time we doubt his innocence, you, the people of Sussex, will be the first to be told. At no time would we lie, cover up or shield him in any way.

"I like so many just pray that one day the truth will come out. Then and only then can we sleep at nights.

"Russell has been given a life sentence. So have we. As his mother I share his torment, his pain and tears."

She continued, on the same theme: "Russell has been sentenced to life imprisonment and now we are being sentenced to the same. I don't care what they do to me but just leave my family and grandkids alone.

"I have no redress against what they are saying about him. We did what we did to protect him. I did not lie for him. I am his mother and he is my son. Someone has to stand up for him."

It was dignified, if rather sanctimonious and self important, but it would have carried more weight and integrity if she had spoken up as publicly when the Fellows' house was being vandalised with graffiti.

In an interesting aside, the *Argus* also unearthed a telling picture from its archives.

During the Devil's Dyke trial, the defence made great play of the victim's claim that her attacker had worn a gold watch. Bishop proudly announced in the witness box that he never wore a watch because it gave him a rash. In 1986, he told police in a statement, "I don't wear a watch and I don't pay much attention to time."

Yet the *Argus* dug out a photo taken of the Bishop family celebrating his acquittal in 1987. There they all are sitting at home with big smiles all over their faces and clearly visible on Bishop's left wrist ... is a large watch.

*

While the police were trying to trace the firebombers, two other legal processes were developing.

The Fellows and the Hadaways were looking into the chances of taking a civil action against Bishop over the murder of their daughters. A criminal action had failed but there was a chance – a slim and very expensive one – of making a civil claim on the grounds that Bishop had been responsible for their deaths.

The advantage was that the standard of proof was much lower than in a criminal case. Instead of having to prove he was guilty beyond reasonable doubt, although judges now use the phrase "so you are sure" to jurors, a civil action would be decided by a judge on the balance of probabilities.

The downside was that it was very expensive – an estimated £40,000, probably more – and, without new evidence, almost certainly doomed to failure.

Lee Hadaway said at the time, "We don't have much money but we will spend every penny we have got. We will do anything to get it. I cannot speak for the Fellows but I know they feel the same way I do."

Maisie Johnson, Karen's grandmother, added, "We desperately want to do it but we are only ordinary people and we have no money."

In fact, their hopes did not get past the first hurdle in Brighton County Court in 1991 when a judge rejected the claim. He suspected it was a back door attempt to challenge the not guilty verdicts in the criminal case – which it was.

But, by now, both families were more interested in what Bishop was up to in his cell in maximum-security Whitemoor Prison in Cambridgeshire.

For, in defiance of all things sane and logical, Bishop was determined to continue his claim for damages from Sussex Police for wrongful arrest in the Babes in the Wood case, false imprisonment pending trial and malicious prosecution.

He wanted compensation for his hurt feelings and the damage to his reputation over a crime he insisted he had not committed.

After the conviction for the Devil's Dyke attack, even a layman could see Bishop had not the slightest chance of success and would leave himself open to all sorts of new questions and allegations.

His solicitor Ralph Haeems had clearly told him as much because he withdrew from representing him, yet, somehow,

Bishop, possibly egged on by barrack-room lawyers on his prison wing, still thought it was a good idea.

Did nobody tell him that the key question to be settled in court if he was to win was not, "Who killed the Babes in the Wood?" but, "Did the police have good reason to arrest him?"

He was also fighting history, as never before had a prisoner serving a life sentence sued the police over a previous allegation.

So, in February 1994, the familiar shambling figure in a grey suit and blue patterned tie shuffled into the dock at the Royal Courts of Justice in the Strand where the Square Mile of the City of London meets the West End.

He still sported his little moustache but his hair was starting to recede compared with the last time he had been seen in public at Lewes just over three years earlier and he looked far older than his twenty-seven years.

He had brought with him a plastic Tesco carrier bag for his papers and, with his head barely visible above the iron bars atop the wooden dock, he set about defending himself because he could not get Legal Aid for such a hopeless case to pay for a lawyer.

In stark contrast to the packed courtrooms at Lewes, the court was almost empty. Just a couple in the press box, nobody in the public gallery apart from his mother Sylvia taking notes and offering moral support, Ian Heffron representing the Fellows family and a handful of police officers and, on the counsel benches, just one bewigged lawyer.

Bishop rose to his feet and called just one witness, himself. Mrs Justice Ebsworth told him he could give evidence from the dock rather than put court staff to the inconvenience of having to have him escorted across to the witness box.

Reading from his notes, Bishop announced that he had been a convenient scapegoat and denied having anything to do with the murders. At this point, he broke down again in tears and his mother called across the courtroom – in defiance of all known court etiquette but perhaps understandably – "Take your time, son."

He told the court the police had only charged him because of the Pinto sweatshirt, which, he said, had no link to him at all.

"They could not afford to lose face, having had the glory of the investigation," he said.

After about twenty minutes, Bishop had clearly finished what he had prepared and started ex temporising, getting more and more rambling and repetitive. Eventually, he sat down with the look of a man thinking, "Right, where's my money?"

He did not expect the imposing figure of Richard Camden Pratt, QC, to rise to his feet, let alone expect that he, Bishop, would now have to answer questions about the murders for the first time in open court.

Camden Pratt has worked extensively for Sussex Police and Sussex CPS in many high-profile trials at Lewes Crown Court, most notably prosecuting Hastings deputy headmaster Sion Jenkins in his first trial over the murder of his adopted daughter Billie Jo. Dogged, rather than colourful, he was now clearly relishing the opportunity Bishop had stupidly given him.

He started by telling the judge that Bishop was a convicted sex offender and attempted murderer and posed the question what possible damage could his reputation have suffered in these circumstances?

Then he came to cross-examine the lone witness and the look on Bishop's face was priceless.

For the next four hours, Camden Pratt had Bishop skewered on a spit-roast, turning him slowly over an open fire. The QC went back over all the old evidence of sightings in Wild Park, the lies he had told the police, how Michelle Hadaway had banned her daughter from going near him, and his actual links to the Pinto – not just the forensics but Jennie Johnson making a statement that it was indeed his.

Camden Pratt did not have to address the fact that much of this had not stood up in court, merely that the police had good grounds for charging him.

It didn't take long for Bishop to splutter, "I didn't expect to come to this court to face allegations myself."

By the end of the day, Bishop was a wreck and Camden Pratt was looking forward to renewing the battle on the morrow. The only people who enjoyed the day as much as Ian Heffron were the Sussex policemen.

But, by the time the court reconvened the following day, Mrs Bishop had stepped in. Understandably unwilling to see her son suffer for a second day she told him the sort of truths only a mother can successfully convey and between them they dropped the case.

Said Ian Heffron: "He was on the ropes under cross-examination from Camden Pratt. When Sylvia Bishop got to her feet to stop the case, I was inwardly shouting, "No, no."

The judge rejected an attempt to seek an adjournment and possibly restart the case at a later date. She described Bishop as not having "high intellectual function" and thanked his mother for her help (i.e. in shutting down the case and saving court time and money).

She also ordered Bishop to pay the legal costs of the police, an estimated £75,000, and granted authority for them to pursue him for his assets.

As Bishop knew, this meant nothing. He had no money to pay, he had no assets to be seized and to this day he hasn't paid a penny, so the whole farce had been funded at the taxpayer's expense.

Mrs Bishop excused her son by claiming he had been overwhelmed by "the wigs and barristers' cloaks" and there was no point in continuing without Legal Aid.

In fact, there were considerably fewer wigs present than in either of the Lewes trials, which had not seemed to phase him. He had come to court thinking he could blackguard Sussex Police without any comeback and pick up a lorryload of money without even having to answer any questions. When he found out that was not the case he turned tail and fled.

Outside court, Assistant Chief Constable Elizabeth Neville accepted the inevitable. "I doubt very much whether he has anything in the way of assets," she said.

"We had ample evidence to arrest Bishop, to charge him and put him before the court. That evidence was independently considered by the CPS and the magistrates at the committal hearing and they too felt there was a case to answer."

She went on: "We are pleased the action has now been withdrawn, although the cost of defending it, in both time and money, has been considerable. It would have been our intention in court to rebut any suggestion of wrongful arrest or malicious prosecution.

"We would have shown that a number of suspects were considered and interviewed and that the case was investigated very thoroughly."

The *Argus*, which had had its hands tied by professional impartiality after the 1987 acquittals, now denounced Bishop in spectacular style as an "odious little creature" and "a wretched man".

"Is there no end to the damage Russell Bishop can inflict on the people of Sussex?" railed editor Chris Fowler on the front page.

The *Argus* also hinted that the police had new evidence up their sleeve that they had been prepared to use in court and that this had been disclosed to Bishop, which had prompted him to throw in the towel.

The Fellows were very intrigued by this. It would not be for another twenty-four years and another court case before they found out what that might be.

They had been waiting for Bishop's case to collapse before pressing ahead with a new plan to sue him for a nominal £15 for damage to Nicola's clothing on the day she and Karen had died.

Again, it would have been an unprecedented civil action against someone found not guilty of murder. But if 1930s Chicago gangster Al Capone could be jailed not for murder but for tax fraud, then could not this work, too?

But first, the family had to deal with another tragic loss. Kevin Heffron died of cancer on 2 January 1997.

Said Ian: "He had just got through Christmas. He said he would never give up on the girls. Nicola was his god daughter, they were very close. He was twenty-three stone, although, when he died, he was only thirteen stone, but he was a gentle giant.

"I believe to this day the trauma of Nicola dying was part and parcel of him getting cancer and dying but we were never, ever going to give up. We were determined to get the right result at the end of the day."

But the year that had started with the loss of Kevin also marked the start of more than a decade of hardships and setbacks for Ian that would have floored a lesser man. Instead, the dedicated policeman battled on through this personal turmoil and still kept at the forefront of the campaign for justice for the girls.

For one thing, Ian took up position as the family's spokesperson against alternative theories and arguments that the mass media interest surrounding the case had sparked. In one instance, they had agreed originally to cooperate with a book authors Christopher Berry-Dee and Robin Odell were writing about the murders.

However, the book, *A Question of Evidence* published in 1991, purported to suggest that Bishop had not murdered the "Babes in the Woods" and made references to two anonymous men as the real suspects. The Fellows family believed this conclusion shattered the book's accuracy and immediately withdrew their support.

Furthermore by 1997, Ian had been a serving police officer for twenty-one years and the call to a Basildon hospital A&E did not appear daunting. However, together with a WPC, he was tutoring he was required to deal with a patient called Peter Allen who had been locked in a cubicle after taking a more than a month's worth of medication in one shot.

Allen attacked Ian so savagely it needs an urgent assistance call and ten other officers to calm the patient down.

The following day, Ian was required to take Allen to a mental hospital. Despite fresh back-up, the patient punched

Ian in the face and was able to crush his wrist in the melee. The injury needed an operation and all the nerves were damaged.

As a result, he suffered an attack of PTSD (post-traumatic stress disorder), his third in four years, originally sparked when a woman had taken a bite out of his arm when he had been set upon by a mob of six people.

But this time, the injuries, physical and mental, were fatal to his career. In May 1998, he went before a medical board and, after twenty-one years and three months, his police career was over. Within two weeks, he received a letter from Essex Police, threatening him with eviction from the police house where he was staying in Wickford. What price loyalty?

Ian moved his family to the other side of the country, to South Wales, "which I had always loved".

As a further cruel and baffling twist during this testing period, Ian was also receiving threats that his new South Wales village in November 2006 would be leafleted with claims that the former policeman was a paedophile.

"This scared the hell out of my wife Mandy," he said.

"One night, she had to call an ambulance when I had stomach ache and they found I had a burst abscess on my bowel, which was threatening to spread to my lungs. This was life threatening; I was knocking on the door!

"A year later, I went back to the hospital at Llantrisant to have the colostomy bag removed and they discovered two hernias and I needed a six-and-a-half-hour operation.

"Within a couple of months, I sneezed and everything flew apart so I was rushed back to hospital to repair the damage.

"In November 2008, it all came undone again, there was a

threat of gangrene and I had to have another op. By this time, my blood pressure was through the roof.

"We moved to Essex and I was rushed to Southend Hospital, blues-and-twos [the police term for flashing lights and screaming sirens]. I was discharged but went straight back two weeks later for bowel surgery. I lost four stones in three months.

"Over the next three years, I needed stomach reconstruction, suffered a massive heart attack, which needed a double-bypass op, and nearly lost my left eye.

"In all, I had seventeen ops in ten years and we were fighting for justice for the girls."

That wasn't all. "Back in April 2007, I was driving through Ferndale on my way home in a thirty-mile-per-hour limit when I was passed by a motorbike doing seventy miles per hour. I did my ex-copper thing and I dialled 999 and reported his reg number. He was caught by the police helicopter doing one hundred and four miles per hour and jumping a red light.

"I was summoned to give evidence against the motorcyclist at trial. That morning, I had my car tyres slashed and from that day for the next nine months I went through the most evil intimidation.

"My tyres were slashed eight times, my windscreen was smashed, my windows were broken I received silent phone calls. The police did nothing.

"By August 2008, we decided we just had to move home. The children were frightened.

"At the time, we were expecting to get £75,000 for our home in South Wales but we sold it for just £21,000. I lost everything. The mortgage company even sent debt collectors after me.

"While I was away at court during all this, I was frightened my house was going to be firebombed.

"I got PTSD again. I attempted suicide. It all got too much for me. It broke my marriage up. It was a very horrible period of my life but I had to carry on with the fight for the girls.

"I got myself back online. I saw a psychiatric nurse who told me that a normal person would go through one major trauma every ten years. I had had thirty-two. My brothers Kevin and Keith died. There was so much going on it was a living nightmare. There was no respite, it was just bad news. My mother-in-law, a nice lady, she died. Everything that could go wrong did go wrong. I was involved in a crash and my car was stolen. I hit rock, rock bottom."

To see this hard working, decent man nursing a cup of coffee and opening up about his life with tears in his eyes was truly heartbreaking. But, and this was in 2018, he was determined to keep on looking forward and putting his family before himself.

"It was the worst time of my life and I'm hoping and praying that we get the result we have been waiting for. We can then take a step back and the girls can rest in peace."

This catalogue of devastating blows inflicted on a single person seemed to epitomised the never ending battle and seemingly impossible odds the Fellows were facing if they were ever to win justice.

Meanwhile, back in 1997, as the hopes of the civil action fizzled out, it seemed that the only way to get Russell Bishop to face justice was a change in the law and a repeal of the double jeopardy rule that no man can be tried twice for the same crime.

But how could that happen when this tenet of law was considered to be one of the golden threads of British justice for 800 years?

Yet, an answer to their prayers was not far away, but there would be many more twists and turns and heartbreaks before their faraway hopes would be fulfilled.

CHAPTER 14

DOUBLE JEOPARDY

Though nobody could have guessed it at the time, the Babes in the Wood breakthrough can be traced back to a bus stop in Eltham, South-east London on a spring evening in 1993.

Stephen Lawrence, a nineteen-year-old student with dreams of becoming an architect, was stabbed to death by a pack of young, white racists for no other reason than he was black.

It was a truly shocking murder but worse was to follow as the police, riddled by incompetence, indifference and alleged corruption, made a botched and pathetic attempt to catch the killers, who were all well known locally.

The CPS could not charge the prime suspects because the police had been incapable or, at least, initially, unwilling to find any evidence. As the years went by, the Lawrence family acted in desperation and brought their own private prosecution, which ended, inevitably, in failure and the suspects walked free, knowing they could never face trial again under the law as it stood then.

189

In 1999, the Macpherson Report into the scandal damned the police as institutionally racist and, among a host of recommendations, suggested the "double jeopardy" law be re-examined.

It was at a time when forensic science and, in particular, DNA or genetic fingerprinting was being constantly refined and had started to bring astonishing cold-case results.

Over the next twenty years, these refinements were to turn into giant strides and previously unsolved cases were starting to be routinely resolved. But only if the culprit had not previously stood trial. Government ministers became increasingly interested in closing that loophole, despite the centuries of tradition.

The Lawrence case first brought the injustice of double jeopardy into public consciousness but it was the tireless lobbying of the Babes in the Wood families, and Nigel and Ian, in particular, that laid the groundwork and steeled the minds of government ministers' minds to turn it into legislation.

The key moment came when David Blunkett succeeded Jack Straw as Labour Home Secretary and brought with him a more right-wing (in Labour Party terms) agenda, with the repeal of double jeopardy definitely on his mind.

But lobbying Cabinet ministers is a lot easier said than done and Nigel had to use the wiles and tricks of his previous life to get an in.

He explained: "Jack Straw refused to see me, he kept fobbing me off, but I got to Blunkett.

"I had taken a job as a tourist guide at the Houses of Parliament. Basically, I would show the coach drivers where they should park in Vauxhall or wherever and then help the tourists.

"Through this I became friendly with the police on duty and the security people who used to let me inside.

"At first, I was campaigning for the death penalty for murder but then I realised that we needed to get rid of double jeopardy.

"I would speak to MPs, but they just asked me if I was a constituent and when I said no they would tell me to speak to my own MP. Then I would gatecrash MPs' press conferences, pretending to be a reporter, but usually got kicked out.

"Then one day I saw Blunkett and I went over and introduced myself and he said I should phone his secretary and book an appointment because he wanted to talk.

"I had my foot in the door. Ian used to joke that we were Cagney and Lacey – I would kick the door down and he would go in and talk. That's metaphorical, of course!

"I told Blunkett that this was a terrible miscarriage of justice and it must be put right and we were getting no help, as a family, to do it.

"Blunkett agreed and it was clear that he had read all about it before he saw me so he knew fully what was going on. I didn't have to explain the case to him as if he was a stranger.

"He said, 'I don't know what support I can give you but I will give you as much as I can.' And that included a say in Bishop's parole situation, which was unprecedented as, officially, we had no standing in that case at all."

Blunkett was now determined to repeal double jeopardy but knew he would face an avalanche of criticism from legal groups, such as the Bar, and from Liberty and other civil-liberties outfits.

What the Fellows family, and other families from all over the country who had suffered in a similar way, could provide was first-hand experience of miscarriages and the pain and suffering they had caused.

These families were doing everything to push momentum forward. Ian and his daughter Lorna went to see the Attorney General Lord Goldsmith, while Nigel met Baroness Anelay of St John's, the Shadow Home Office Minister.

Said Ian, "Goldsmith invited me to make representations for fifteen minutes at the House of Lords. I leaped at the opportunity. I took Lorna. She had been seven at the time of the murders but she is a very intelligent lass.

"Ann Ming, who was another key figure in getting rid of double jeopardy after her fifteen-year-old daughter was murdered in 1989, had her say first.

"I listened to what she had to say and it was heartbreaking. I broke down and started crying. They gave me a ten-minute break to recover then I presented our part of what we wanted to say.

"We wanted them to make an amendment to the new law. They agreed and we were amazed."

The Fellows believe these meetings helped in a crucial change to the wording of what would be allowed in terms of new evidence to quash old acquittals.

At first, it was to be just "scientific" evidence but by the time the bill came before the House of Commons, it had become the far more favourable "new and compelling" evidence.

Their hard work was paying off and fresh impetus was provided by Neville and Doreen (now Lady) Lawrence, who came forward to speak out about the racist murder of their son.

The Lawrence's case caught the public imagination and convinced more and more MPs that this cause was a vote winner.

The bill was on its way through Parliament and, for the Fellows, there was now no time to lose after the threat suddenly arose that Bishop might be getting out.

Ian went on: "Bishop was eligible for parole in two thousand and three or four when his fourteen years was up taking into account the year he spent inside awaiting trial. We got a tip off that the probation department were looking to re-house him in Southampton.

"I wrote to the Southampton house department telling them what Bishop was like and warning them what sort of a person would be coming to their area should they agree. That quickly put a stop to that.

"Lord Faulkner, the Lord Chancellor, allowed me to be the spokesman for the victims and to have involvement when Bishop made his applications for parole. I said that whatever Bishop says, he is a danger to children and I quoted the judge's sentencing remarks.

"In the following years I was invited to speak at meetings and a rally in Trafalgar Square, by a group campaigning against child abuse. There were about 1,500 people there.

"Bishop started appealing for parole on human-rights groundsand naming me as one of the people harassing him.

"We were very, very worried he would be released and abscond by going off to France or somewhere. We were saying you can't allow this man to go free."

An end to double jeopardy was finally incorporated into the 2003 Criminal Justice Act, which came into force in 2005.

The act stated that three major stipulations had to be met to bring about a second trial. There had to be "new and compelling" evidence not available at the first trial, the application had to have the personal approval of the Director of Public Prosecutions, and you'd only get one shot – in other words, the CPS couldn't come back every couple of years to have another go if their first attempt had been rejected.

The families were overjoyed. Said Barrie, "I had always thought it would be impossible. But then I didn't know about little Nigel and his genius.

"Nigel, Ian, Kev and the rest, they all worked tirelessly for me and for themselves to put that bastard away.

"Doreen Lawrence deserves all the accolades she has got. I would love to say thank you to her.

"I never thought double jeopardy would be revoked. The law [stated] once tried you can never be re-tried. I knew Nigel had it all in hand, I knew he was probing, I knew what he was up to but I didn't know the details and I left him to it."

Reflecting to the *Argus* in 2006, Nigel said, "When we found the fresh evidence [about the Pinto] in 1989, we were told, 'Sorry, nothing we can do.' But we campaigned and my brother Ian and I went to London and were told we would get ninety-eight percent of our wish list with the wording of the new legislation.

"We started pressing the police and we got respect. You stick together. You are family. That's the way it has always been. When anyone asks me why I am still doing it, my answer is always, 'You have never gone through it [the murders]. It's the most horrible thing."

In the Lawrence case, two of the suspects were finally convicted of murder in 2012 thanks to new DNA evidence not available in the 1990s. One of them, Gary Dobson, who earlier had been acquitted had his case referred back to the Appeal

Court, which ordered the new trial. Originally, the second, David Norris, had been charged alomgside Dobson but his case had collapsed before it came to trial so he wasn't subject to double jeopardy.

*

Sussex Police had never given up on the Bishop case even during the long years of double jeopardy being in place. As long ago as 1993 – eight months after the Lawrence stabbing – the Pinto sweatshirt had been sent back to the Aldermaston labs for renewed examination on possible blood stains but under the technology of the time nothing new could be determined.

Nine years later, the police, alarmed at the prospect of Bishop's first parole-board hearing fast approaching in 2004, tried again with the experts at the Forensic Science Service (FSS).

In August 2003, the FSS had reported that they had found traces of DNA from two separate sources but that they were too complex and uncertain to pinpoint further. Tellingly, scientists were already warning that the way the police had stored and opened and resealed the packages containing the Pinto may have allowed contamination and transference that could call into question the findings.

Undaunted, and with the repeal of double jeopardy now looking a certainty rather than a possibility, the police pressed ahead and, in 2004, Operation Salop was officially launched with a cold-case review some seventeen years after Bishop's acquittal.

Not only the Fellows and Hadaway families but most of Brighton, it seemed, had their hopes raised to new levels by the prospect of a combination of a new law and new technology finally unlocking the door to putting Bishop back on trial.

Forensic scientist Raymond Chapman re-examined the Pinto and found new fibre evidence, and also looked again at taping from the sweatshirt taken in 1986 and 2002.

In December 2005, with the Criminal Justice Act now in force, he reported that he had found very strong support for the fact that the Pinto had been in contact with Bishop's home environment.

Similarly, another forensic scientist, Carole Evans, found that DNA from hairs taken from the Pinto showed moderate support that they had come from Bishop or a maternal relative.

Promising, but the CPS understandably decided that this was not enough to take back to court. The memory of the forensic disaster of 1987 was still too raw to risk a repeat.

In September 2006, a month before the twentieth anniversary of the murders, Assistant Chief Constable Nigel Yeo announced publicly that the new inquiry had failed to find sufficient new evidence to warrant fresh charges.

It was a bitter blow for the families and those who had built up their hopes. There was talk of trying to raise money for a judicial review of the decision not to bring charges but nothing came of it.

The police, battling to keep the families onside, pleaded for patience and hinted to them that there was more to come.

Barrie, speaking now with perhaps the benefit of hindsight, was more sanguine than most at this turn of events. "When the police said there was no new evidence to bring new charges I was not too worried because I had heard there was a little bit of evidence that could not be submitted until they were ready," he said, looking back.

In October 2006, on the actual anniversary of the murders,

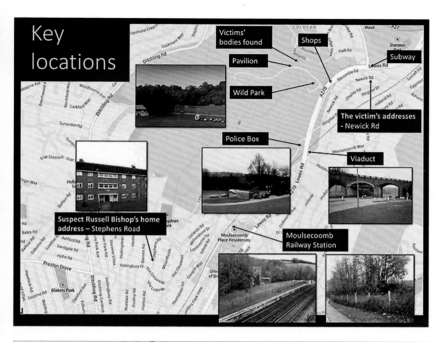

Key locations

Victims' bodies found

Shops

Subway

Pavilion

Wild Park

The victim's addresses - Newick Rd

Police Box

Viaduct

Suspect Russell Bishop's home address – Stephens Road

Moulsecoomb Railway Station

Above: Wild Park and the Moulsecoomb estate. © *Sussex Police*

Below: Newick Road, on the Moulsecoomb estate, where the Fellows and the Hadaways lived. © *Rex Features/Shutterstock*

Above: Police and forensic scientists set up camp on the slope in Wild Park, below the den in the woods where the bodies were found. © *PA Images*

Below: The hawthorne tree in Wild Park where an impromptu memorial was set up after the bodies were discovered. It was as near to the murder scene as the police would allow the public. © *PA Images*

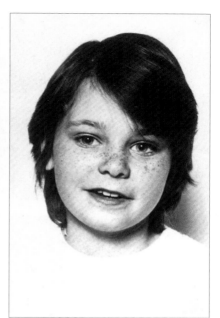

Above: Nicola Fellows (left) and Karen Hadaway (right). © *Sussex Police*

Below left: Russell Bishop as he was when charged for the first time with the murders, in December 1986. © *PA Images*

Below right: Marion Stevenson in November 1986 © *Argus Archive/Brighton and Hove Stuff*

Left: The funeral cortège led from the Moulsecoomb estate to St Andrews church for the service and on to the cemetery in Bear Road.

© *PA Images*

Right: The coffins outside the church: Karen's in the foreground and Nicola's behind. Barrie Fellows can be seen beside the St Andrews church sign.

© *PA Images*

Left: The murders hit everyone hard on the Moulsecoomb estate – especially the young.

© *PA Images*

Above left: Barrie Fellows, cigarette characteristically in hand, at the Seafarer fish and chip shop in Barcombe Road. This is where the girls had bought chips the night they died, and was one of the last places where they had been seen alive. © *Argus Archive/Brighton and Hove Stuff*

Above right: Michelle and Lee Hadaway in Wild Park.

Below: Barrie Fellows arrives at Lewes Crown Court with his brothers, for the first trial of Russell Bishop. On the right is gentle giant Kevin Heffron. To the left, Ian masks Nigel from the camera's view. © *Rex Features/Shutterstock*

Left: Lee and Michelle Hadaway and Barrie and Susan Fellows either side of Brighton MP Andrew Bowden outside the House of Commons, with the petition to reopen the 'Babes in the Woods' murder inquiry.
© *PA Images*

Right: Russell Bishop's Pinto sweatshirt, bearing the treasure trove of forensic evidence which played such a crucial role in both trials. Note the traces of red paint which matched the paint on the car he had been spraying.
© *Sussex Police*

Left: Brian Altman QC, the brilliant Old Bailey prosecutor, on the jury site visit to Wild Park in October 2018. Behind him is the bearded figure of Mr Justice Sweeney.
© *PA Images*

Inset: The den in the Wild Park woods where the bodies were found. © *Sussex Police*

Above left: Barrie Fellows, his gait unsteady because of persistent leg problems, arrives at the Old Bailey to give evidence at the second trial. © *PA Images*

Above right: Russell Bishop as he is now – a very different figure to 1986. An artist impression of him appearing on video link from Frankland prison to the Old Bailey at a pre-trial hearing in January 2018 (© PA Images) and, inset, the custody picture after he had been rearrested for murder in 2016 *(© Sussex Police)*.

Below: Michelle Hadaway and Susan Fellows consumed by emotion outside the Old Bailey after Bishop was convicted of double murder. Behind them is Michelle's daughter, Lyndsey. © *PA Images*

Left: Nigel Heffron at the Wild Park memorial in 2019. © *Mike Alsford*

Right: The graves in the children's section of the cemetery in Bear Road, Brighton. Proceeds of this book paid for repairs to the masonry, which had damaged by weather erosion and subsidence – and has now restored it to the exact state it was in 1988. © *PA Images*

Left: A banner erected at the entrance to Wild Park after the Old Bailey conviction epitomise the relief and satisfaction of the estate after decades of hurt and anger. It was put up by Nigel Heffron and his nephew Peter Burrows, beside a flower arrangement by Nigel's wife Christine and his niece Emma. © *PA Images*

the families staged a protest march and Nigel and Ian issued a press release indicating the families' anger and despair:

> The families of Nicola Fellows and Karen Hadaway are to march from Brighton police station to Wild Park on Tuesday, 10 Oct 2006, starting at 2 p.m.
>
> They are asking if anyone would like to walk with them, if so, could they either carry a photo or a teddy bear to show support.
>
> They hope to arrive at the park around the time the girls were found at 4.30 p.m.
>
> A judicial review has been commenced and the police have been invited to initially respond.
>
> The families are shocked that ACO Nigel Yeo wrongly advised the media that his force has fully reviewed all evidence. Neglecting to contact SEVEN witnesses whose details had been provided to them at the outset of the new investigation
>
> This is unacceptable, he then compounds the error by saying the case remains open and evidence coming forward would be investigated. Why wasn't it done before?
>
> It is now 20 years since these awful crimes were committed, the girls will never be forgotten.

That afternoon, at the hawthorne tree shrine close to the murder scene, Michelle stood with Susan and their families. They had brought a teddy and red roses.

"All we want is justice for those girls," Michelle said. "We haven't had justice in the past twenty years."

The police were coming under increased pressure. The

public, fuelled by press allegations, were casting round for all sorts of other suspects. Could it be Roy Whiting, who was jailed for life for abducting and killing eight-year-old Sara Payne near Littlehampton after being released from a sentence for a kidnapping and sex attack on another girl also aged eight in Crawley?

Could it be Peter Tobin, the Scottish serial killer, who had lived off and on in Brighton from 1969 to the late eighties? Or even Levi Bellfield, who abducted and killed schoolgirl Millie Dowler and two other young women in South-west London and Surrey?

An unsolved murder is a gaping wound for any police officer. The Babes in the Wood was the highest-profile unsolved murder in Sussex and it hurt the most. Something had to be done, and fast, because if Bishop was released here would be trouble, serious trouble.

The public pressure on the police was cranked up another notch thanks to a man who used to be one of their own. Soon after the protest march former DS Phil Swan, once a key figure in the Bishop inquiry and later a pub landlord in Chichester, decided to speak out.

In a double-page spread in the *Mail on Sunday*, Swan said he was convinced Bishop was guilty of the murders and blamed Sussex Police for preventing him giving evidence at the trial.

"If I'd been allowed to give my evidence against Bishop, he might have gone to prison for the Babes in the Wood murders," said Swan, described as a "security specialist".

"Then he wouldn't have been free to attack that next little girl [on Devil's Dyke]. I've felt terrible for years. It's time I stood up to be counted."

Swan told reporter Eileen Fairweather that Bishop had ducked and weaved in interviews until he was shown the Pinto sweatshirt and told Jennie Johnson had confirmed it was his. Swan said he then placed photos of the dead girls in front of Bishop looking exactly how he had described them.

"I said, 'You only knew about the blood, the dirt, the foam, because of how you left them: for dead,' Swan told the paper. 'He pulsated. He went absolutely white, there was water in his eyes, they were bulging, and he was shaking like a leaf. I thought he was going to pass out – or cough it. "Over the years, experience tells you when they're on the verge.

"But then he started screaming, 'Get him away from me!' and his lawyer said, 'I'm ending the interview,' and got him out of the room. After he was brought back, he wouldn't say a word. He just stared above our heads."

Swan had an important role in the inquiry but three months before the trial, the detective had been suspended by the police, and later sacked, allegedly for matters relating to an expenses claim.

Swan now said the allegation was "Mickey Mouse stuff" and the expenses for petrol and a meal at a motorway service station had been incurred during police business.

He then claimed that he could have turned the trial if he had been called as a witness. However, the prosecution had little option but to drop him as a witness. How could they have called a police officer who was suspected of falsifying an expense claim and be certain the jury would view him as an honest witness? The prosecution had enough trouble convincing jurors of its case based on witnesses who were above board and of unimpeachable integrity.

In the *Mail on Sunday* article, Swan went on to make two astonishing allegations.

First, he claimed his suspension was apart of some conspiracy to sabotage the case by a senior officer in the force whom he suspected of being involved in a child pornography ring.

Second, he claimed that Bishop had written to a fifteen-year-old girl who thought she was pregnant by him, saying that he hoped the baby would be a girl "because I want to be the first to have her". Allegedly meaning to sexually abuse the baby.

This claim had been circulating privately among a number of police officers. As was disclosed decades later, Bishop had written to a young girl from prison but all the letters would have been inadmissible at the 1987 trial.

Swan's intervention was deliberately timed to make the police look bad. They were under acute pressure and were unwilling to reveal that they all they could do was wait in the hope that the ever-evolving new forensic techniques would still win the day for them.

For the Fellows and the Hadaways, the hopes of justice were as far away as ever. They did not know that a reviled figure from the past was about to return to make their mood even darker, though.

CHAPTER 15

———

BREAKTHROUGH

W hile the scientists were still beavering away with the murder exhibits, in the summer of 2007, Marion Stevenson was back talking to the police and repeating her claims about Barrie Fellows and that video.

At this time, she was in her mid- to late-twenties, in a new relationship and had children of her own. But she refused to put the days of 1986 behind her.

In July, she made a fresh statement to the police, making the same allegation about Barrie and Dougie Judd (albeit with some differences to her 1988 account).

In her new statement, she describes going to the Fellows house a few months before the murders. "It was a school day," she said.

"Dougie was there with his brother, Timothy [first time he was mentioned] and Russell Bishop.

"There was a bottle of Pernod [first time mentioned] and we shared it between the four of us. I was mixing it with blackcurrant, we smoked [pot], drank and listened to music.

"I decided to go to the kitchen to get a drink of water, the drinking was making me thirsty. You have to go through the sitting room to get to the kitchen. There was a sofa and two armchair. You have to walk around the back of the sofa to get to the kitchen.

"There was quite a big TV standing on something wooden and it [the TV] was on top of a silver-coloured video recorder. There were two people in the room [first mention of a second man].

"Barrie Fellows was sitting on the sofa and to his left was the other man who I have not seen before or since. He had short dark brown or black hair with little bits of grey."

She said that what they were watching on the screen was two figures having sex, adding that by 1986, she had seen a few pornographic films and that the pictures had been in colour.

"I saw Nicola Fellows lying absolutely naked on her back on a single bed [previously, she said Nicola was topless with a blanket covering her lower half]. She had her legs apart and I saw her face clearly. I immediately recognised her. It looked like Dougie Judd's bed in his room.

"When I first saw the man he was withdrawing his hand from between her legs. I have no doubt at all it was Dougie Judd. They were about to have sex [in the other statement, she said they appeared to be having sex].

"I could not believe what I was seeing." Stevenson said she watched for about one to two minutes. "I turned and went back to Dougie Judd's room. I said I didn't feel well and I was going home to bed. I left the house and I never said anything about that video to anyone."

The police re-interviewed her in December of that year and confronted her with her earlier newspaper story, to which she had to admit "I must have spoken to a newspaper reporter" but said she had given the money they paid her to charity, claiming she was unhappy at profiting from the murders "unlike Barrie Fellows". More accurately, she should have said "unlike Russell Bishop".

Stevenson said that at the time of her relationship with Bishop she had been scared of him and that now she thought that he, Barrie Fellows and Judd were all responsible for the murders, having "been in it together".

Having denounced Barrie as a paedophile and a murderer, she then created even more anguish for the family by claiming she had seen Nicola "flirting when men were around, which suggests to me that she must have been abused".

This time, Sussex Police took the claims seriously enough to head north and arrest Barrie and even though he was soon released and never charged it severely damaged the bond between officers and the Fellows.

It was 7.30 on an April morning in 2009 when Barrie, by now fifty-nine and a father of eight, was woken at his home in Great Sutton, Cheshire, by *eight* police officers.

The supermarket worker and his wife Karen had to watch as police seized two laptops, a desktop computer, a stack of videos and DVDs and his mobile phone, before he was led away for questioning.

In an interview stretching over twenty-four pages, Barrie was informed of the renewed Stevenson allegations.

He replied, "The lady is a liar, I promise you she is a liar, she is a fantasist, she fantasises about Russell Bishop.

"Nothing untoward happened in my house, why should it? I have never done anything like that in my life, why should I?"

Barrie asked the officer if they had got the alleged video and on the reply "No," snapped back: "Exactly! It's a myth, it's always been a myth, you understand where I'm coming from, I know it doesn't exist. For the sake of my daughter's memory, the first I knew of this was when the *News of the World* printed it. That woman did it for the money.

"I don't have any recording equipment either. I have never had a camcorder in my life, I don't understand the technology of it."

Barrie was so confident that he had nothing to hide that he didn't even want the comfort of a solicitor by his side, even though one was routinely offered, during the police interviews.

Within twelve weeks, Barrie, and Dougie Judd, now forty-four and who had also been arrested at his home in Brighton at the same time, were told no charges would be brought.

If that sounds all pretty straightforward, the memory of it even now brings Barrie close to tears when he tells of what he had to endure: "It really hurt. It brought memories flooding back of when my little girl was murdered. It's like I'm reliving it all over again. All I did was lose my little girl."

"When the Sussex police officers arrived, I thought they were going to tell me they had caught my daughter's killer. Then I feared it was something to do with my son [Jonathan], who still lived in Brighton.

"But then they said I was under arrest but they didn't say why. They said they could not tell me. I was taken to a police station in Blacon and they took my glasses, my laces, my shoes. It was as if they were trying to humiliate me. I was that angry it was unreal.

"They had no sympathy for me or the situation they had caused, dragging me out of my bed. If they had rung me I would have voluntarily come to see them.

"At the police station, they said it had come to light that I had sexually abused my daughter and watched her in porn videos. I said, 'That sounds like 1987 and what I was accused of then. Why the fuck are you doing it now and investigating something that allegedly happened in 1987?'

"They said it's an offence that has been reported. I said, 'I know who this is and it's Marion Stevenson. Are you going to tell me.' They said, 'No.' They never confirmed who had made the allegation against me at all.

"But Bishop was coming up for parole and he and her wanted to muddy the waters and turn the limelight away from him. Then Sussex Police had the temerity to release a press statement. Nobody knows what that did to me, not even Nigel knows, it fucking destroyed me."

But the people of Ellesmere Port stood by Barrie in a way that those in Brighton never did. It was as if they collectively felt that this is not the bloke they knew, it must all be wrong, in contrast to Brighton, who thought it must be true, no smoke without fire.

Morrisons gave him time off to recover from the blow and offered him a new job in Chester, but Barrie declined and, until the 2018 trial, nobody raised the matter – behind his back or otherwise – again.

"When I was arrested, the whole of the town was behind me. The positivity of the people of this town was incredible. I had text messages, phone calls and cards from people all saying that they knew I was innocent," he said.

His now ex-wife Susan lent her full support, saying, "I just don't believe these allegations. I don't believe Barrie would be involved in anything like that."

Also, Michelle pointed out, "Barrie and Susan were our neighbours and their house was always open to friends and family.

"I would walk in there and my kids would go in there regularly and we never saw anything untoward."

Meanwhile, in a statement, Sussex Police said: "When there are serious allegations made – in this case alleging that sexual crimes had been committed against a child – the public rightly expects us to investigate. After receiving information, we arrested and interviewed two men. That process, and the inquiries that followed, have enabled us to decide we will not be taking action against either man."

Barrie asked the police for an apology, but is still waiting. "They put me through twelve weeks of hell and not once did they say sorry. Apart from the death of my daughter twenty-three years ago, this is the worst thing that has happened in my life. They sent Social Services round to my house after my arrest, to interview my daughter – suggesting that she was at risk of sexual abuse because she lived with me."

But sometimes, one step back can be followed by two forward. From the dark days of 2009, more hopeful signs were emerging, albeit slowly. As Bishop sat in his cell feeling ever more confident that parole was just around the corner, the police decided in 2011 to make one final concerted push and all the forensic evidence was sent to the labs of LGC Limited in Abingdon, Oxfordshire, for a complete review.

Armed with their preliminary results, Detective Superintendent Jeff Riley was then appointed senior investigating officer in November 2013.

Now there was a need for urgency. Bishop was the longest-serving prisoner held behind bars for a crime other than murder – the Devil's Dyke attack being only attempted murder.

He had already served way more than the fourteen-year-minimum sentence imposed, the Parole Board having judged him a continuing danger to the public.

But how much longer could this continue? Would his lawyers turn to the European Human Rights Act and mount an attempt to win his freedom in the European courts?

Even the worst killers can find a way of getting out. David McGreavy was jailed for life for murdering a baby and two toddlers in 1979 – far more serious than Bishop' Devil's Dyke conviction – but was cleared for release in 2018. The difference was that McGreavy – and other released lifers – had shown remorse. Bishop never did.

The police and the CPS could not afford to wait much longer to re-charge Bishop. The clock was ticking. An online petition calling for Bishop to be held in prison for the rest of his life had been signed by 3,000 people in 2013.

However, time was running out. In October 2014, Conservative Justice Secretary Chris Grayling approved his case for review – in Bishop's eyes, the first step towards his freedom.

Ian Heffron spoke of the mounting fears of the families that Bishop could be back on the streets. "This is something that stops us from being able to get on with our lives even after this long," he said.

"Every two years, we have to go through this. We need him to be locked up for life and to get justice for Nicola and Karen."

The terms of the Criminal Justice Act, which had repealed the double jeopardy defence, demanded that the police should gather evidence and act with due diligence or their request for a retrial would fail.

But, knowing they could only had one shot at a retrial and justice, detectives and prosecutors were determined to resist the pressure, keep their nerve and hope that the ever-evolving scientific techniques would produce new, even stronger forensic evidence.

In 2013, Roy Green, a senior scientific adviser at LGC, told the police he had found an almost full DNA profile of Bishop on tapings taken from the right cuff of the Pinto sweatshirt.

The profile had been found inside the doubled over material of the cuff and would show that it was more than a billion times more likely to have come from Bishop than any other person outside his family.

Hallelujah! A meeting was set up in December with Green to timetable a review of every single scrap of forensics they had – fibres, blood, DNA, hairs and paint etc. – by the new techniques, including the hyper-sensitive DNA-17 testing.

But within months, the hopes came crashing down to earth again and, once again, the perennial problem of contamination was the cause. Green's fellow scientific adviser Rosalyn Hammond – brought in to specifically highlight any potential contamination – reported that she could not conclude that the right-cuff DNA profile was more likely to have come from the wearer of the Pinto as opposed to having been inadvertently transferred from some contact during handling and storage.

The right-cuff profile could not be used in court. The search for new evidence had to continue.

"It was a dark day for the investigation," Riley admitted later.

In June 2015, Green reported that his re-examination of the 2005 evidence showed that fibres taken from the Pinto matched a sock and two sweaters at Bishop's home in Stephens Road, fibres on Karen Hadaway's T-shirt, and a fibre snagged on vegetation near the girls' bodies.

Fibres taken from Nicola Fellows's clothes also matched the Pinto and a skirt belonging to Marion Stevenson.

Green was able to put these findings into much sharper context than before. He found that there was "extremely strong support" for the link between the Pinto and Bishop's home and "at least very strong support" for the link between Karen's clothing and the Pinto.

As testing continued into 2016, Green was able to examine skin flakes taken from the outside of the Pinto and DNA processes on tapings taken during the 1986 post-mortem from Karen's left forearm.

Green found that the DNA from the skin flakes indicated two people and it was one billion times more likely that they were Bishop and an unknown person rather than two people unknown to Bishop.

The taping from Karen's arm revealed that what could be either skin flakes or dried bodily fluid bore DNA 58,000 times more likely to be from Karen and Bishop than from Karen and somebody else. Another technique showed that the probability of a man other than Bishop having the same DNA profile was one in 2,900.

There was further good news in the examination of hairs found on the Pinto, which provided "moderate support" for a link with Bishop.

Meanwhile, Dr Louisa Marsh had been working on fragments of paint found on Karen and Nicola's clothing. She found there was strong support for the girls coming into contact with the Pinto and maroon paint on the sweatshirt originating from paint on the Mini Bishop had been working on at the time of the murders and red paint from outside his and his neighbour's homes where he had also been working.

In conclusion, Green reported, "When all the findings to date are considered together this is what I might expect if Russell Bishop, while wearing the Pinto sweatshirt, had close contact with Karen Hadaway and Nicola Fellows at or around the time of their deaths."

That was all that the police and CPS needed and it was all that the families had been waiting for.

Said Susan: "We had a meeting with the police at Littlehampton. That's where they had set up their operation HQ to keep it out of Brighton and possible leaks.

"They told us, 'We are going to arrest Russell Bishop in the next month.'

"Nigel was there with me, John, Lorna, Emma and Michelle. They told us about all the new evidence, and the timeline would be: one, get the Director of Public Prosecutions to sign off the double-jeopardy bid and the anticipated new charges; two, arrest Bishop; three go to the Appeal Court; and take it from there."

Nigel added, "The fact they had this evidence was down to Ian West, who took the original tapings back in 1986 and they were kept. If he hadn't of done that, and it was before DNA was invented, then there wouldn't have been the evidence to charge Bishop again. It would have been no good going back to the Pinto because it had been so contaminated since the trial."

But Barrie had mixed feelings: "There was a little bit of elation but also I knew I would have to go through it again. I had hoped they would do without me, I didn't want to go to court but it was not to be."

The approval of the Alison Saunders, the DPP, was a given. It was time to nick Bishop again.

CHAPTER 16

"HELLO, RUSSELL, WE'RE FROM SUSSEX POLICE"

Russell Bishop was feeling quite chipper on 9 May 2016 as a prison van pulled out through the gates of HMP Frankland in County Durham. He hadn't been told where he was going but he suspected he was being moved to a new prison, a change of scenery, possibly even a slightly easier regime. Perhaps his parole plans were looking rosier, maybe his luck had changed?

Soon afterwards, he realised he had been hopelessly optimistic as the van pulled into Durham City police station and, after a night in the cells there, he was led into a room full of people he had never seen before who announced themselves with the dread words, "Hello, Russell, we're from Sussex Police."

Det Super Jeff Riley later described the scene as Bishop's face fell.

"When we arrested him he was really, really surprised. He thought he was going to be moved to a new prison but when the van pulled into the yard he saw all the police vehicles," said Riley.

"We introduced ourselves and explained we were from Sussex Police, and it's fair to say he probably wanted to go straight back to prison. You could see from his reaction, he would not have been used to coming out of prison, particularly to a police station and he indicated, without saying anything, that he wanted to go back."

Once the shock had worn off, he sat next to his solicitor, Mark Styles, and Claire Warren, an appropriate adult (it is a routine step for an outside independent to be involved, in order to monitor fair behaviour on all sides) and opposite DCs Gary Patterson and Richard Slaughter, for four interviews.

To start the first thirty-one-minute interview, he produced a signed statement: "I completely and utterly deny any involvement in he deaths of Karen Hadaway and Nicola Fellows. I was tried and found not guilty by a jury after two hours deliberation. There was evidence of clothing and paint put to the jury and I was found not guilty."

The police persisted but Bishop stonewalled "no comment" often interrupting before the officers got half way through each question.

"If you didn't touch Nicky or Karen this is your opportunity to tell us that."

"No comment."

In the second interview, lasting just over an hour, in between his "No comment" replies, he suddenly hit out: "The only evidence on that Pinto was them fibres. The [girls'] clothing and the Pinto were examined on the same table by the officers, it's on the record, you go away and look at it. It's got nothing to do with me. There no evidence.

"It's all been before the jury, all the hairs have been before the jury, it's not new, it's been planted and I hope that's not the case. I'm sorry, I want the case resolved but you are looking in the wrong place."

In the third interview, Patterson told Bishop about the one billion to one DNA on Karen's forearm. He interrupted to reply: "I'm sorry I have no more comment. I know what you are going to say."

Patterson: "Let me finish. It was found on a taping taken at the post-mortem by Dr West."

Bishop: "I have no more comment at this stage. I can assure you I am totally innocent of this case but no more comment."

Styles (his solicitor): "He is entitled to give the answer he has given."

Bishop: "I have nothing more to say."

Patterson: "You keep saying you are innocent so help us to establish that you are innocent."

Bishop: "I have really got no more comment."

Patterson: "Can you give us any explanation at all."

Bishop: "I have no more comment at this stage. Here some fucking stuff genied up thirty years later. I have no comment to make."

In the fourth interview he spent twenty-five minutes just saying, "No comment."

Bishop did indeed go back to Frankland but only after agreeing to give evidential samples of his blood and DNA for the Crown scientists to cross check against their forensic findings.

Bishop's arrest had had the secondary effect of freezing his application for parole.

A press blackout was imposed on any reporting of the new

developments and a date set for a hearing at the Appeal Court for the Prosecution to convince the judges that the 1987 murder acquittals should be quashed and fresh charges brought.

*

A month earlier, the Nicola and Karen memorial bench placed close to the murder site in Wild Park was vandalised barely six months before the thirtieth anniversary. The combined efforts and resources of the police and council were to replace it but, again, it left an unsavoury reminder of what Moulsecoomb could be capable of.

Said Ian Heffron, "Its heartbreaking to think that someone could damage the memorial knowing it's significance. It's there to show how much we miss the girls."

On the anniversary in October, the two families gathered to light candles and release balloons in their annual vigil at the memorial plaque in Wild Park redolent with the nagging pain that yet another year had gone by without justice.

Ian Heffron told the *Argus*, "It was highly tinged with sadness. Nobody can bring back the girls but we all have our memories that we will cherish on the day.

"We will never give up in our hope for justice and closure. We live for the day we can truly see them rest in peace. Nicky and Karen are the brightest stars in the night sky, sending down live and hope to us all.

"They are constantly in our thoughts and hearts, God bless you both, our little angels."

But that sadness was transformed into hope by word from the police that Bishop had been rearrested.

Looking back, Susan said, "I never thought I would see

Bishop back in the dock again. I never thought the situation would arise where double jeopardy would be repealed.

"I didn't really think very much at the time. I tried to put it out of my mind. All I wanted was just the memories of Nicky. I thought about it more when I was at home on my own.

"I just hope we have got him this time and he will be put away again but this time, for ever. Then Nicky can go back to her little angel bed and can rest."

Ian added: "We had a meeting at the CPS when they told us they were going for a retrial. It was tea and biscuits when just a few years earlier they would have had us arrested if we had tried to speak to them. How times change!

"We were never ever going to let this drop, never in a million years. The only way I would have stopped was if I was carried away in a wooden box. It's the same for my brothers even though we are all in our sixties now.

"Nobody could doubt our determination. We would not go away. We would not take no for an answer."

*

In December 2017, the Fellows and the Hadaways travelled into London to sit in court again as Russell Bishop appeared in public for the first time for twenty-three years. Not in person but via a video-link from Frankland Prison in County Durham – and what a transformation.

Bishop looked unrecognisable from the weedy, fresh-faced, lightweight figure who had sat in the dock at Lewes thirty years earlier and in his subsequent farcical appearance at the High Court in 1994.

This time, he sat four square in his seat with arms folded across what was now a barrel chest. He wreaked of self confidence and was strong and resolute in his replies. When asked to confirm he was Russell Bishop, he replied gruffly, "I am, yes."

He had clearly hit the gym and, in contrast to his self-imposed diet on remand in Brixton in 1986/7, he had obviously found a new taste for prison food. His hairline had receded to the back of his head and what little hair was left was dark not light brown.

Gone was the wispy moustache, while dark-rimmed glasses now sat on his nose. He was not fat but thick-set, with massive biceps stretching the fabric of his short-sleeved black-and-white-hooped shirt.

As the hearing began, he leaned forward in concentration. But that had the effect of taking half his domed head out of the spotlight so that his face was partly in shadows giving him a distinctly sinister appearance.

The other major change was in the prosecution team. If anyone had ever doubted how seriously the CPS was taking the case their fears were dispelled by the selection of Brian Altman, QC, in my view the greatest prosecutor of his generation.

Altman has a gentle but implacable style in front of a jury and he is a renown winner with an unparalleled success rate as a prosecutor. His win record includes three murder cases where the body was never found, which are notoriously difficult to prove.

Brought up in the far-from-Establishment boroughs of North London, he went to school in Chingford and graduated from King's College, London. He has an astonishing mastery of detail. In 2008, he kept in his head every facet of two complicated murder trials he was prosecuting that came to overlap. Not only did he win both cases but serial killer Levi Bellfield was to receive a full life means life tariff, and Mark Dixie, who killed a beautiful aspiring model in Croydon, also received a life sentence with a minimum of thirty-four years.

Altman has such safe hands that he was drafted in as lead counsel to rescue the troubled Independent Inquiry into Child Sexual Abuse, which had run into serious problems.

He was supported by Alison Morgan, nicknamed Freckles in the press room, a diminutive but rising star at the Old Bailey, with an infectious smile and throaty laugh. Her successful record includes murders and terror trials.

Bishop's third different QC was Joel Bennathan, a friendly approachable man, who, once wigged and gowned, is transformed into a steely-eyed competitor renown for a clever tactical approach to defending murder, robbery and especially terror trials.

In court, his quiet, authoritative and persuasive style is well liked by juries and judges. Alongside him was the experienced and online-crossword-loving Nicholas Peacock.

The three judges to decide this historic case were headed by Sir Brian Leveson, best known for the public inquiry into Press standards in the wake of the *News of the World* phone-tapping scandal. Before becoming a judge, he had been an accomplished criminal barrister, prosecuting the comedian Ken Dodd over his tax affairs, and Britain's most prolific woman serial killer, Rosemary West.

Now, as the President of the Queens Bench division, he was sitting in judgement with Mrs Justice Nicola Davies and Mr Justice Picken.

The key question the judges had to decide was not, "Is

Bishop guilty?" but "Does the prosecution meet the demands for a retrial in producing 'new and compelling evidence' not previously available at the first trial and in keeping with the requirements of the Criminal Justice Act?"

Altman produced not only the new forensic evidence but also Bishop's 1990 Devil's Dyke conviction as evidence that Bishop had a propensity to abduct, strangle and sexually assault young girls.

Referring to the Devil's Dyke victim by the letter "R", the QC pointed out that both she and Nicola and Karen had been pre-pubescent girls targeted after school time in Brighton before dusk. All three were strangled into unconsciousness, sexually assaulted in a similar manner and left in wooded and concealed areas, although R had survived.

After both attacks the suspect had tossed aside incriminating articles of clothing and attempted to destroy evidence on himself, his clothing and his car.

Altman also made an important change to the time the prosecution alleged the murders took place. In 1987, Brian Leary, QC, had fixed it at between 5.15 and 6.30 p.m. but the defence had produced witnesses to say that the victim's were alive and eating chips – later found in Nicola's stomach – at 6.30.

Now, Altman said the prosecution would allege Bishop must have headed home but doubled back and returned to Wild Park and killed the girls after 6.30.

Bennathan argued that there should be no retrial because the threat of contamination made the new forensic evidence invalid, he said the Crown had failed the due diligence test because it had waited so long after the possibility of new results first came to light in 2005 and, for a variety of reasons, Bishop could not possibly get a fair trial now.

He pointed to the random and careless storage of exhibits bags and even contents being "dumped in disgust after the 'Not guilty, trial verdict" as revealed in an internal police email of November 2014. The Pinto for instance had been thrown in a boiler room at the police station.

He put the scientists under pressure in the witness box but, after a day-and-a-half-long hearing, the judges rejected all the defence submissions, quashed the 1987 "Not guilty" verdicts and ordered that Bishop must appear at the Old Bailey to enter pleas to a new indictment of two counts of murder.

"In our judgement, the interests of justice point very strongly to that conclusion," they said.

In their written judgement released a month later, Sir Brian pointed out: "There is, in short, no necessity that the new scientific evidence should be conclusive or unanswerable.

"We have considered the points which Mr Bennathan has made, both in submission and when cross examining. Our conclusion is that none of those matters undermine the conclusions which we have arrived at. They are all matters open to Mr Bennathan to explore at a retrial."

In rejecting the defence claim of a lack of due diligence, the judges fully backed the CPS decision to wait for the best forensic evidence and they praised the scientists for their "assiduous and painstaking work".

"The prosecution only had one shot at making an application for retrial," said Sir Brian.

"It is understandable, therefore, particularly in a case as sensitive and high profile as this, that the prosecution would regard it as crucial to ensure that the evidence in support of its application was not only new but as compelling as it could be.

"We would observe that, in a very real sense, events in this case, specifically the DNA findings matching Bishop to the taping taken from Karen's left forearm, have demonstrated that the prosecution was right not to make an application earlier, since the evidence now relied on is clearly stronger now than it would have been in 2005 or at any stage before that DNA was obtained."

Finally, Sir Brian turned his attention to the two families: "We conclude by commending the dignity shown by the families of Nicola and Karen during the course of the hearing of this application."

"Whatever the merits of this application [and whatever result a retrial might bring], we are very aware that those families have had to endure enormous distress over more than three decades, and that this distress will never leave them."

Bishop would face a new trial. Susan was pleased but did not go overboard. "By then we had had a lot of disappointments so when the police told us he would definitely be found guilty my reaction was well we'll wait until the jury foreman says guilty before I get my hopes up."

So it was that Bishop, appearing again via video-link from prison, was arraigned at the Old Bailey in February 2018.

Two hearings were needed because the Prison Service had forgotten about the video link on the first occasion.

To the charges of murdering Nicola Elizabeth Christine Fellows and Karen Jane Michelle Hadaway, Bishop replied each time, "Not guilty, ma'am," as they were read out by the woman court clerk.

Mr Justice Edis, another former formidable prosecutor in his days at the Bar, agreed that the trial should take place at the nation's most famous court and not back in Lewes because of "the notoriety of the case and the defendant in that geographical area" and the difficulty of finding a jury capable of "approaching the case without preconception".

Altman put forward 15 October as the date the trial should start and suggested it would last six to eight weeks – twice the length of the original trial – because "the case is not without its complexities, it is voluminous and involves a number of witnesses".

Finally, the judge rejected defence submissions that the media blackout should remain until the trial and allowed a limited amount of reporting.

The *Argus* the next day ran the front-page-splash headline Russell Bishop in the Dock over the familiar black-and-white pictures of the two girls. Inside, they printed a court artist's impression of Bishop on the video screen with his chin resting on his left fist and a smaller custody picture of Bishop released by the CPS.

Wearing a light blue prison shirt, he stared directly at the camera with the eyes of a long term prisoner – hooded, threatening but, ultimately, dead.

The stage was set. Would Justice finally be done?

CHAPTER 17

SIR IVAN

So if Russell Bishop was going to dodge justice once again, how was he going to do it? What kind of ratlike cunning would his defence team adopt?

Who better to ask than the man who masterminded the not guilty verdicts in the first place.

Three months before the retrial started, I drove up to one of the Surrey suburbs of London often described as "leafy" to meet Sir Ivan Lawrence at his beautiful Victorian cottage on the green.

In his autobiography, *My Life of Crime* (published by the Book Guild), he described the Babes in the Wood case as "horrifying" and "one of the most sensational cases of the decade".

The murders were close to his heart for more than the obvious reason. Sir Ivan was born in Brighton, lived with his parents in Montpelier Road and went to Brighton Hove and Sussex Grammar School (he is now president of the school's Old Boys Association) before heading to Oxford University,

During the trial, he had accompanied the jury on the site visit to the murder scene and realised that Wild Park was where he had a football trial for Brighton and Hove Boys (it was also where Bishop, Fellows and their friends used to plat Murderball).

In 1987, he was a major figure at the Criminal Bar with a client list of some of the nation's most notorious rogues.

He had defended Ronnie Kray in the Old Bailey trial of the murder of Frank Mitchell, the Mad Axeman, and in a blackmail case that the twins both won, and also in the murders of George Cornell and Jack the hat McVitie, which the gangsters lost.

He also defended the serial killer Denis Nilsen and attended some of the 1960s Profumo-related hearings, which were to eventually bring down the Macmillan government. As an MP his private members bill had encouraged John Major to launch the National Lottery. He was knighted for legal and political services in 1992.

Now in his eigthy-second year, I found him, as I expected, sharp, enthusiastic, charming and calculating as his brain ticked over the lessons of 1987 and how they could be applied to 2018.

Settling back in what was clearly a favourite chair with his back to a lovely view of the green he reflected on that first Bishop trial, the not guilty verdicts, and why the jury came to that conclusion.

He insisted he had not known then, nor knew now, whether or not Bishop had been the murderer but, with the scent of the past battle in his nostrils, the old war horse re-fought every argument and reanalysed every item of evidence with the same certainty and conviction that he had presented then to the jury.

He voraciously assimilated every aspect of the new evidence, as I related, from the Appeal Court and remained steadfastly unimpressed – apart from the Bishop DNA on Karen's arm.

He pointed out that the mistakes over contamination of the forensic evidence that had done so much to undermine the Crown's case in the first trial would still constitute a powerful basis for the defence case in the retrial.

For instance, the Pinto sweatshirt had been handled by 15 different police officers, slung across seats in a police car and examined on the same police station table that had been used to look at one of the victim's garments, he said.

The Crown would have to explain in 2018 how the forensic failings came about, which, even by 1987 standards, were "many and inexcusable".

Sir Ivan also made great play of two issues that, over the passage of time, had faded into the background.

He insisted there had to be at least one other killer because one person could not have held and subdued both girls while he carried out the sexual attacks.

He also highlighted the evidence of two people helping the search who said that at 6.20 a.m. the morning after the disappearance they had heard girls' screams coming from the area where the bodies were later found.

I remain unconvinced by both points, particularly the latter, which would imply that the girls were still alive during the search and had, probably, been taken away from the park and brought back and killed in the early hours of the morning.

But doubt and confusion is the friend of the defence. Which brought us to the role of Barrie Fellows in the trial.

Sir Ivan said there were question marks about Barrie and Dougie Judd – and the timetable of them coming home from working together on a swimming pool in Hove on the day the girls went missing.

"There were inconsistencies in their statements. It was a very suspicious, odd feature of the case. But the idea that Fellows was in on the killing of his daughter is very unlikely," said the barrister.

"But once I read about the video porn on the estate it became an issue, it opened up a whole new world."

When I pointed out that the *News of the World* had published an apology and paid damages to the Fellows family, Lawrence seemed disappointed that a possible new lead had been undermined.

But he would not be drawn on whether he would have used that in court and he repeated that he never thought Barrie could have killed his daughter.

"When I read [in] the *NOTW* about the porn thing, I remember thinking, 'Oh, my God, here could be something to the puzzle.' I don't think I ever thought the father would have killed the child."

I asked whether Barrie's behaviour in court had helped the defence case and was surprised that Sir Ivan had forgotten the attention-grabbing outbursts.

"I don't remember it as such," he replied. "I only raised the porn thing because it was another anomaly in the case and the more anomalies you set before the jury the more doubt it creates in their minds.

"The key is there had to be more than one person, somebody must have taken the girls to the den. There were no signs of a struggle with the girls unless chloroform was used, which is unlikely."

The point Lawrence makes about anomalies and court craft is typical of an experienced defence barrister. The suggestions he raised might neither prove nor disprove Bishop's guilt or innocence but it might cloud case and that would always mean good news for the defence because it created uncertainty.

Lawyers are bound by rules of confidentiality when it comes to discussing their clients but it is clear that Bishop, as a person, made much less of an impression on his QC than the Krays, Dennis Nilsen or many others that Sir Ivan had previously represented.

"I dealt with Bishop on a strict fact by fact basis. I didn't get to know him. When one case was over you moved onto the next like a hired gun. It's different now and the leader has to go through the case line by line with the defendant."

Not that Sir Ivan would ever use such an inelegant word as no-brainer, but the decision not to call Bishop to give evidence in his defence before the jury must have been one of the easiest in his career at the Bar.

"I did not call Bishop to give evidence. There was no need to do so. There was no evidence to link him with any of the garments.

"There was no evidence to link him with the den. There was the clearest and strongest evidence that he went home – in the opposite direction to that of the little girls.

"The prosecution had no idea what time the killings had taken place. Their case was a complete mess. Bishop had, by his plea, denied his guilt, he had already given fifty hours of interviews [to the police] and explanation, and in any event he was a normally dishonest man who often said anything that came into his head.

"There were more reliable witnesses than Bishop who were called to give evidence establishing his innocence."

So, after the success of the Lawrence/Conway/Haeems team, was he not tempted to mount a replay for the Devil's Dyke trial?

"I was not considered to represent Bishop in the second trial because I was otherwise engaged. I though it might have been because I was preparing for the general election but it must have been some other case."

I pointed out that the Devil's Dyke attack took place in February 1990 and the trial in December of the same year while the general election was not until the spring of 1992. At that trial, the whisper in the press box was, "Where is Sir Ivan?"

"It wasn't the case that I didn't represent him because I didn't believe him, it was just I was not available to do it," the QC replied in some bemusement at the implication.

Nevertheless, Sir Ivan looks back with fondness at the old team.

"Ralph Haeems was a very good friend and he briefed me on a large number of cases," he remembered.

"In every dealing I had with him, he was honest and respectable. He was very shrewd and hard working. If anyone was in serious criminal trouble and asked around who he should have to advise him, the answer would always be Sampson, which meant Ralph Haeems, or Kingsley Napley.

"Charles Conway is a very good man. Ralph knew that Charlie and I got on well together. It was Ralph and Charlie who decided I should be the leader [in the Bishop case]. I must have led Charlie half a dozen times.

"He carried out all the ground work for the case. I came in and dug the knife in deeper. He did much of the principle stuff.

"When I read the case papers after getting the case once it had been committed from the magistrates court I thought we would be onto a winner here, mainly because of what Charlie had achieved at the magistrates court in the way he challenged all the prosecution case."

In his book (published in 2010), Lawrence pays glowing tribute to Conway.

"Good juniors, who are prepared to help a leader by grinding through the boring and detailed bits, and who bring experience, flair and wisdom to a case, are a joy," he wrote.

"Charles Conway's cross-examination in the magistrates court laid the foundation for the acquittal of an alleged murderer [Bishop]."

Was the prosecution of Bishop really so bad, and was Brian Leary, QC, to blame?

"I didn't know him personally. He was a nice looking fellow with a nice manner and when he was cynical he did good cynicism and he was honourable," said Sir Ivan, striving as the honour of the Bar would dictate, to be fair and generous.

"It wasn't his fault that the pathologist didn't take the body temperatures of the victims, which would have fixed the time of death, which was so important. That led to the disaster of the prosecution case."

However, he repeated to me his one personal criticism of Leary that he makes in his book.

"At the start of the trial, in the presence of the jury, I asked Brian Leary what time he was alleging that the murders had actually taken place.

"'I do not propose to respond,' was his lame and surprising reply.

231

"That underlined early on the fundamental and enduring weakness of the prosecution's case. They did not know the answer, although they should have done."

As I drove home after a day in the company of this fascinating man, I dwelt, not for the first time, on the job of a defence counsel and how that must appear to the families of victims.

Every case turns on the evidence and how it is presented to the jury, just as every barrister has to defend his client to the utmost of his ability regardless.

Sir Ivan's job was to defend his client and test the prosecution's case at every turn. That case was found wanting.

The truth was, as Sir Ivan concludes in his book: "The jury... must either have believed him [Bishop] to be innocent, or had come to the conclusion that the police and the forensic scientists had together made such a mess of the evidence that they could not be sure of his guilt. Either way the verdict was the only possibility on the evidence."

CHAPTER 18

HEART ATTACK

The new trial date had been set, the timetable mapped out, there would be a verdict before Christmas. What could go wrong?

On the night of 2 and 3 August, Bishop suffered chest pains so severe he was taken from HMP Frankland to the University Hospital North Durham, where a possible heart attack was diagnosed.

When the police told the Fellows they were aghast. Said Susan: "When I heard he had had a heart attack I thought, 'Oh, no, he is going to go sick, is he going to cheat justice, are we not going to get a trial and an actual verdict?' My heart sank. I did feel for a little while that he was going to pull out."

Nigel added, "There was part of me thinking I hope you have a painful death, but then we would not have got justice in court."

Barrie felt he same way: "I didn't want him to pop his clogs before justice."

The following day Bishop discharged himself, against medical advice, and was taken back to prison.

Back in his cell Bishop, clearly recovered, saw a way to paint himself as a victim and put himself in the spotlight once again. If all went well, he figured, he might even be able to escape prosecution on medical grounds.

Little more than a month later, he put the plan into operation when his QC, Joel Bennathan, informed the Old Bailey of the "heart attack" that he described as "shooting pains, breathlessness, close to collapse".

Behind the QC, on a CCTV screen, sat Bishop himself, looking remarkably fit and unconcerned, wearing a navy-blue-and-white-hooped short-sleeved top, the sort favoured by the yachting fraternity, which had become the go-to item in his cell wardrobe for court appearances.

As he waited for the hearing to begin he lounged back with the same self confident ease he had shown earlier, arms spread out across the chairs either side of him with the disinterested insouciance of an institutionalised inmate.

On the arrival of the judge, he confirmed his name and rested his chin on his fist with the elbow on his right knee.

In fact, the identity of the judge striding into court was another surprise. Mr Justice Edis was a respected figure but his replacement, who had found himself with a three month gap in his diary perfect for the case, was Mr Justice Sweeney, possibly the only red-robe judge with even greater experience as a prosecutor than his predecessor.

Sweeney, who sported a grey beard grown since his days at the Bar, was an interesting choice for this case. As a judge, he was not shy of making potentially controversial statements that embarrassed the authorities.

In 2013, he had ruled that the prosecution of John Downey should be terminated as the defendant had received a "letter of comfort", a form of amnesty, from Tony Blair's government.

Downey was suspected of involvement in the 1982 Hyde Park bombing that had killed four soldiers. He was one of a number of suspected former IRA terrorists to receive such a letter under the Good Friday Agreement. The prosecutor on the wrong end of that judgement was Brian Altman.

With rigid reporting restrictions in place, Bennathan told how his client had been taken off to hospital after his breakdown and monitored for twenty-four hours.

The hospital had wanted to keep him in for four weeks of tests but Bishop had decided he had a better chance of recuperation back in his cell and wanted out. Why? Well, as a Category A inmate, he had been laid out on his hospital bed with double handcuffs and two prison officers watching over him.

His lawyers believed that Bishop was unable now to properly discuss his case, give instructions or focus on the trial as he had done before. "Bishop says he has better days and less good days. If he walks a hundred yards he has to sit down and recover," said the QC.

"Bishop is anxious to get the trial out of the way but he is more than interested in knowing what has happened to him and what is to be done about his heart attack.

"He is anxious about going from the North-east [Frankland is in County Durham] to a prison [in London] for the trial and travelling to and from court on a daily basis. We need to know as soon as possible what is going on."

Bennathan said Bishop had been told at the hospital that he

needed to be seen by a specialist who would decide how serious his condition was – raising the threat of possible surgery. But the prison authorities were dragging their feet and, weeks later, no appointment had been made.

The QC asked the judge to – if I can paraphrase – tell the prison to pull their collective finger out and get this man seen by a specialist. Bishop had volunteered to allow his medical notes to be made available to the court to put pressure on the prison.

The prosecutor, Brian Altman, QC, rose wearily to his feet with an air of a man sensing impending doom for the trial schedule. He admitted that "the worst of all worlds" would be for the trial to start on time and Bishop suffer a relapse, which would mean aborting the case and starting again on a future date unknown.

This would effect the large number of witnesses who were, by now, old and expected to trawl back to thirty-year-old memories, he said. No doubt raising in Bishop's mind a possible escape root out of the trial.

A further hearing set just two weeks before the trial date to make a decision on whether the trial would start on time, or at all.

But by the time that day dawned, the prosecution was convinced he was up to his old tricks of lying and swinging the lead.

Altman read from Bishop's hospital notes that the defendant had actually turned down a transfer to a specialist unit at the James Cook Hospital in Middlesbrough. There was no mention of any further appointment with a consultant cardiologist, merely a suggestion of seeing a nurse and returning if the chest pains persisted.

"We suggest, with a fair degree of confidence, that since early August there has been no recurrence of his chest problems. It's been two months since his self discharge and it can be concluded that his condition is no so serious as to require invasive surgery. One has to assume that Bishop is fit and sufficiently well enough to stand trial," said Altman.

Once again, the facts had exposed Bishop's lies and his protestations of life threatening ill health and look-at-me victimhood.

Bennathan told the court that his client now wanted the trial to proceed as soon as possible on the agreed date. The judge was happy to go along with that.

*

A day or so before that last court hearing and back in Brighton two large pictures of Russell Bishop are projected onto a screen.

One is the slim, carefree, fair haired figure from 1986, the other is the bald, beefy, intense, threatening custody snap taken thirty years later.

"As you can see, he has aged somewhat – and they say prison doesn't work," joked Detective Superintendent Jeff Riley to laughter.

We are in an upstairs room of Brighton police station in John Street less than a month from the start of the trial.

Sussex Police and the CPS have invited the media to a "confidential and embargoed briefing" about the impending trial and we have all signed papers pledging not to reveal a word before the end of the trial.

It's not an unusual event before a big trial and is often used by the police PR operation to flag up big case they are expecting to win and try to focus press interest on the positives for the families and, in particular, the police and prosecutors. Or in their words "to assist news media in collating and understanding information that will enable balanced and accurate reporting of the investigation and case for the prosecution".

For the next hour and more, much is said about the expected defence attack on possible contamination of the forensic evidence but not a word about police, scientific or prosecution failings that led to the, in the first place.

Present are Riley, Nigel Pilkington, Deputy Chief Crown Prosecutor CPS South east region, and Libby Clark, senior Crown prosecutor and from the off they are all in bullish mood, typified by Riley's joke.

It was a good one but unexpected for a copper in front of a group of reporters, most of whom he had never met, in an on the record briefing, albeit one embargoed until the end of the trial. Might it come back and haunt him if Bishop was to be actually cleared for a second time?

Riley runs through the basic scientific evidence from 1986, the results of what was discovered in 2005 and the new, triumphant details unearthed now, plus the Devil's Dyke conviction, concluding: "The key thing for me is that we have never forgotten or given up on this case."

He outlined the impact not just on the victims' families, but also the whole community in Brighton. By implication that included Sussex Police and the stain on its reputation l eft by the acquittals although he did not mention that specifically.

Riley also sought to stress the close link and decades long

bond between the investigators and the two families. He didn't mention that they had arrested Barrie Fellows ten years previously on Marion Stevenson's allegation of child porn.

"The families have been really, really patient. We explained that we had the new evidence and we took them into our confidence and all of them were on board immediately with what we were trying to do," he said.

"They were very relieved, they realise it's not over yet, they want to see Bishop on trial again. They want justice that they have campaigned and fought for thirty years. They have been very supportive of the investigation."

So far, the account of the police investigation that never gave up and the breakthrough of the forensic-science results all rang true but then two points they raised about the families set off a klaxon of uneasiness in my mind.

First of all, police press officer Tim Mahony, who had actually been at the first trial in 1987, announced that a *cordon sanitaire* had been set up around the two sets of parents and no one would be allowed to approach them without the permission of the police.

Secondly, the CPS pair boldly and unhesitatingly announced that they were certain none of the three surviving parents would be called as witnesses in the trial.

What? How could the CPS not realise that Barrie had to be a key figure for the defence just he had been in 1987. At that stage little did we know exactly how crucial ! And as it turned out the defence were particularly keen to have Michelle called so she could be cross-examined, too.

Two weeks before the trial was due to open and I had a terrible nagging feeling that the CPS were way, way too complacent.

It was as if as soon as they had got the DNA results they all headed off to the chicken coop to start the counting.

I was not alone in being concerned by the atmosphere of uber-confidence being radiated. When it came to questions, Fiona Thompson, of the Press Association, pointed out, "You are pretty confident that you have got this one in the bag."

All three, Riley, Pilkington and Clark, looked a bit taken aback. Pilkington eventually responded by gulping: "I don't think we are that confident but we are confident that we have a really, really strong case. But in 1987, they thought they had a strong case so you never think you have it in the bag.

"It's a circumstantial case with a lot of science. We have got lots of other evidence, the DNA is just one part of it."

Once the trial had opened and before any of that evidence had been called before the jury, that self-confidence would be well and truly wiped from their faces.

CHAPTER 19

"OVERWHELMING, COMPELLING AND POWERFUL"

At 10.15 a.m. on 15 October 2018, Russell Bishop finally slouched into Court 7 of the Old Bailey to face a double murder trial jury for the second time.

It was just six days after the thirty-second anniversary of the murders – marked with the usual mournful and intensely emotional gathering first at the graveside and then at the girls' memorial bench in Wild Park.

It was there that a BBC TV documentary crew filmed Michelle, saying, "I just don't want to be let down no more." Barrie, who was standing next to her, added: "I don't want to be accused no more."

Inside the Old Bailey was the sight they have been waiting thirty-one years to witness – Bishop stood between prison officers. He was wearing a dark grey round necked T-shirt over light grey tracksuit trousers and trainers.

As jury selection started he sat back with his hands clasped on his lap and round his expanding gut.

Between the dock and Joel Bennathan sat solicitor Mark Styles, who had sat in on the Durham interviews. A friendly Geordie, Styles was to develop a painful limp early in the trial. "A stick across the kneecap," he winced, which turned out to be a hockey injury not a gang-related punishment beating.

The following day, the trial was moved one floor down to the much larger Court 16. Michelle arrived in a wheelchair and was helped to her seat at the back alongside the dock but out of sight of Bishop. She sat with daughters Lyndsey and Kimberley and two witness support volunteers.

After the jury was finally selected and sworn in, Brian Altman, QC, opened the Crown's case shortly after midday. His speech was seventy-five pages long and took the rest of the week to deliver.

Bishop kept his head down, following the words in a copy of the speech supplied by his solicitor.

Altman immediately spelled out the case in plain terms: the two girls were killed by Bishop "who sexually assaulted them for his own gratification... the main motive, if not the only one, was sexual and paedophilic."

As Altman spoke, Bishop started to raise his head to stare at the jurors possibly trying to divine their thoughts as they heard for the first time what, to him, was a familiar story.

Michelle sat four square in her chair, her tattoo-ed forearms thrust in front as she gripped her walking stick.

When the QC described how the bodies were discovered and the jury were shown the upsetting photos Michelle sat rigidly forthright determined not to be beaten, even though Lyndsey and Kimberley headed for the exit in tears.

Altman also laid down the prosecution's new approach to

the time of death, which is now after 6.30 p.m. This meant that the chip shop witnesses discarded by the Crown and who gave their persuasive evidence for the defence in 1987, were now very much part of the prosecution case.

On day three, Susan Fellows arrived in court for the first time and sat with Michelle and Lyndsey. Altman told the jury about the 1990 Devil's Dyke attack and the seven similarities with the 1987 murders and then moved onto the science, first detailing the forensic evidence as it was in the first trial.

Interestingly, he said that Dr Anthony Peabody, whose evidence at Lewes had ended with him being pinned to the wall by a frustrated police officer, would be called again but only in a limited way.

"The prosecution is not relying on him as an expert witness as such, as things have moved on substantially in the thirty years or so since his examinations," said Altman.

How substantially became plain to the jury when the QC unveiled the new findings – the DNA, the fibres, the paint stains, the hairs.

Even apart from the one-billion-to-one DNA found on Karen's left forearm, time after time, each piece of evidence was marked by scientists as "extremely strong support" for proof that Bishop was the killer.

As Altman explained, that level of support was 7 out of 7 on a scale used by scientists ranging from inconclusive (the lowest), through limited, moderate, moderately strong, strong, very strong, to extremely strong support (the highest).

There was no reference to Jennie Johnson, nor to her original statement confirming Bishop had owned the Pinto, nor to her subsequent performance in court in 1987.

It was clear that the Crown was convinced that the forensic evidence was enough to prove the Pinto was Bishop's regardless of his predictable denials or what anybody else might say.

Finally, the prosecutor told the jury how, in anticipating the defence would argue contamination, a specialist, Ros Hammond, had re-examined all the exhibits with just that threat in mind, and to rule out anything potentially compromised.

Said Altman, "For each piece of evidence she considered, there was, she says, either no possibility that the evidence arose through inadvertent transfer [i.e. contamination], or the probability that it had occurred in that way was so small that it could effectively be discounted as a realistic possibility."

During Altman's speech, the court had taken a day off for a site visit to Wild Park. It's a sign of these austere times that the 1987 jury were provided with packed lunches for their visit but the 2018 panel were told to bring their own.

So, judge, jury, counsel and court staff – but not Bishop, who elected to stay in Belmarsh, nor Bennathan, who had a date in the Appeal Court on another case – set off by coach for a day out in Brighton.

It is always amusing to see court figures in their civvies away from the formal wigs and gowns. Trudging through Wild Park, the judge sported the country gentleman's uniform of Barbour jacket, while Altman kept his spectacularly bald dome warm under, not greying horsehair, but a flat cap.

On their return, the opening was completed and the jury sent home. In their absence Bennathan gave notice to the judge that there would have to be "substantial" legal argument before the trial could continue.

Nothing had been said at the pre-trial hearings and Altman

was furious at this apparent ambush. The judge was also angry at the delay in the case, which would mean the jury not returning to court for another week.

Bishop, no doubt, rejoiced at their discomfiture. This was his chance.

The following Monday, and with the jury sent away, Bennathan opened by claiming that there was "credible evidence" that Barrie Fellows had been party to the sexual abuse of his infant daughter.

He said he intended to call Marion Stevenson, who had made statements to the police in 1988 and 2007 about the Barrie video, and to the *News of the World* in 1987.

The QC said he intended to ask her about DS Swan and the bug in Bishop's flat, he would also accuse Barrie of being a "more likely candidate" than Bishop as the murderer and he would question Michelle Hadaway, Susan Fellows and Teresa Judd to this effect.

Bennathan said that if the judge refused to allow him to call that evidence the jury would feel "cheated" when they found out about it after the trial.

Legal argument is always conducted in the absence of the jury and a reporting ban imposed so that what is said in court during that time is not published or broadcast until the trial was over.

Altman hit back immediately by pointing out that whether the jury felt "cheated" or not was "neither here nor there" in a matter of law.

He said the Dice report proved that the video allegations were completely uncorroborated and her statements contained important differences.

Her claims about Swan telling her to have sex with Bishop was a clear lie because the defendant's home was never bugged.

Altman warned Bennathan that if he called Stevenson as a witness the prosecution could cross-examine her about her other statements, which might not be to the defence's advantage. Not only that but if he was allowed to produce bad character evidence against Barrie then the prosecution could do the same against Bishop and, he hinted intriguingly, there were some letters not able to be produced at the 1987 trial that the prosecution might bring out this time!

Sweeney gave his decision three days later and, to the astonishment of the prosecution, and even the defence, agreed that the Stevenson video allegations should be allowed to go before the jury.

In his written judgment extending to nineteen pages and handed down a few weeks later, the judge criticised Bennathan's failure to raise the issues much earlier.

Nevertheless, he ruled that in relation to Stevenson, "I do not consider it appropriate to find, at this stage, that her evidence is such that no court or jury could reasonably find it to be true."

He went on: "The fact that Barrie Fellows is said to have been watching it [the video], is capable of demonstrating that he had a paedophile interest in Nicola [the key point being that the evidence was only "capable", not proven. The judge can not rule on what the evidence means as long as it is lawfully put forward, that is down to the jury].

"In my judgement, Stevenson's evidence about the video has substantial probative value to the issue of who the murderer was or might have been, and that issue is of substantial importance in the context of the case as a whole."

Altman was furious, Bennathan cock-a-hoop, Bishop even more so, once it had been explained to him.

The prosecution felt they had been well and truly ambushed but had still not expected to be beaten on this evidence, which was bound to cause serious emotional hardship to Barrie and the entire Fellows family, let alone what impact it would have on the jury in giving a glimmer of credence to Bishop's only line of defence.

The trial was two weeks old, the first witness hadn't even been called yet and already the prosecution was on the back foot and the families' morale was at a low ebb.

Surely, it could not go wrong again?

CHAPTER 20

FACING BISHOP

Thanks to the child porn video hiatus there was a 10 day gap before the jury could return to court and the first witness called to give evidence.

But first, Bennathan was allowed to give his own opening and in just ten minutes laid out the defence case in clipped and punchy detail. He concluded by pointing the finger straight at Barrie Fellows.

"He has a guilty secret that he has been complicit in the sexual abuse of Nicola and therefore has an interest in paedophilic sex," the QC told the jury solemnly.

"He is not on trial but once you have looked at the facts surrounding him, we suggest that those facts should lead you to accept that the police and prosecution have spent thirty-two years building a case against the wrong man."

The court was cleared to give the first witness, Michelle, the privacy of dealing with her infirmity and manoeuvring herself across the court and into the tight witness box.

Dressed in a black coat and grey scarf, she thrust her heavily tattooed forearms forward and perched her reading glasses on her nose as she was patiently taken through her family history and the painful last moments of life with Karen and the heartbreaking search.

She broke down in tears as she described the moment she realised her daughter was dead.

After twenty-four hours of searching, a pregnant Michelle was exhausted. "I sat on a seat on the grass by the pavilion in Wild Park," she said. "I was all upset and confused and did not know where I was. I was just terrified about my little girl, worried about both them children."

Suddenly, there was an intensity of activity, a swarm of police officers and a helicopter hovered overhead.

"As soon as I saw the police tape go up, I knew what had happened," she said.

"I saw Russell and I shouted at him. I shouted at him because I wanted to know what was happening. He looked at me and put his hand over his face" drawing her own hand over her face to illustrate the look and then reached for a box of paper hankies.

In cross-examination, she was asked about a letter she had written on 18 September 1989, to be passed to the police, which resulted in a visit by Councillor Gordon Wingate and a man she didn't know but who introduced himself as "Michael Dawes".

In the letter, she said she had wanted to list the number of times Barrie's behaviour had caused her concern.

She wrote: "I came into contact with Barrie about 11.40 p.m. [on the night the girls went missing]. He was outside his house and by this time there were a lot of people, searching. Barrie asked me what I was doing. I said to him: 'What the fuck do you think, I'm searching.'

"Barrie said, 'Michelle, the police are doing everything they can.' I told him, 'I can't wait for the police I had to keep searching for my daughter.' He put his hand on my shoulder and said, 'There's nothing more we can do, the police are doing everything. Why don't you do what I'm doing and go home and get a good nights sleep?' I rejected that.

"I'm afraid that Barrie's strange and unnatural behaviour once my daughter was murdered has not got any better. I got quite upset when on one occasion he said to me that it was lucky that Karen had not been beaten before she died. I thought that was strange because it was not long after she had died and we had not been told at that stage what had happened to out daughters."

Questioned by Altman, Michelle confirmed the letter had been written two years after Bishop had been acquitted.

Asked about Wingate, she said, "It wasn't any of his business but he jumped on the bandwagon like everybody aide for that length of time there was a very bad vendetta against Barrie. People accused him of being the murderer and a number of other things. People were saying awful things in the local community.

"The other man Dawes didn't tell me who he was at first but said he had a lot of information. I invited him in and he sat down and told me he was Russell Bishop's uncle.

"He asked me if I was suspicious of anybody. I said a number of people including Barrie but that doesn't mean to say he was involved. I handed the letter to them. They didn't tell me any of the information or evidence that they said they had that would prove somebody else was involved."

She admitted she had not known that Barrie had identified Nicola at the mortuary when he made the beating comment and would have seen his daughter's bruises.

Asked about the wrong place, wrong time comment, she replied, "Looking back now he wasn't the only one who said it, I can remember it was an off the hand comment that he came out with. I think he opened his mouth before he put his brain in gear."

Evidence over, Michelle left court and bumped into Susan Fellows. They embraced. A sign of reconciliation and a shared bond of stress and grief.

Susan entered court dressed in a yellow round-neck top and black leggings and told jurors she had been married to Barrie for sixteen years by 1986.

"Dougie Judd was the lodger, a friend of Barrie's, who had come to stay temporarily. He was only going to stay for three months before moving on but ... He had a key to the house but not his room, which was on the ground floor on the left as you enter the front door," she said.

"Nicky was funny, she spoke her mind, she would tell you what she was thinking and, for a child, was outgoing to the point of embarrassing me sometimes.

"Nicky was really dotty over her father but was also wary of him. She knew that what he said went. Nicky and Barrie loved each other, she loved him in a child's way."

Asked about Marion Stevenson, Susan said, "Once, I saw her with her hand down Bishop's trousers. I was in my kitchen and I saw them in the back garden. I once saw her sitting on his van outside my house. She was in a tracksuit and he was leaning between her legs. It didn't bother me but it did bother me that the children were out there.

"She had a foul tongue, always using foul language in front of the children and Nicky and Karen had a habit of picking that up."

Bennathan asked her about an incident in which her grandmother, Mabel Prior, had ended up with her nose broken by Barrie.

"My nan was quite outspoken and she said something about not liking him and he raised his hand up in the direction of my nan and struck her directly on her nose and he stood up, and threw something at me and my mother but it missed. Nan didn't want to press charges and she was taken to hospital with a broken nose.

"Barrie said it was an accident. The police were called, I don't know who called them. My nan said she didn't want to press charges for my sake."

Throughout her evidence, Susan kept her eyes on the QC asking the questions and the jury when delivering her answers and only allowed herself two glances at the dock.

She had not seen Bishop since 1987. She said later, "I thought, 'Oh, my God, he looks different.' I couldn't see much of him because he was on my left side, my bad side because of my eye. When I left the witness box I looked straight ahead, I didn't look at him."

After the first day of evidence, the defence had had a good day in their attempt to turn it into a trial of Barrie and not Bishop.

The long awaited arrival of Barrie in the witness box was

delayed for more than two weeks as a result of the video porn judgement.

Five months earlier, he had told me that this time he would be prepared for what would be thrown at him – but that was before the judge had opened the door for the defence to throw a whole lot of new, and far more damaging, allegations at him.

Would he react in the same way as he had in the first trial? If so the retrial could go the same way. Hearts were in a lot of mouths as he stepped forward and took the oath.

He actually looked slightly trimmer than when I had last seen him that summer, and was dressed in grey trousers and a short-sleeved pink shirt that showed off his tattoos, which were less extensive than Michelle's.

As he gave evidence, Bishop made notes and glared at him from the dock but Barrie refused to respond.

He was clearly nervous as he told of his new life away from Brighton with his second wife Karen, now dead, and Amber and his stepchildren. "I don't call them stepchildren but MY children," he emphasised.

But he settled down and, with the help of his thirty-two-year-old police statements, ran through the events of the fateful day.

"I got up about seven forty-five, when Sue, Jonathan and Nicky were already up and Nicky was getting ready for school.

"Dougie Judd was our lodger at the time and as far as I was aware he had to go to sign on at the Labour Exchange that morning.

"I left home at eight. It was the last time I saw I Nicky. She was in her way to school and she was dawdling slowly. I said to her, 'Hurry up.' I caught the Number Twenty-five bus to Woodruff

Avenue in Hove, where I was cleaning out a swimming pool and doing a bit of gardening

"Dougie Judd turned up about ten a.m. to help and we worked until five p.m., when we stopped and went home.

"Dougie and I walked back through Shirley Drive and Hove Park to George Street where I went to the butchers for some ham because I knew we were having salad that night and I like a bit of ham.

"Then Dougie and I went to Church Road and waited for sometime for a bus. We caught a Number Forty-nine to East Moulsecoomb and got off at about six p.m.

"I went to see Teresa Judd who was a friend of mine through her husband Steve, who is Dougie's brother.

"She lives at one hundred and thirty-eight Moulsecoomb Way. Dougie came with me to the house initially. I went in and had a cup of tea at some stage. He left to visit his girlfriend Jackie."

The exact timings of Barrie's homecoming were to be hotly disputed in court over the coming hours. Was there or wasn't there a missing hour in his alibi?

Barrie said that he got home, ate his salad, watched the end of *Top of the Pops* on TV [7–7.30 p.m.] and went out looking for his daughter between 7.30 and 7.40 p.m.

"When I got home, Susan was not in. Edna was in and told me Sue was out with Michelle because Nicky and Karen were missing.

"After eating my dinner, I went looking for Sue and Michelle to see what the scare was with Nicky. I saw a couple of kids and I asked if they had seen Nicky, but they hadn't. I went back to Teresa's, to see if she had seen Nicky. She had a two-year-old child with her called Adam. She got him dressed and came back with me to Number 26.

"Sue and Michelle were there and I got really worried because Nicky should have been in and it was getting dark.

"I went out again alone and spoke to other kids in the street. I heard that Nicky had had an altercation with young Lyndsey over roller skates – they were always having some sort of argument.

"I went back home and saw Dougie who said he had called the police and about twenty minutes later uniformed officers arrived. They took me for a tour around the immediate area in their car.

"I was frantic with worry. I was worried sick.

"At ten thirty, I went to Wild Park with the police and they gave me a torch. I suggested going to that area because it was a favourite of hers during daylight hours. I had warned her that the bogeyman lived up there in the park. I said that to make her not go there and I knew she wouldn't.

"I was taken home by the police at about eleven. I looked in at Michelle's but Sue was not there. I was instructed to stay in by the police."

Bennathan rose to cross-examine Barrie, knowing he had to break his alibi and get some sort of reaction from him to back his claims that this now sixty-nine-year-old man was a violent paedophile.

The QC started by pointing out that it was three miles from Woodruff Avenue to Newick Road, "so how come it took him two and a half hours?"

"It's a long way, it's quite a hike," he replied.

Barrie told Bennathan he had walked from the bus stop in

Moulsecoomb to Teresa Judd's house in Moulsecoomb Way and he had stayed there for fifteen or twenty minutes, then it was an eight-to-ten-minutes walk from her house to his home.

Q: "If the bus stops and you get off about six p.m. and you left Judd at six twenty-five, you should have been home at six thirty-five, but you got home just before seven thirty."

A: "You are trying to mislead me but it's not happening. I believed he times are correct at the time."

Bennathan left the point there in the air so he could claim afterwards that it was unanswered.

Q:"Even by your own account you should be home at six thirty, but actually you got home a whole hour later."

A: "I suggest you are wrong."

Bennathan asked why Barrie had gone to see Teresa Judd the second time when he was searching for Nicola?

"I knew her husband was away and I was worried about her and I wanted somebody to sit with Edna."

Q: "It was not to get her to give you an alibi?"

A: "No, why would I do that?"

Bennathan turned to the allegations of violence against Nicola.

"Did you slap her for not doing her homework?"

"I don't think so, no."

"She ran crying into the house holding her head."

"I have hit her, yes, it's commonly called a thick ear back then."

Moving onto to the grandmother-in-law incident, Barrie admitted: "I broke my grandmother-in-law's nose, it was an accident. She was quite an outspoken woman, there's no doubt about that?"

Bennathan: "You were in such a rage you threw an ashtray

towards Susan and your mother-in-law, which smashed a window."

Barrie: "I don't know where you are getting all this from. I stood up at the same time as her after a small altercation and [waving his right arm up and sideways] her nose was broken, it was an accident, that's true.

"Susan and Edna panicked and said I had done it deliberately but, in fact, I just swung round and I didn't see her, seriously sir. I don't deliberately punch old ladies in the nose."

Bennathan: "Did you break a window?"

Barrie: "I might have done."

Bennathan brought up the headmaster's claims about Barrie threatening to cut his daughter's fingers off if she stole again.

"I know exactly what you are going to say," Barrie said, interrupting the QC before he had barely begun the question. "I said I would cut her fingers off if I ever caught her stealing but I would not do it."

With Barrie looking sheepish in the witness box, Bennathan threw in his three hand grenade questions.

"Were you party to Nicola being filmed in a pornographic video film?"

"No."

"Were you in the front room of your house watching a home made pornographic film of your infant daughter?"

"No."

"Did you have anything to do with her death?"

"No."

The QC left it there with no follow up questions at all. It was clear he was worried how the badgering of the father of a murdered child would look to jurors when it was based only on one dubious witness.

Barrie's straight bat and composure under fire disconcerted Bennathan, whose cross-examination was rapidly running out of ammunition.

Finally, he tried to skewer the witness with his comment to Michelle Hadaway that Karen had been "in the wrong place at the wrong time".

"I probably did [say that], but so was Nicky – they should not have been in Wild Park. I said they both should not have been in Wild Park, anyway, after dark; it's not safe, which has been proven."

Bennathan made one last throw of the dice. "You said to Michelle Hadaway that Karen had been lucky not to be beaten?"

"Only in comparison with Nicky who had bruises on her face."

"The only person who would have known that was somebody who had been there when they died."

"I don't know what you are saying, I don't like it."

Bennathan sat down. Barrie had beaten him. The comparison with Lewes in 1987 could not have been more profound. It was only left for Altman to rise to his feet to ram home the advantage.

The alleged comments to Michelle had come after he had had to identify his dead daughter's body at the mortuary – "just how awful was that".

The stress finally began to show, as Barrie's face crumpled and his lips wobbled. "It was he hardest journey I have had to make. It's not nice. You go into this clinically white room. I walked in. There was a sheet over my little girl up to her neck [he had to indicate where with his hand as words started to fail him].

"I tried to ask the man there why it was like that. She had

been examined apparently. I said I needed to give her some pocket money. He said you are not allowed to touch her. I said why? I put the fifty pence I had in my hand into her hand."

This was not a poet nor a politician, no actor nor archbishop, this was an ordinary man who had suffered an unimaginable loss and in recalling this short and simple moment Barrie encapsulated the depth of his suffering and hearts almost visibly sailed across to him from the jury box.

Unsurprisingly, the emotion caught in Barrie's throat as he fought to hold back tears but in the silence of the stunned courtroom no one begrudged him a second.

Altman followed up: "Lest nobody is left in any doubt, you are being accused [by the defence] of having killed Nicola and Karen and you are being accused of sexually assaulting your own daughter and Karen and punching Nicola in the face."

Barrie, still in turmoil, nodded an acknowledgement.

"Nicky had bruises to the left side of her face. I didn't know what it meant that it had happened to Nicky, the police told me later but I'm not sure. They came back and told me they had been sexually abused. I had to run into the street."

Altman told him quietly: "I have to ask you more questions because of the questions you have been asked [by Bennathan on the instructions of Bishop]."

After clarifying one or two minor points, Altman's last question was about a letter Barrie had written to the police in 1988 demanding they reopen the case and, among other things, stating, "I want the police to publicly state that I was not guilty of murdering my daughter."

Barrie replied simply: "That's what I wanted in 1988 and what I want now."

After less than ninety minutes, his ordeal was over and he left the witness box slightly unsteadily due to what appeared to be cramp but seemingly never once making eye contact with Bishop in the dock.

Outside court, he immediately broke down in tears, heaving sobs, as he was overcome by emotion and was comforted by his daughter, the Hadaways and the witness support staff at the Old Bailey. But in his mind, and in those in court – especially the few of us who had been there in 1987 – he had triumphed.

Nigel agreed: "I thought Barrie was going to get a rough ride and Bennathan would give it one hell of a run but he didn't. We were very pleased that Barrie came out of it with dignity. For once he did what he was told!"

Barrie told me later: "I put him [Bennathan] in his place; I wasn't having him trying to mislead me. I wasn't on the Number Twenty-five bus, as he thought with his missing hour, I was on the Forty-nine and there is a different bus stop to get off.

"That's why the timetable was wrong. There wasn't a missing hour, maybe a missing five or ten minutes but nothing more."

CHAPTER 21

TURNING POINT

After the drama of Barrie and the parents' evidence, the police and scientific evidence, which was to take a long three weeks threatened to be deadly dull in comparison.

But, in fact, a series of unexpected quirks and cameos were a surprise and it marked the movement when all Russell Bishop's hopes came crash down around his head.

A number of mostly retired ex-policemen had to explain how the Pinto had been kept in unsealed brown paper bag and passed through a variety of hands between store rooms.

With Scenes of Crime officer Eddie Redman too ill too come to court, It was down to Cormer Det Insp Christopher Bentham to explain how Redman and his colleagues had not realised the sweatshirt's significance until 30 October 1986, twenty days after the murders.

Then the scientists explained in painstaking detail every aspect of the findings (already detailed in Chapter 14). It soon became apparent that the defence was not contesting what was found both in 1987 and in the later testing in the 2000s, but what those findings meant and whether they could be trusted was the battle ground.

One scientist eagerly, if slightly ghoulishly, awaited was Dr Anthony Peabody and the question of how his evidence would compare with his performance at Lewes in 1987.

Now grey haired and in his seventies, he wore a crimson bow tie, matching his vivid socks, above a blue striped shirt and dark suit.

He started with a confident air his hands clasped in front of his chest, fingers entwined and thumbs tapping together, telling the jury he had been a Home Office forensic scientist from 1967 until 1999 when he left to act as a consultant before retiring in 2007.

Sensing where the fight over his evidence would take place, Alison Morgan took him straight to the nub – the threat of contamination.

"We forensic scientists believe it to be of primary importance," he said proudly. "Cross-contamination was something we took every step we could to minimise."

He emphasised that Nicola and Karen's clothing were examined in a different room to the Pinto and Bishop's clothes.

In fact, they had arrived in different deliveries three weeks apart. All of the girls garments had been examined and returned to their sealed containers with the results recorded long before the Pinto had even arrived at Aldermarston.

When Joel Bennathan rose to cross-examine Peabody's self-confident expression narrowed with suspicion. His mind must have flickered with dark memories of his mauling by his nemesis Ivan Lawrence, QC, thirty-one years previously.

Bennathan smiled beguilingly and told him there were other experts he would challenge on the evidence so wouldn't waste the jury's time now.

"Do you remember that as you left the witness box at the trial in 1987 you were pinned against the wall by a senior police officer?" Was his surprising first question.

"As it happens, yes," Peabody replied cautiously.

"I don't want to go through the rights and wrongs of that, probably wrongs, but he was not happy about the way your evidence came out."

Peabody: "A great deal of work had been put into this [case] and emotions naturally ran high."

Bennathan: "The police officer's emotions?"

Peabody: "Yes."

The QC continued with memories of 1987 for another's nasty reminder. "You were cross-examined by a barrister representing Mr Bishop then – it wasn't me."

Peabody gave a nervous laugh and responded with a heartfelt, "No."

Without looking up but registering the subliminal shudder of dread recognition from the witness box, Bennathan sailed back, "Thank you."

Peabody rallied from this defensiveness and sought to return fire. He invested his responses with a tone of slightly unnecessary irony. They were never impolite but his "Thank you" and "Not quite" and "I certainly did" answers started to niggle the QC.

Bennathan asked, "If a forensic scientist examined an exhibit without making a note, how serious would that be?

Peabody quickly responded: "If there's a follow up statement, I would like to hear it first."

Adopting his best laconic accent, the QC snapped back pointedly but ever so politely: "Could you answer the question please."

With his victim suitably chastened, Bennathan decided now was the time to drop the bomb from the first trial, it was time for exhibit IEW 55 to rear its ugly head again after thirty-one years.

He reminded the jury that the now deceased pathologist Dr Iain West had removed three hairs and a piece of fibre from the vulva of Nicola at the post-mortem, placed it in an exhibit bag to such effect and despatched it to Aldermaston for forensic examination.

At the trial at Lewes, it had gone missing in a massive and ultimately fatal blow to the competence of the prosecution.

The judge had ordered Peabody to find it and return to court.

Bennathan asked the scientist: "You were criticised for not opening the bag and given the opportunity to do so you made a witness statement and came back to testify. What did you state was in it?"

Peabody. "One white curly hair twenty-five millimetres long, one brown desert hair nineteen millimetres long, no other fibres loose in the bag, a small piece of solid debris."

Bennathan: "You appear to have lost a hair?"

Peabody: "I can't speak to what Dr West might have placed in the bag, I can only speak to what I found in the bag."

Bennathan: "That's right but is it possible you missed a hair?"

Peabody: "I can only speak of what I found."

In fact, the hairs in the bag, which of course West had not been able to examine under a microscope, turned out to be animal hairs but Bennathan had made his point about the breakdown between the police and pathologist and the forensic scientists in addition to the mistakes over the Pinto.

After further skirmishes over contamination Peabody was able to leave the witness box having given evidence for the best part of four hours, a gruelling episode for a seventy-year-old.

As he left court, he could pride himself on a more convincing performance than at Lewes Crown Court and there wasn't a policeman to pin him against the wall.

The key scientific witness was always going to be Ros Hammond, the specialist on contamination. On her shoulders rested the integrity of the core of the prosecution case.

Dressed all in black, she crossed the courtroom to the witness box emanating professionalism, her tied-back hair and dark-rimmed glasses giving her a "schoolmarm" look.

She passed through her evidence in chief to Altman's promptings radiating confidence in her forensic findings and explaining why she ruled out other results that may have been open to dispute.

The test would come from Bennathan. He threw everything he had at her. His best points being that all the significant results (such as the one billion to one DNA link to Bishop on Karen's left forearm) had come from Sellotaped exhibits taken in 1986 that had either been cut, damaged or eroded over time.

He also pointed out that there was no DNA from Nicola or Karen on the Pinto as would have been expected , and the sweatshirt itself should have been covered in blood had it been worn in the killings.

All of these points Hammond batted back back safely, her lips getting tighter and tighter in her determination not to be bested on her specialist subject.

Even when Bennathan chastised the police's handling of the Pinto in 1986, Hammond hit back with a stout defence.

"All the police officers had an understanding of contamination. They understood the importance of evidence such as fibres to the case," she said.

"Items would not have been taken out of their bags and handled. That is based on my experience and understanding of working as a forensic scientist for nearly 30 years and dealing with police officers."

Bennathan told her that, such was the anger and frustration of the police at the failure of the 1987 trial, that the Pinto, and other exhibits, had been thrown into an old boiler room and left there for years before the case was reopened after the repeal of double jeopardy.

Totally unphased, Hammond responded: "Nothing has altered my conclusions and evaluations. In my view, they were not compromised. We took the condition of them into account in assessing the findings. We have particular expertise in dealing with cold cases."

Hammond left court with a smile – modest but unmistakable – just starting to play on her face. Outside court, that small smile broadened into a grin and her eyes sparkled as she chatted with police officers in mutual satisfaction.

Finally, it was down to Roy Green, the senior scientific adviser for the forensic specialist company LGC (later renamed Eurofins), to bring the entire scientific evidence together into one, easily understood, bite size chunk for the jury.

His key message was: "Its important to consider these links not in isolation but in conjunction with each other. Bear in mind the totality of the evidence."

In other words, whatever darts the defence can throw at the integrity or possible contamination of the Pinto, of the girls' clothing or the DNA, or irrelevance of the ivy or randomness of the paint, the possibility that all of it is in some way wrong is *so* infinitesimally small as to be entirely impossible.

He went through each segment from the one billion to one DNA on Karen's forearm, to the fibres linking the Pinto to Bishop and his home, and the fibre and paint findings linking Bishop to both girls and every scrap was designated "extremely strong support" the highest level of proof a forensic scientist can bestow.

The impact of the concise summery of the evidence was so damning that Bennathan was on his feet complaining bitterly that this was evidence the jury had heard four times over and was just a further waste of court time.

Sweeney glared at him and slapped him down with a judicial straight right to the jaw. Presenting the evidence in his form was "eminently sensible", he said, inviting Altman to continue underlining Bishop's agony.

Green concluded, "In my opinion, when all the findings are considered together I would expect that Russell Bishop, while wearing the Pinto sweatshirt, had close contact with Nicola Fellows and Karen Hadaway at or around the time of their death."

As he left court the prosecution metaphorically leaned back in their seats and puffed out their cheeks.

That was it. That was the turning point. Bishop and his defence was finished.

A day later, and after Barrie Fellows had completed his evidence, a senior source at the heart of the prosecution confirmed their belief that the defence, so perky in the early days of the trial, was now "flat-lining".

The defence had been riding high sniping at the police and scientific failings in the eighties from a thirty-year perspective and flying the kite of Barrie being the killer without, as yet, producing the only, discredited, witness to back it up.

Now the prosecution had put forward all its damning evidence without any damage to its core, significance, the defence had nowhere to go.

Somehow Bishop and Marion Stevenson had to go into the witness box and convince the jury. And, in the face of hours of cross-examination by such a master as Brian Altman, that was never going to happen.

The source also described Bishop's defence as "pulling every trick straight from the Levi Bellfield playbook", adding, "I wonder if they were in Frankland prison together?"

This was a reference to the serial killer who killed three young women, most notably the schoolgirl Milly Dowler, and attempted to kill another. In two trials, also prosecuted by Altman, Bellfield had run the most disgraceful defence, which reduced parents to tears of rage and frustration and repeatedly threatened to derail the entire proceedings. He is now serving "a life means life" full-tariff sentence.

The figurative smile on the prosecution's face got even broader when they produced their final piece of evidence before closing their case – and Bishop finally cracked.

Altman told the jury that Bishop had written letters from Brixton Prison, while awaiting his first trial, to N, a schoolgirl then aged thirteen and fourteen years old.

Suddenly, Bishop leaped to his feet in the dock and with his face jammed to the toughened security glass yelled "stop it right now, this is not agreed evidence."

A horrified Mark Styles, defying his hockey injury, raced over to the dock to calm his client. But Bishop was not for calming. "No, no, no. I am not having this shit. If it's not done I'm having a retrial," he hissed at his wide eyed brief.

Bennathan hastily tried to repair the damage in front of the jury by telling the judge: "There has been discussion with the prosecution about various letters, written by various people and there some confusion with Mr Bishop about which letters."

Sweeney called for an adjournment and the jury filed out and the court cleared while Bennathan hurried over to join the argument that was continuing through the dock screen.

So what were jurors to make of that?

It would have taken no great leap of imagination to have pictured this aggressive, angry-faced man with his hands around the throats of two nine-year-old girls. He had exposed his brutal self to the very people he had to convince he was innocent.

Jurors would be very eager to know, here and now, what was in those letters that Bishop so desperately did not want them to hear.

How frustrating it must have been for the police to have had those letters in 1987 but be unable to use them in the first trial. They would have been inadmissible then and remained so until Bishop had insisted that his lawyers accuse Barrie Fellows of being a paedophile killer. At that moment they became admissible, as Altman had warned Bennathan three weeks earlier.

Fifteen minutes after Bishop's meltdown, the jury filed back into court and the letters were read in full.

They were written on prison notepaper with his number B82594 in the corner and in his semi-literate mixture of upper and lower case and misspellings, such as won when meaning one and wall for while. To avoid confusion I am reproducing selected passages in normal rather than Bishop English.

The first began, "Dear N, how are you, my love?" Bishop comments, "I hope to be out at the end of next week. I cannot do no dirty rhymes as this letter will go to the police." It ends "Love from Russell xxxx."

In the second, he wrote, "N love, you must not tell Jennie a thing what I put in my letters to you as she had a go at me ... as she thinks something is going on.

"I think it is the best thing for you to tell Jennie you are not getting letters from me as she will want to see them.

"The last time when you saw me was at the bus stop twenty weeks ago. You did something I cannot say what it was but you will know what it was. The times when we were in a B&B, the times when me and Jennie come up to see you. I know that you love me and I love you but you must not let Jennie know a thing about it and when I get out I think you know what we will end up doing."

In another extract, he wrote, "But if I can get a way out of it so you will have to go on the pill.

"So, are you a [he draws a blank line], or not? I hope you know what I mean; if not, I have put the first letter of the word at the end of this letter [there is a V at the bottom next to 'love from Russell xxxxxx']."

In the third, he wrote, "Its been 115 days, I've not had a thing now so you can help me out. That's if you want to have a good time when I am out. If you play your cards right you could have a good time, all day, no stopping in a B&B somewhere just for the weekend out of the way."

The letter ended with fifteen x's written in an inverted pyramid ending in a heart.

Each letter got longer and the fourth included the passage: "How old are you, baby? 'Hee', 'Hee'. Don't matter. No worries about that. Well N 16-17 more weeks and I will be out and up to no good as before. I just hope you can handle it as I am a man not a boy. I know you have been longing for it for a long time for me so have I and its all working out now. All I have to do is get out of here so it can happen and we can stop putting it on paper.

"N can you put a picture of you in your next letter and it can go on the wall with the ones I have of Victor and Hayley [his children]. I will make you one happy girl when I get out."

He added later, "Hove in B&B was the first time and its gone on from there. Well it won't be long now."

It ended with a large heart containing "N R J H V for always" and six x's.

In the fifth, Bishop wrote, "I still say you wont handle 12ins, you see Jennie, she said the same and she was [he draws a blank line] she's not no more."

Much of the rest of the letter and the next was taken up with Bishop's thoughts and sometimes complaints about Jennie Johnson.

The last letter contains the excerpt: "It is about time you got yourself on the pill if you want to have fun so you'd best see to that?!"

As this was clearly an attempt to groom the young teenager for sexual purposes, she cannot be identified.

As the court broke up for the day and Bishop headed back to his cell in Belmarsh, he must have thought the trial could not get much worse for him.

He was wrong about that, too.

CHAPTER 22

"BELITTLE AND SHAME"

At 11.25 a.m. on Friday, 23 November, Russell Bishop was led in manacles from the dock to the witness box.

The tension in the air was almost breathless. What was he going to say twenty-seven years after he had last spoken in public? How was he going to react?

Bishop had both wrists handcuffed together and was separately cuffed to a prison officer.

Once the cuffs were removed and he stood with his hands resting on the front of the wooden structure, one officer sat two paces behind him and two more guarded the door that was locked – a very rare move – with no one allowed in or out.

In fact, the precautions could have been even heavier as Sweeney had rejected an application by the prison authorities for Bishop to give all his evidence in handcuffs.

What was he going to say? Well we were treated to exactly the same version of events he had put forward in 1990 and 1991 –

Bishop the victim, Bishop the sensitive flower and Bishop the shameless and practiced liar.

For the first time he publicly admitted he had carried out the Devil's Dyke attack and had lied at his 1990 trial. But, as we were to find out later, the confession came only on his warped terms.

Bennathan got straight to the 1990 issue and, predictably, it cued the first bout of choked words and wobbly lower lip.

"I'm ashamed to say I was given a life sentence after my conviction. I was in a bad state," he mumbled.

"What had you intended to do that Sunday morning?" asked the QC about the day Bishop had snatched R from the streets.

"I had planned to go to my brother's house and try and put up a satellite dish. I intended to drive up there but my brake pipes had been cut – not for the first time. In three years, they had been cut eight or nine times after I was found 'Not guilty' [at the first trial] in 1987 up to 1990. Many things happened in that period of time.

"By the time of my offences, for which I'm now convicted, I was in a bad, bad state.

"I fixed the brake pipes and drove to my brother's. He was not in. My intention was to drive away but I had a puncture. I changed the tyre and threw everything into the car.

"But as I was tightening the wheel nut with my hammer I struck my hand and lost my temper. I just blacked out through pain. It was the straw that broke the camel's back.

"I started going mad, screaming and shouting. The victim was standing within arm's reach and I grabbed hold of her. I accept everything that was said in this courtroom [about the 1990 case]. I feel deeply ashamed."

Bennathan: "You gave evidence in that case, did you tell the truth?"

Bishop: "I didn't tell the truth in any way, shape or form."

Police officers and the CPS watched silently, no doubt anticipating what Altman would conjure up in cross-examination. Michelle sat equally passively, churning inwardly, next to Lyndsey while Nigel Heffron and his niece Emma sat upstairs in the public gallery.

Bishop was then taken through his early life and soon he was rolling up the sleeve of his T-shirt to show off his gym-perfected guns during a question about his shoulder operations.

Moving on to the fateful day, Bishop started sniffing and mumbling prompting Bennathan to bark at him to speak up.

Bishop went through the familiar story of trying to steal cars at the university car park, buying cannabis from Angie Cutter, seeing the girls when talking to the park keeper before walking home, putting on the washing and running a bath.

However, he also told how an insurance man had arrived, getting him out of the bath, although he couldn't say who he was, then he cooked a meal and switched on *EastEnders*.

The first he knew the girls were missing was a knock on the door at 2.30 a.m. by the police. Later that day he made a witness statement and helped with the search.

He described how he had been standing with PC Smith in Wild Park when the alarm was raised and he raced to the scene.

"I went straight to the victim's and felt for a pulse. On Nicola I felt for a pulse on her neck and on Karen on her right arm. At school a young lad had died suddenly when I was thirteen or fourteen and we were told about taking a pulse in first aid," he said.

Asked about the accounts of the two who had made the discovery that the defendant had gone nowhere near the bodies, Bishop said "that's incorrect, it's a lie", adding, "I felt shocked, totally sickened and numbed" and gave a loud sniff into the witness box microphone.

He then reminisced about clashes with the police in the past – in addition to his criminal record of petty thieving – and why he was naturally suspicious of them.

"In the Grand Hotel bombing [1984], I had been arrested briefly. I was nothing to do with it in any way, shape or form," he announced.

"A couple of years before this [the girls murders], a young lady called Margaret Frame was walking home from Falmer school, I might have been about twelve, when she was abducted and found a week later brutally murdered buried in a shallow grave [in Stamner woods near Wild Park].

"My father was wrong arrested for that while minding his business in the wood, he was hunting at the time. He was stopped by the police and arrested and we sat around for days waiting for him to come home from the police station. He was finally exonerated by the police more than six weeks later.

"The house was searched, fingerprints were taken, all the normal stuff that goes on with this kind of high-profile thing."

Over the following days, Bishop had given a number of witness statements and three interviews under caution as a suspect. So why did he give so many different accounts? asked Bennathan.

Bishop replied that it was all down to the "unpleasant and nasty" atmosphere, which "wasn't normal" at the police station.

He was only twenty and bigger older policemen were

"bullying" him, he claimed, so, "I started getting, all distracted, tired and tied in knots."

"I was being called a liar, they had been downright nasty, I was basically being kept prisoner when I wanted to leave. Two police officers destroyed me in that room. I was dyslexic, I had problem solving skills, I lied and said I had not checked the pulses, It was literally the only way I could get out of it."

Despite his serious predicament, he continued to tell the police that he had not felt the pulses "because I didn't want to complicate things so I carried on telling the lie."

He was released on police bail and "I was advised by them to leave Brighton. For a time I went to Nottingham and Wales. Jennie was here for some of the time and some of the time I was by myself. I got fed up being away from home and went back to Brighton."

Soon after, he was charged with murder and this prompted another bout of sobs, choking on words and sniffs into the microphone, which were almost ear-splitting.

"I was devastated. I was remanded to Brixton Prison; I was Cat A [the highest level of security for suspect murderers], so I had to sleep in a cell with a red light on [and] I was on remand for twelve months."

This brought Bennathan to the prison letters to N, and Bishop said he thought his pen pal was fifteen or sixteen.

"Jennie said somebody wanted to write to me. I didn't pick up the name. I said, 'Yes, it'll give me something to do, let her write.'

"I was writing to quite a few other people and people wrote back to me. N sent letters to me virtually every single day."

Bennathan then turned to the SOCO (scene-of-crime officer), Edward Redman, who had been responsible for the

Pinto sweatshirt at Brighton police station but had not realised for three weeks how important it was to the inquiry.

Bishop said that he remembered Redman telling the 1987 jury that the Pinto had been examined "on the same table in the same room" as the dead girls' clothing. (Interestingly, Sir Ivan Lawrence, Bishop's QC at that trial, also remembered the phrase and included it in his autobiography. But the police and the prosecution are absolutely adamant that it had never happened.)

After the trial and the "Not guilty" verdicts, the police issued a statement saying they were not looking for anyone else in connection with the murders, which, Bishop claimed, implied the jury had got the wrong decision and led to a backlash against him.

In a monologue with tears never far away, he told the jury: "When I got home the first of many bricks came through my window. There were too many to count, you just gave up in the end and I just boarded up the window.

"It happened dozens of times, there was never a day that something didn't happen, the car was taken from outside my house, rolled down the hill and set on fire. My home was firebombed on several occasions- there were basically people trying to kill me and the children [by this time he had two with a third on the way].

"When I took my son Victor to school the other parents didn't like it so I had to get someone else to take him to school.

"After the first firebombing at the flat the police were called. They told me they did investigate people but nothing happened from that and I just stopped calling them."

Bishop said that in October 1989 he had taken his children to the swings at Saunders Park, near his new home in Preston

Barracks, only for someone to call the police and he was "pinned to the ground" before they were conceded he was not trying to molest someone else's kids.

Sobbing now, Bishop went on to tell of the incident already described in Chapter 10. "Somebody threw a firebomb through my children's bedrooms window."

As a result of all this, he claimed: "I drove to Beachy Head in January 1990 [which, if correct, would be just days before he carried out the Devil's Dyke attack], I had my children with me and I intended to end my life and my children's life because I could not bear it any more.

"But on the way my son said something in the car and it made me rethink. I went to the beach to clear my head and I went for a walk with my children.

"It's hard to put into words but I didn't recognise then the symptoms of mental illness but I certainly suffered mental illness at that time."

In the public gallery I could see Nigel wide-eyed with disbelief. Outside court he told me: "So, remind me, what is Bishop saying he is? A convicted paedophile? A suspected terrorist? A car thief? Mentally ill?"

It was a Friday afternoon and as Bishop was taken back to his cell he had the weekend to prepare himself for the ordeal by Altman to come.

*

It's the nature of bullies, murderers, those who pick on those younger and weaker that they are cowards. Today, Russell Bishop ran away from the firestorm he had created for himself.

A day of drama, as dramatic as any day I can remember at

the Old Bailey, started with a laugh and ended with the broadest smiles imaginable on the faces of the Fellows and Hadaways alike.

Susan Fellows was back, and looking much happier and healthier than on her last visit to court, as she sat with Michelle and Lyndsey Hadaway.

Upstairs was Nigel Heffron and his nieces Emma and Lorna.

Led to the witness box again in manacles, Bishop handed his court papers to the prison guard as they undid his cuffs.

The uniformed officer turned to look for a suitable place to park the papers for a few seconds and absentmindedly put them on the nearest surface, which turned out to be prosecuting counsel's lectern.

"Don't give them to them," yelped the defendant to laughter unreflected in Bishop's alarmed expression.

With the jury in place, Altman rose to his feet to almost audible anticipation around the court. And so began the forensic dissection of Russell Bishop.

First his self-confidence was picked to pieces, then his defence case, then his ego and finally his will to fight.

Altman started off on Bishop's weakest ground: His lies, the 1990 conviction, the decades of no remorse and his letters from prison in 1986/7.

No doubt, Altman was hoping for a quick kill, even though he had prepared for a long haul and intended to keep Bishop in the witness box for three days if necessary. He told me that morning that he had spent sleepless nights preparing ninety pages of questions but even he would not have expected how quickly it was to be over.

As the Fellows and Hadaways looked on savouring how the

tables had been turned since 1987, it is worth chronicling step-by-step how Russell Bishop surrendered to Brian Altman.

To start with Bishop adopted a confident, even cocky, pose leaning on his right arm on the side of the witness box and looking sideways at the QC, who, behind his lectern, was so close he was almost in touching distance.

Altman warmed up with a few probes about lies and why Bishop had wanted to kill his children at Beachy Head.

Then the QC produced a parole board report in 2001 prior to Bishop's first application in which he had stated he believed the Devil's Dyke attack in 1990 had been caused by his own sense of "misplaced revenge" for the hate campaign allegedly conducted against him in Brighton.

This prompted – less than ten minutes and barely a dozen questions into cross-examination – Bishop's first hissy fit.

Annoyed at being questioned about the 1990 convictions, he suddenly appealed: "I don't know why you are not objecting Mr Bennathan, I don't want to be tried for what I have already been convicted of, I'm facing different charges here."

Bennathan kept his head down intent on his papers. The cavalry had no grounds to ride to the rescue.

Altman carried on eagerly, pointing out that, far from the "deep shame" Bishop had told the jury he now felt, the defendant had claimed in the 2001 report that he was not guilty of attempted murder of the seven-year-old because he hadn't strangled her.

What's more (in Bishop's twisted version of the evidence), Dr West had not even seen R and had lied and "fabricated and falsified" the evidence against him while two defence doctors had agreed with the Bishop theory.

"I only put my hands over her [the victim's] mouth when she struggled, I admit that," he said.

Astonished at this volte face from Friday's position, in which Bishop had "accepted everything" about the conviction, Altman said the two doctors had not stated what Bishop had just claimed and West had carried a full examination.

"I don't bloody agree with that," Bishop replied with his temperature clearly rising.

Altman pointed out that from being ashamed, in 2003 Bishop was still appealing against the 1990 convictions. The Appeal Court has thrown out his appeal in 1992 and the Criminal Case Review Commission had done the same.

A probation report in 2003 stated that Bishop had planned an immediate application as soon as he became eligible for parole and "is hopeful he will win an appeal against his conviction for attempted murder and, having served the ten-year sentence for the other offences, will therefore be released."

"This was all about getting out early," suggested Altman.

"Who wants to stay in prison? I bloody don't," replied Bishop.

Altman: "In the 2003 report, you were claiming you were not sexually motivated in the assault on [the 1990 victim]."

Bishop: "I wasn't fucking sexually motivated, no."

Altman: "In 2006, Sally McKenzie, in a post tariff parole assessment, said, 'Mr Bishop's main concern remains his solicitor getting statements from R saying that Mr Bishop had not strangled her during the assault. Mr Bishop said he had no sexual interest in children and has never had sexual fantasies about children.'

"Do you have sexual interest in children?"

Bishop: "No. I don't have any sexual interest in children."

Altman, continuing to read from the 2006 report: "'We discussed why he would choose to assault a seven-year-child if he had no sexual interest in children. Mr Bishop replied he had been accused of this type of offence 'so he might as well do it.'"

Bishop: "I did have those kinds of thoughts."

Altman: "So was all this about revenge?"

Bishop: "Partly, yes."

Turning again to the attempted suicide claim, Altman asked whether it had been true or whether "you are seeking sympathy [from the jury] or trying to?"

That really angered Bishop, who was really ticking now, and he launched into a harangue, "You have come with a few selective reports, you have not read all the reports. I could bring reports to court tomorrow and totally blow this out of the fucking water so don't make me look like an idiot."

Altman stood very still and very quietly reminded Bishop that he was telling the jury that he denied attempting to murder the 1990 victim, denied having any sexual motivation and had only attacked her "out of three years of harassment and losing it."

Bishop, now calmer: "That's correct."

Altman: "You are the victim in all of this by the sound of it?"

Bishop, very angry again: "No, I'm not the victim."

Altman: "And that's exactly what you have been trying to portray yourself to the jury, as a victim."

Bishop: "No, in no way or shape or form."

Altman turned to the agreed facts, accepted as true by the defence, that semen on the 1990 victim's vest was found to be a one in 19,000 chance to be anyone else's but Bishop's.

He responded with a convoluted explanation that the

semen had come from his tracksuit bottoms onto his own children's discarded clothes in the back of his car and then onto the victim.

Altman: "This offence was all about sexual gratification- you are a paedophile are you not?"

Bishop: "You have to understand what the word paedophile means."

Altman: "You enjoy controlling children and one aspect of that is sexual gratification ."

Bishop: "No, not in any way, shape or form."

Returning to the McKenzie report Altman read the author's comment that Bishop "did not show any concern for the victim and how it may have impacted on her [R] when she would be approached by his solicitor for a statement [that he had not strangled her]."

So why did he choose a young girl to attack, especially when he claims he wasn't interested in children sexually?

"The victim in 1990 could have been anyone. The behaviour came out of the experience I had been though before, through psychological trauma going through the head, I carried out in that behaviour," Bishop replied ungrammatically and illogically.

"You bundled a young girl into the boot of your car, drove fourteen miles to remote woodland countryside on Devil's Dyke," said Altman, "and you didn't have a sexual interest in girls?"

"I was bloody angry," said Bishop, getting seriously heated as well. "At anyone. I wanted to belittle and shame her because I was bloody angry at her and everyone and everything that I had gone through."

This was another key moment not lost on anyone in court. Angered by Altman's relentless questioning, Bishop had let slip an insight into the evil within him. He had admitted that he had wanted to shame and belittle a seven year old girl just because she was there.

"Why not pick on somebody your own size, a man?" Altman immediately followed up.

"Because there wasn't one at that particular time when I lost it," he replied lamely.

"Why did you dump her in gorse bushes?"

"I left her on a pathway."

"Why did you strip her naked?"

"Because I had realised then, after she had started screaming, what I had done," was the confused reply.

"That's rubbish and lies," snapped he QC.

Clearly frustrated and angry at the incessant questioning and his own weak responses, Bishop appealed in desperation to the judge. "Excuse me, your honour, is this legal?" Meaning the questioning.

Sweeney, who as such a senior judge should have been addressed as "your lordship", told him instantly: "It is and if it wasn't I would stop it."

Altman was straight back at him. "You have told us that what you said to the 1990 jury was a load of lies."

"Yes."

"This is what you are doing now."

"You are entitled to say that."

"Your defence was an alibi in 1990, your case was that you had arranged to fix a satellite dish at Alex's house and you said you could not have been at Devil's Dyke because of that alibi."

"I lied anyway, I said a bloody lie. Are you deaf?"

"You told that jury those lies to try and get them to acquit you, do you agree?"

"Yeah, whatever."

The defendant who had started his evidence "oh, so politely", calling Bennathan "Sir" and apologising for misplacing the right document, was now swearing and insulting. It was everything Altman would have hoped for, and he wasn't going to release the pressure.

"Do you agree that much of what you did in February 1990 is very similar, if not identical, to what the killer of Nicola and Karen did in 1986?"

"I totally disagree."

"You strangled Nicola and Karen."

"No."

"You removed Karen's clothing."

"No."

"Did you remove and replace Nicola's knickers?"

"No."

"Punch her in the face for good measure?"

"No."

"Because you have a sexual interest in children you [abused] Nicola and Karen."

"No."

"Why did you drive your [1990] victim to Devil's Dyke?"

"I just ended up there, I didn't have no plans or anything."

"On 9 October 1986, you didn't have a car because your Ford Escort had broken down on the Ditchling Road."

"Yes."

"Three years or so after you had killed two girls on your own doorstep, you decided to drive your victim 14 miles from the local area."

"No."

Now the QC turned to the prison letters, which was to prompt Bishop's final meltdown.

He reminded him that he had told the jury how he had started writing to the girl, at Jennie Johnson's suggestion, without knowing who she was or her age.

"A complete stranger? How did you know her?" Asked Altman.

"I don't remember now," Bishop replied.

"Was there a time in late 1984 when Jennie Johnson moved in with Victor into bed and breakfast accommodation in Saint George's Terrace in Kemp Town, Brighton?"

"I can't remember."

Altman gave the name of the friend Johnson moved in with and the name of that friend's daughter who happened to be N, the young girl Bishop wrote to from prison. Occasionally, N would look after Victor while Bishop, Johnson and the friend would go out together, he said.

"My suggestion is that you knew who N was because you had lived in the same B and B as her."

"No. I didn't recognise the name but that's not to say that I didn't know her."

"You knew that she was nowhere near sixteen in 1987."

"No. The second I found out how old she was I stopped writing straight away."

Altman quoted seventeen sections from the letters focusing on how they had started with just a smutty element of dirty rhymes, then escalated to clear sexual innuendo about his twelve inches, references to him hoping she was a v, an obvious code for virgin suggested Altman, to out and out grooming with his talk of getting out of prison and getting together in a B&B.

Each time Bishop tried to play a straight back repeating over and over that he had thought she was fifteen or sixteen and repeating his favourite mantras "I don't remember," "I haven't a clue" and "in no way, shape or form".

But the hounding was unceasing. Altman pointed out that Bishop had asked for a photo of the girl and begged her not to tell her mother or Johnson what they are writing to each other.

Bishop was now getting more and more flustered. He lashed out that Altman was "prejudicing the jury", he tried to talk across the QC, which prompted the judge to intercede and tell him to calm down, and the witness even tried to stop the questioning with a "Whoa, whoa, whoa!" reminiscent of Peter Kay's character Brian Potter in *Phoenix Nights*.

Bishop actually sounded quite proud in his responses to questions about the reference to twelve inches, which as Altman pointed out was obvious bragging about his penis, and then suggested it had all been taken out of context because he had only been replying to what N had written to him.

The digital clock below the court clerk's seat showed it was almost twelve noon and time for the usual mid-morning break.

After the jury filed out, Bishop turned to the judge and complained: "I think he is giving evidence," meaning Altman.

The judge ignored the comment and told him he should go back to the dock.

Then Bishop in a quiet voice said: "I'm sorry but I'm finished."

The handcuffs were replaced and he returned to his seat in the dock.

The judge was straight on it. "In the light of the defendant's last comment I'm going to have a fifteen-minute cooling-off period, during which he can think very carefully about what he wants to do. I will then sit again and invite him to come back into the witness box to discover how he feels having had a break.

"If he declines to answer any further questions at that point I'm minded to allow you [the defence lawyers] to speak to him about the inferences that can be drawn from a refusal half way through giving evidence not to answer any more questions."

The judge gave Bishop two hours to see if he would change his mind.

At 2.05 p.m., Bennathan told him: "The position remains what it was earlier, he declines to continue to testify."

Sweeney: "In your judgement is there any point in any further cooling off period?"

Bennathan: "No."

The jury was brought back into court and the judge told them that Bishop had decided he would give no more evidence. "I will give you directions in due course as to how to approach that."

Bishop had been broken by the remorseless logic of the questioning. A man spoilt by his mother through childhood and who had become used to getting his own way was overwhelmed by his public humiliation and came to the conclusion that the only way to stop that humiliation was to run away.

Altman's victory was complete – without even mentioning Barrie Fellows, the Pinto sweatshirt, nor DNA, let alone ivy hairs or paint stains or practically anything that had happened in 1986.

Bishop had faced Altman's questions for not much more than an hour before he threw in the towel.

I had seen Altman pressure another defendant in a double murder trial into refusing to answer any more of his questions, but that had taken a day of cross-examination. So to achieve breakdown in an hour? That is what Olympic athletes call a personal best, or PB.

Later Bishop claimed he could not stand another night in maximum security Belmarsh prison where unspecified "things" had gone missing from his cell and asked to be allowed back to Frankland in County Durham. He said that if he didn't go that week he would not get another chance into the New Year.

The judge was uninterested.

Two days later, after Marion Stevenson had given evidence, Bishop decided he didn't want to go into court at all (another one of Levi Bellfield's tricks, by the way) and the dock remained empty for the rest of the trial.

Altman was delighted to hear later that as Bishop was led from court for the last time he muttered "scumbag" in the QC's direction. A badge of honour from such a man, he beamed.

CHAPTER 23

"HE WAS MY
FIRST LOVE."

Marion Stevenson cut a tragic figure. The once pretty, young, vivacious teenager was now in her late forties, bloated and gammy-legged. Her face betrayed the ravages of her wretched childhood.

The court was cleared so she could make her way to the witness box and a large green curtain pulled across that end of the court so she was shielded from the sight of Bishop in the dock.

There she sat, wearing severe black-rimmed glasses and a black cardigan over a black-and-white low-cut dress that showed off some of her tattoos (when she pushed up her sleeves, her forearms revealed even more tattoos).

She had been brought to court by defence lawyers straight from a doctor's appointment and a three hour drive and she made it clear she didn't want to be here.

I never thought I'd feel sorry for Marion Stevenson but this was a dispiriting sight.

She was there because Russell Bishop thought her evidence

would help him blindside the jury into acquitting him. But she was also there because of what she had said in 2007 (as well as in 1988 and in the *News of the World*). You reap what you sow

So, why had made her speak out again in 2007? She answered, cryptically, "Because of an incident to one of my children. That led me to want to talk to the police about the issue again. At that time I knew he [Bishop] was locked up."

Asked about the child porn video, she said it had taken place two or three months before the murders and repeated her account of that day in Number 26.

Thirty years on, she was clearly distressed and took deep breaths and plentiful sips of water.

Altman rose to his feet for what was going to be a tricky cross-examination. Stevenson wasn't on trial but he had to expose how far her claims were from the truth by accusing her partly of lying but mostly of being a victim of false memories.

He asked her about her falling out with Barrie Fellows.

"The dispute was over me seeing Russell and Barrie sympathising with Russell's ex girlfriend Jennie," she said.

"You called Jennie Johnson his ex girlfriend," said Altman.

"That's what I wanted to believe at the time," she replied.

"I had been to Russell's flat on several occasions when Jennie was there and on more than one occasion I saw him hit her in the course of a row. He would punch and slap her face and kick her even when she was pregnant with Hayley [their second child].

"It seemed that Jennie did everything for him."

After the murders she and Bishop were sitting in the park, she said. She started crying and asked him: "How could anybody kill two little girls?" He replied: "They deserved it. I blame the parents for letting them out that night."

He went on to say that she would not see him for much longer because he was going "to be put away for the murders."

She replied: "Don't be silly." But Bishop told her that he had found the bodies, they had been cuddled together, he had felt their pulse and they had been strangled.

Weeping in the witness box, Stevenson went on: "Bishop said 'They looked so lovely lying there.'"

She also said that Bishop told her that the police had taken all his clothes "except for ones hidden at my mum's house."

These were staggering admissions, why didn't she demand more answers? "I felt that was strange but I didn't want to say anything because it would have developed into a row."

Stevenson had not been called as a witness in the first trial and the defence had summoned her because of her video-porn allegation, yet that tactical decision was now backfiring spectacularly.

After Bishop's arrest, Stevenson made further statements. She told detectives: "Russell told me he loved me and asked me to wait for him. He asked me what the police had said about him. I said that they thought he had done it. I said I didn't believe them."

On another occasion, Bishop had pointed to a jumper and said that the police had got the wrong one and he was going to make sure they didn't get the right one. He said they had found some fibres from his clothing on Nicky and Karen's clothes.

"He said there could be some fibres of his on Karen and Nicky's clothes and that he had been in contact with Karen when she had her [school] uniform on."

*

Stevenson returned to the witness box the following day and Altman cut to the chase about the alleged child porn video and her allegations that DS Swan had tried to get her to sleep with Bishop and get him to confess into a bug planted in his flat.

She repeatedly said she could not remember details from so long ago, but did say that the *News of the World* had interviewed her in a hotel four days before the jury had cleared Bishop at Lewes.

She said that she had not mentioned the video in any of her police statements "because I was too young and scared".

Between sobs and sniffs she had to agree that she had believed Bishop to be innocent and if she had told the police or his solicitor Ralph Haeems about the video it would have helped his case.

"I was scared. I was only sixteen. I wasn't going to school any more but I was not working, she said.

Had the then teenager reported what she claims to have seen at that time, i.e. before the murders, she might have saved the girls' lives? Pressed Altman. "Yes," was all Stevenson could reply.

Altman listed nine occasions when Stevenson could have reported her claims, yet she only chose to speak out to he *News of the World* more than a year later.

In tears, she replied: "It was Sylvia Bishop's idea. She didn't have nothing to do with me before but she used me, everybody used me, Bishop's family, the police, everyone.

"She was a domineering mother, she was like that with all her children. I didn't mind her until Russell got arrested for the murders.

"He told me not to cross her but I never saw the nasty side

of her because I was sticking up for her son at the time. She was using me and she took charge of everything.

"The *News of the World* wanted a story from me and I wanted to say that he was innocent because at that time that was what I believed. Sylvia said 'make sure you are paid for it' because I had suffered. She said 'this is going to happen' she was in charge. She was a very domineering person and liked to get her own way.

"I was besotted with Russell. He could do no wrong in my eyes. He was my first love."

In her statements, Stevenson claimed that first one then two bugs had been found in Bishop's flat.

Altman: "Seventeen Stephens Road was never bugged, and if it wasn't, then Bishop could never have claimed to have discovered one."

"There was. You are just trying to make me out to be a liar," she replied.

But Altman pointed out that with her parents permission the police had put a recording device on the telephone at her own house in Barcombe Road to record Bishop's phone calls.

"My parents gave permission, not me, I didn't know that," she retorted.

"You transposed one story for another," said Altman quietly but tellingly.

"No," was the monosyllabic answer.

Altman followed up by suggesting Stevenson had hated Swan and had falsely accused him personally because he had told her that she had to come clean to her parents and admit she was still seeing Bishop after they had banned him from the house. When she refused to tell them the police officer informed them himself sending her into a rage.

"No," she replied again.

Turning to the video Altman wanted to know why Stevenson had not immediately confronted Dougie Judd, whom she claims had been having sex with Nicola?

"I loved him like a brother. I see it now but I didn't then. I'm ashamed I didn't," she replied.

Why were there so many discrepancies in her accounts of the alleged video over the years?

Because, even though she was only sixteen, she had been drinking spirits heavily and smoking "joint after joint", she replied, although this had not created hallucinations but merely affected her memory.

"When I made the statement in 1988, I was smoking pot heavily so my memory was not so clear as it was in 2007 when I was not smoking it. As the years went on, it got clearer to me."

Stevenson left the witness box in tears having given evidence for the best part of four hours. She had been exposed to questioning, much of it hostile, for far longer than Bishop. He had been her first love yet he looked entirely unperturbed at her distress.

And that, apart from a few minor matters, was the entire defence case. All that was left was closing speeches and summing up.

But first the judge had to tell the jury why the dock was empty.

"The defendant is not here today because he has chosen not to attend. You must, of course, treat that as providing no assistance to the prosecution. We shall simply continue in his absence, said Sweeney.

No assistance to the prosecution? Well Altman cleverly

linked Bishop's absence from the dock on which the law says he could not comment, with Bishop's absence from the witness box, on which he could and would.

Altman told the jury: "The defendant chose to give evidence but within a relatively short time of my cross-examination he refused to return.

"During that time you may have concluded that he showed his true colours. He is an abusive, aggressive, controlling man who could not continue to give evidence on his own terms so decided to refuse to go on.

"He was a coward to refuse to continue his evidence, a cowardly paedophile who though nothing of attacking a seven-year-old child and killing two nine-year-olds for his own sexual gratification, and a coward who, in pursuit of a successful acquittal for a second time, was quite happy to see Barrie Fellows put through the ordeal of being accused of the sexual killing of his own daughter but was not prepared to give evidence himself."

Altman pointed out that Bishop had refused to go on when he had been caught out lying about the age of N to whom he wrote the prison letters.

"These grubby letters are a window into his sexual interests ... grooming N for sex on his eventual, hopeful release, he is a violent predatory paedophile."

It was a strong start by Altman who moved on to hammer home the message of Bishop's cowardice and hypocrisy by bitterly condemning the decision to subject Barrie Fellows to the concerted character assassination with the claim that Barrie was "a better candidate" to be he killer than Bishop himself.

"He didn't have to take that course to try and bolster his

defence but he, and his defence team, have chosen to do so," said the QC.

Altman speech showed exactly why the prosecution had to abandon Leary's disastrous adherence to a 6–6.30-p.m. time-of-death timetable.

In the first trial, eye witnesses had clearly put Bishop and the girls in the same part of Wild Park, between the bus stop and the police box, at around 6.30 p.m., the QC pointed out.

Bishop insisted he had been on his way home. In fact, the paedophile had spotted his opportunity to attack, the court heard.

"Bishop did see the girls and he never went home but turned back and engaged with them. He turned back and he took those two little girls with him," said Altman.

"We may never know if there was some promise to have fun and games or the idea that Marion Stevenson was waiting in the woods that he knew so well.

"We may never know what artful process persuaded them to go with him, but go with him they did. Stevenson said Bishop was one of the people the girls would have gone into the woods with."

Altman concluded: "I ask you to put right a thirty-two-year injustice by returning verdicts of guilty."

Bennathan opened his closing speech with the absurd suggestion that Altman was to blame for Bishop refusing to answer questions by winding the defendant up.

He finished it with an attack on Barrie Fellows, which left the grieving father so profoundly upset his large frame heaved with uncontrollable waves of emotion, completely inconsolable in the arms of his daughter Amber, the Hadaways and Witness Support staff.

Every defendant deserves the best defence, and Bennathan is unquestionably one of he best criminal defence barristers in the country. But counsel only acts on instructions and, notwithstanding the confidentiality of the client lawyer relationship, it's not difficult to imagine the scene at Belmarsh or one of the Old Bailey cells in which Bishop orders his QC to throw everything, good, bad or downright disgraceful at the only surviving father of his victims, whatever the cost.

He started by describing Barrie as a violent paedophile and a liar. He told the jury that we live in a bad world and "we know that sometimes parents do kill their children."

He described the Nicola/Barrie relationship as a weird mix of lust and violence.

He pointed out that Nicola had had her knickers replaced on her lower half, unlike Karen, even though she had been the victim of the greater violence so the killer cared enough to redress her.

The QC claimed that Barrie's suspicious comments after the murders were far worse than anything the prosecution can point towards in Bishop's case and concluded to the jury: "Let's be clear. If someone else is implicated that's the end of the case against Russell Bishop."

Apart from that line of attack Bennathans speech contained more of the same old story. Bishop, or the semi literate car thief as his own counsel described him, was a victim of the nasty old police and the nasty old spirit of Moulsecoomb.

He also blackguarded the character of Rowland and Marchant who had found the bodies and rolled out the old canard that none of the forensic evidence could be trusted because of contamination.

The expression on the jurors' faces was polite, but uninterested.

CHAPTER 24

ENDGAME

The end, when it came, was swift and surprisingly sudden – to everyone apart from Brian Altman, that is.

He had told the jury how Bishop had "boasted" that he had been acquitted in 1987 in just two hours. Altman had hoped jurors would take up his subliminal challenge to beat it.

And they very nearly did. They retired to start their deliberations at 12.21 p.m. and were back in court at 3.06 p.m., which, taking into account the adjournment at 1–2 p.m. for eating their sandwiches, amounted to the most contemptuous dismissal of Bishop's lies.

Said Nigel: "Barrie got a phone call to say the jury was coming back and we all thought, 'Oh, no, not another two-hour verdict, not another rerun of 1987.'"

In the well of the court, Michelle, Lyndsey and Kimberley held hands with Barrie. Susan clutched John's widow Sarah and their children Megan and Tyler. Upstairs in the public gallery, Nigel, Ian, Amber and others did likewise.

The first "Guilty" verdict from the jury foreman elicited gasps and a great suppressed hiss of "Yeah," followed by tears and emotion, bottled up, as best they could, in a dignified and respectful silence. Such was the relief that Susan missed the second verdict and was briefly concerned before being reassured.

Barrie struggled to his feet and left court engulfed in a tsunami of emotion. It was 10 December, exactly thirty-one years to the day that Bishop had been cleared at Lewes Crown Court. What a contrast to the mayhem and Bishop triumphalism of that bitter, bitter day.

Mr Justice Sweeney announced he would sentence at 2 p.m. the following day and, with an eye on the empty dock, said that although he could not force Bishop to attend court he would require him to be here and, if not, he would be sentenced in his absence.

He then thanked the jury for their efforts over the past eight weeks and exempted them from further jury service for the next ten years.

Turning to the Fellows and the Hadaways, every one of them in tears, he said he wanted to pay "a heartfelt tribute for the extraordinary dignity in which they have conducted themselves throughout these traumatic proceedings. If I may say so, they have the court's admiration and thanks for the way in which they have conducted themselves throughout."

He exited and the court broke up with more tears, handshakes and hugs. Nigel muttered to himself, "Job done, Nicky. Rest in peace now."

My memory will be of Susan and Michelle, both of roughly the same height, age and suffering, totally immersed in each other' arms, red faced with tears and eyes shut entirely given over to mutual solace.

Every day of the trial had showed the bond strengthening, previous wariness forgotten, until finally they were like two sisters tied together by loss but also hope for the future now that justice had been served.

While the families composed themselves the media gathered outside the entrance to the court building for the main players to address the cameras for the night's TV news bulletins.

Forty or so minutes later with the families now in the foyer of the Old Bailey, a huge cheer erupted from them as members of the jury filed passed them on their way out of court. The jurors emerged looking sheepish at the reception, but inwardly proud.

When they were ready for the cameras Det Super Jeff Riley described Bishop as "a deeply wicked man" and a "predatory and vicious killer".

He praised the courage and persistence of the two families and noted that Lee Hadaway had passed away before he could see justice for his daughter. He commended the jury for "seeing through" Bishop's disgraceful defence, which had caused Barrie Fellows so much pain and anguish.

Nigel Pilkington of the CPS outlined the key points of the "overwhelming" case against Bishop and then it was Lorna's turn on behalf of the Fellows family, and she pulled no punches.

"Nicola and Karen are beautiful girls who will never be forgotten – their smiles that would light up a room, their laughter, their cheekiness. During the past eight weeks we have had to endure reliving the horrific details of the murders and the true meaning of heartbreak all over again.

"We stand here as two families united in our grief. United in our fight for justice. And now united in our elation at today's "Guilty" verdict.

"Russell Bishop remains behind bars, which is where he belongs. The guilty verdicts do not bring Nicola and Karen back but other children are now safe. He is a monster, a predatory paedophile, he is totally evil personified."

But the star turn was Michelle, a picture of defiance as she grasped her stick in one hand and a sheet of A4 paper in the other, telling the cameras: "After thirty-two years of fighting, we finally have justice for Karen and Nicola.

"Time stood still for us in 1986. To us them beautiful girls will always be nine years old. They will never grow up.

"We've been deprived of a happy life to watch them grow into adults. What people like Bishop inflict on the families of their victims is a living death. They take the lives of children but they also take the lives of the families left behind.

"Kaz and Nicky, as they were affectionately known, were friends playing out together only to have their lives wiped out by a sexual deviant, a monster.

"What's been hard, horrendous and heart-breaking is to hear that they were murdered by a disgusting paedophile, who we actually knew and them two girls liked and trusted. He abused that trust.

"Bishop doesn't deserve to breathe the same clean air as we do. After all, he decided that day to strangle the life out of our two angels, leaving them no air to breathe.

"What makes a man want to squeeze the life out of two innocent children with his bare hands? Unbelievable, when he had a child himself and another on the way.

"He's a coward, without a conscience. I don't believe you can rehabilitate evil. I think Bishop was just born that way.

"People talk to me of forgiveness, but I can never forgive or forget what that evil monster did to my beautiful Kaz and Nicky.

"I'm trying so hard to get my head around this but I will 'cos I'm a fighter and I'll never stop being strong for my family."

Then it was off to a nearby hotel for a pre-arranged pooled interview conducted by Daniella Relph of the BBC and Emily Pennink of the Press Association.

Awkwardly perched on a sofa with his ex-wife and Michelle, Barrie allowed his true self to escape from the emotionally disciplined cage where he had parked it for the duration of the trial.

Asked about how he had faced up to being accused openly in court of sexually abusing and murdering his own daughter, he replied through the tears: "What have I done? All I have done is lost my little girl.

"It's the worst thing that can ever happen to anyone. You sit or stand there and you take so much crap off one person through his barrister. He had no evidence, none whatsoever.

"I just wanted to jump out that box and get him but I was told I had to keep my cool. Thirty years ago he would not be living now."

When he heard the guilty verdict, Barrie had to rush from court. He said: "It's hard to comprehend that we finally got him. We got him bang to rights as well."

Asked if he ever harboured doubts that the day would come, he said: "None whatsoever. The man is a complete pig. He does not even deserve to breathe the air we breathe."

Barrie, Susan and Michelle would have more to say on the following day.

*

Sentencing hearings are the happiest occasions – particularly when the defendant doesn't turn up.

Gone are the gaunt, haggard faces, the fear, the stress, the dread in the eyes. Now the tension has disappeared, there are smiles, more handshakes, more hugs and a sense of looking forward to warm words and harsh punishment from the judge.

Bishop, predictably, refused to leave his cell in Belmarsh or even enter the prison video suite for a live link to the court.

First Altman had to read the victim impact statements. I have listened to dozens of intensely moving statements of this kind over the years, but few have brought a lump to so many throats as these three.

Michelle told how she had tried to attend every day of the 1987 trial and had been devastated by the verdict.

"Since then I had resigned to there never being any justice for those little girls. Our fight for justice never stopped even though I knew Bishop could not be tried again and there was never any shadow of doubt that he was he one responsible," she said.

The repeal of double jeopardy gave hope. "This is the result we should have had thirty-one years ago. Having to go through a second trial has been traumatic and heartbreaking.

"Having to listen in graphic detail to what those two little girls went through is heart wrenching. It is hard to sit in court knowing that everyone can see you and not be able to outwardly express how you're feeling and the distress it causes.

"I had to be doubly strong so that I could support my daughter Lyndsey who was having to hear for the first time exactly what her big sister had suffered. I have always protected Lyndsey from this but I couldn't do so in court and this tore me apart.

"She should not have had to listen to that and now has to learn to live with that knowledge.

"I am not in good physical health, it has taken its toll, getting up early every day and the journey to and from court, which sometimes has been a six hour round trip – but it wasn't optional.

"Finally justice has been done and Bishop has been seen as the evil monster he really is. I was twenty-nine when Karen was killed and I am now sixty-one years old. Karen's death destroyed my husband Lee and I had to raise my family on my own."

Susan wrote not only about the devastation of Nicola's murder but also losing her second husband Peter Eisman and, while preparing for the retrial, the death of her son Jonathan.

"Peter died in November 2016 of ill health and Jonathan died only weeks before the trial. The cause of his death is not yet fully known but I know he never got over Nicky's death and the anxiety, stress and worry over the forthcoming trial was all too much for him.

"In many ways, I blame Bishop for his death also.

"Jonathan and I were going to face this trial together and we were going to be strong for each other. Sadly that didn't happen. I am sixty-nine years old and I have had to go through this on my own, it has been a lonely time for me.

"I have been to court, had to hear all that happened to my little girl and then go home alone and try to deal with that. I try to go to sleep at night without those dreadful images keeping me awake. It has been so hard to do that and now I have to start my life all over again.

"Bishop has now been found guilty, and I'm grateful, however I should have been in this situation thirty-one years ago.

"Bishop is a monster and should never be given his freedom. Everyone needs to feel confident that their children can never be hurt by him. Any sentence will never be enough for what he did to Nicky and Karen."

Altman then turned to the statement of Barrie. "Thirty two years is a long time to be suspected of murdering your daughter," he wrote.

"When they arrested and charged Bishop I thought that would be the end and we would get some closure. It didn't pan out like that.

"My brother Kevin Heffron died in 1996 at the age of thirty-seven and never got to see justice for the girls. Other family members have been deeply affected. It had a devastating impact on my marriage to Susan. It tore us apart and we were never able to build those pieces back together."

Barrie spoke of the demeaning way he was treated when he was arrested by Sussex Police in 2009 on the spurious allegations by Marion Stevenson and the child-porn video.

"After I was released in custody, a social worker came to my house and interviewed my then fourteen-year-old daughter Amber. They asked her if she had ever been abused by me.

"She still has nightmares now about that day. It effected her GCSEs dramatically as she didn't have any form of computer indoors for her studies as it had been seized (by the police).

It not only effected her but my five children I had taken on through my late wife Karen.

"For my children and grandchildren, this was their first proper experience of the whole ordeal first hand. It nearly broke us, as they had never experienced such turmoil and crushing pain of watching the man they all love go through such a traumatic ordeal. For myself it brought back all the pain and paranoia again."

Barrie spoke of how his health had been hit by the stress of the trial, which could clearly be seen by his unsteady gait. He has been mentally drained and listless, prone to chest infections and in need of ECG exams on his heart.

"Unless you have lost a child, you cannot imagine the heartbreak. It's like your heart has been ripped from your chest, over and over again, day in and day out.

"To be then accused of being involved in the loss and harm of that child is emotionally and psychologically damaging. For the past thirty-one years, I have lived with constant paranoia and dread of what everyone thinks of me, even those close to me.

"To look up Russell Bishop's name on google and see my face as the first picture to come up with headlines such as 'Father watched sex tape' has caused me many sleepless nights, not just for me but for the whole family.

"Being accused by him has affected the way I interact with both my children and grandchildren. I feel people may see normal things such as a hug or a kiss as me doing something inappropriate."

There was a fourth victim impact statement made by N, the thirteen-year-old Bishop had tried to groom from prison in 1987 who had identified herself from press reports of the trial and come forward to the police. Altman passed it to the judge to read privately.

Sweeney paused, reached for his script and addressed the empty dock.

"Russell Bishop, I have no doubt you were a predatory paedophile," he intoned slowly.

The judge described Bishop's movements on that day thirty-two years ago, supporting every scrap of the prosecution's case. "The terror that each girl must have suffered in their final moments is unimaginable," he said.

The 1990 attack on R "clearly shows you to be a violent paedophile who carried out another sexual attack on a pre-pubescent girl for the pleasure of doing so."

He went on: "During this trial, you falsely pretended that you were innocent and made allegations – which you were able to do in law- that Nicola's father Barrie Fellows could have been the murderer instead.

"That will not add a day to your sentence but it underlines that you have no remorse whatsoever for what you did.

"Indeed I observe that Barrie Fellows stood in the witness box and dealt with all the questions that were asked of him despite the understandable distress that it caused him whereas, after your initial cross-examination by the prosecution had exposed you as a paedophile and a liar, you refused to answer any more questions and have subsequently refused to attend court at all."

The judge said the personal-impact statements "speak with great dignity and force of the extent of the loss suffered by each of the families and of the suffering that they have endured over so many years.

"The court pays humble tribute to them for their fortitude and determination to see justice done."

On the question of a minimum term Bishop had to serve under his mandatory life sentence, the judge noted that he was bound by the law as it was in 1986 and the fact Bishop was aged under twenty-one at the time.

Today, he noted, "the minimum term would be in the order of forty years or more."

But taking into account that two children were murdered with a sexual motive and with premeditation and the attack on R, "I have concluded that the minimum term would be one of thirty-six years."

The arithmetic – he would be eighty-eight when theoretically eligible for parole – was academic. Bishop is never coming out as he remains in denial about his violent paedophilia and will forever be a danger to children.

Outside court, I was was astonished yet again in this astonishing trial. There was Barrie Fellows being hugged by members of the jury – all twelve of whom had turned up to see sentence passed even though they had been released from their duties by the judge the previous day.

Not only that, they surrounded Michelle in her wheelchair with solicitations, warm smiles and comfort.

Then the twelve were off to the Magpie and Stump across the road from the Old Bailey, where they stayed for some hours. "They all seemed to get on very well together," said John, the usher. Which is not always the case in criminal trials.

CHAPTER 25

PEACE

You can't help but be affected by the plethora of graves and memorials to the tiny fallen in the city cemetery on Bear Road.

It was a bright day with a keen breeze as I trod carefully through the children section on the southern slope. Behind me was about 30 yards of grass to a stone wall, the hum of traffic and the the crematoria beyond.

The two girls lie beneath a marble angel with heavenly gates, cherubs and messages, some handwritten on weather-beaten paper and others engraved in stone alongside stone cats, dogs and teddies. There's even a unicorn with its mane and tail picked out in pink.

Obviously well-tended, recently cut flowers stand in vases that have been knocked about a bit in the wind.

"All of me loves all of you" is inscribed at the feet of the angel.

On the left side, as I look, lies "Karen Jane Michelle Hadaway. Born 21st December 1976. Died 9th October 1986", and the words, "There's a place in our hearts for you alone. A part of our life no others can own. Deep in our hearts your memory we treasure. Loving you always forgetting you never."

On the right, "Nicola Elizabeth Christine Fellows. Born 22nd February 1977. Died 9th October 1986", followed by, "Go to God sleep safe in his arms and carry you. Your bright young charms. Sleep forever in his loving embrace with all your childlike qualities and grace."

Next door, is the grave of her brother, "Jonathan Barrie Fellows (John). 7th December 1971 – 5th September 2018". Somebody had thoughtfully placed a copy of the order of service from his funeral on his sister's plot and there was some flowers tied up in the claret and light blue colours of his favourite team, West Ham United .

His funeral had been held on September 28 at the Downs Crematorium behind me, barely two weeks before the Bishop retrial started. Mourners had entered to the sound of UB40's classic "Red Red Wine" and departed to the stains of the West Ham song "I'm Forever Blowing Bubbles".

At time of writing, the full inquest into his death has yet to take place.

On his grave there is a picture of him happy, smiling, even carefree with Sarah in a striking red dress and Megan and Tyler. Happier times.

After reflection, I walked to the top of the rise for an astounding panoramic view of Brighton. Looking down the hill to the left is the racecourse grandstand towering over Whitehawk and the marina. Pan to the right and there's the sea, the i360 bagel on a stick and Shorehan power station's lone tower with Lancing and Worthing in the distance. And then turning further right I gaze out across the dozens of tight terraced roads towards Moulsecoomb and the Downs beyond. A quiet, fitting spot.

My thoughts turn from the graves of the two little girls to imagine a cell in Frankland prison. What is Russell Bishop thinking about now? No need to waste too long on him, but what about his victims?

Nicola and Karen are in their graves, as is John Fellows, Lee Hadaway and Kevin Heffron, who all died unable to see the justice that finally befell Bishop.

What about those who fell under Bishop's spell? Jennie Johnson and Marion Stevenson have new lives having met new men and had children. Marion Stevenson got married and had her new identity protected in a court order by the trial judge. Jenny Johnson also got married and lives near her old home with Bishop.

At the time of writing the Fellows family is asking the police to look at Jennie Johnson's evidence again. They are also doing the same with Stevenson.

Barrie, of course, has been hit hardest by Stevenson's evidence and feels his own life has been ruined in the aftermath, saying 'Bishop took my family away, piece by piece, over the last 30 years', and the suspicion he has had to face following Stevenson's evidence has taken a huge toll on him.

Nigel also is keenly aware of the hurt Barrie has had to endure over the decades: 'Some people in Brighton still think that Barrie did it and was some sort of threat to his children. That's why we have got to prove one hundred per cent that the video never existed.'

Barrie tells his own story of why he has to keep on proving

his innocence. A month after the Old Bailey verdict, he told me: 'Only yesterday I was sitting on a bus and a man looked at me and said, 'You're Barrie Fellows'. I said, 'Yes' and he said, 'You're a fucking nonce'.

"I reported it to the police. They said it was a hate crime.

" It goes on. There are fucking idiots who are convinced Bishop is not the killer, they don't read the news properly. There's a lot of people who go off half-cocked."

After the conviction, Stevenson spoke to the *Sun on Sunday*, the same paper (under a different title) that had paid her for her story in 1987 and that caused so much trouble.

It was an appalling piece of hand-wringing along the lines of, "I am just so sorry that I didn't see him as the predator that he is and I couldn't keep those little girls safe."

No need to waste time on those two women, who, brought all their troubles on themselves.

But what about R and the tragic and hugely avoidable tragedy of her life. She steadfastly refused all contacts from the media during and after the Bishop trials but her parents did speak to the *Daily Mail* on the condition of complete anonymity for their daughter.

Now aged thirty-six, she was referred to as "Daisy" even though she had always been identified over the years as R.

Fairweather recalled how she had met Daisy in 1990 when she appeared to be recovering well, seemingly "cheerful and carefree, muttering only that if she ever saw that 'horrible man again' she would 'hit him with a big stick'".

Now she recounted how Daisy had phoned her father as soon as she had found out to say, "Dad, he has finally admitted what he did to me."

The father, described as a gruff military man with a kind face, told the reporter: "She was a mess. She couldn't take it in. Bishop and his family have spent decades denying what he did to her and her memories from when she was seven have naturally, thank God, faded.

"But it meant that she had gone through a stage where she feared maybe they were right and she had identified the wrong man. She felt shame and guilt and would run herself down.

"I had to explain to her that his admission meant you were right. And if he hadn't been convicted because of your evidence, how many other children would have been attacked? You should feel strong and proud."

In 1990, Daisy's mother had accompanied her daughter to the identification parade at which the little girl had unerringly picked out her assailant.

"No one prompted her and she never hesitated. She knew straight away it was him, it was Bishop. She was just a little girl. She didn't know his picture from the papers. But she has always been very good at detail, very precise."

Daisy continued her astonishing recovery, which had been commended at the trial, for years to come and married and settled down quite normally before the forgotten memories and flashbacks took her down.

A series of relapses have currently been reduced to just "bad days" but she has been paralysed by panic and agoraphobia when she cannot bring herself to even answer her front door for fear that her attacker might return to strike again.

Said her mother: "She has had to struggle against becoming a prisoner in her own home. There were times, on and off, when

THE BABES IN THE WOODS MURDERS

she wouldn't go out of her front door. That is what Bishop's denial had done to her."

She added, "Daisy is a tough cookie, but we know how much it affected her."

Her father said, "Inside sometimes she is like jelly. She suddenly has releases. Just the words 'Russell Bishop' can bring it back.

"She can come across as brusque but she needs her protective shell. Her husband is very calm and that helps. He knows her background but neighbours, colleagues and even most friends don't.

"We're all private people but that doesn't mean you don't feel it. Just that pity and gossip don't help anyone."

Her parents are determined not to lapse into bitterness about how Bishop had been free to attack their daughter in 1990. Her mother would only say that the evidence in 1987 had been "mishandled".

Her father snapped, "Only one thing would make it better, if the police had bloody got [Bishop] in the first place.

"The verdict was what we expected. Now let's hope everybody can be at peace and that it's over."

The Fellows and Hadaways know exactly how they feel.

*

Looking back, Detective Superintendent Jeff Riley spoke of the shadow Bishop had cast over Brighton for a generation.

"Any murder has has a massive impact on the victim's family and the community," he said.

"But the murder of children particularly has an impact and I think there has been a shadow over Moulsecoomb, which lasts to this day."

He also paid tribute to the families, Nigel, Ian and Kevin, in particular, whose hard work in pressing for a change in the law enabled the police to mount its outstanding second investigation into the double murder.

"The families have waited thirty-two years for justice. There have been meetings with the families in 2006 [when the possibility of new scientific evidence first came to light] and they have been pushing since the acquittal for the reinvestigation of the case," he said.

"The Heffron side of the Fellows family were involved with pushing forward the agenda around a changing of the law."

David Blunkett, now Lord Blunkett, also commended the Fellows family and spoke of his personal pride in the repeal of a law that had allowed "extremely dangerous people to walk the streets".

"As a tour guide, Nigel Heffron was able to have a word with me as well as give me written material. He was pushing at an open door [with me] in terms of double jeopardy and I'm just relieved that justice has been done," he said.

On Christmas Eve, two weeks after the verdict, Michelle laid out a stocking for the first time since 1986 for her daughter, who would now have been forty-two.

She told the *Sunday Mirror* after the verdict: "I've never been able to look at my daughter's photo and say she was at peace.

"But now she can finally rest with Nicola in their angel beds in heaven. I came home after the verdict and looked at her picture and said to her, 'We've done it, darling. You and Nicola can rest – and now mummy can rest.'

"Bishop took my first-born, my husband and my soul. I had nightmares about him almost every night, waking up screaming.

"But now, I can finally grieve. I've never stopped fighting. I did it. I took on evil and I won.

"On our Christmas tree, I'm going to put heart decorations with photos of Karen and Nicola. There will be lots of tears but also tears of joy."

Susan Fellows tries hard not to let bitterness blight her everyday life but the memories keep on impinging on even the most routine family moments.

"It took a long time even for me to be able to cuddle my nieces because they were little girls. I didn't want to be nasty but I could not have other little girls coming up to me and giving me cuddles because that is what she [Nicola] should be doing," she said.

"I'd go to my bedroom and I think she should be here and I wonder whether she would be married and have kids of her own. I imagine her nagging me to baby-sit, I wonder what marks she would be getting in school exams. I have been robbed of those things.

"I had two children and I lost two children. One person took my life and my happiness away from me.

She added, "The worst thing is when I go out shopping and I always look at the children's clothes and I can't help thinking, 'Oh, that's nice' and 'Nicky would love that' and 'Nicky would look good in that'. It's still in your head, it's still there.

"I'm thinking would she get married, would she be a nurse? She had wanted to be a nurse, she liked helping people. I was in hospital and Nicky said she wants to be a nurse and this nurse gave her her hat to wear. Nicky was eight then and the following October she was gone.

"Nicky would have made a great nurse, she was always asking people how they were.

"Nine years of life. It's no life at all."

And there's the rub. Bishop is convicted of double murder and will never be released from prison. That has brought the Fellows and Hadaways peace and justice. But the searing sense of loss will remain for ever.

APPENDIX I –
TIMELINE

9 October 1986: Nicola Fellows and Karen Hadaway go missing in Moulsecoomb.

10 October: Their bodies are found strangled and sexually assaulted in Wild Park.

31 October: Russell Bishop is arrested and later released on police bail.

3 December: Bishop is charged with double murder and remanded in custody.

10 December 1987: After a trial at Lewes, Bishop is acquitted of the murders.

February 1988: Marion Stevenson first alleges to police that she saw Barrie Fellows watching a video of his daughter being sexually abused by his lodger Dougie Judd.

4 February 1990: Bishop abducts a seven-year-old girl and sexually assaults and strangles her at Devil's Dyke. She survives.

13 December 1990: Bishop is convicted of attempted murder at Lewes and is sentenced to life imprisonment with a minimum term of fourteen years.

February 1994: Bishop abandons his attempt to sue Sussex Police for wrongful arrest and false imprisonment in 1986/87 after being humiliated at the High Court.

23 July 2002: The Babes in the Wood exhibits are re-examined at the Forensic Science Service (FSS) using ever-developing new techniques.

2003: The Criminal Justice Act repealing double jeopardy is passed and becomes law in April.

August 2003: Results of DNA testing on the Pinto sweatshirt herald hope for new evidence but years of further work are still needed.

February 2004: Bishop eligible to apply for parole for the first time.

2005: paving the way for Bishop's acquittal to be quashed and a possible new trial.

September 2006: The victims' families are informed that, as yet, there is insufficient evidence to recharge Bishop.

April 2009: Barrie Fellows and Judd are arrested after Stevenson makes a second statement in 2007 about the alleged porn video of Nicola. They are released and never charged.

2011: A further forensic review is undertaken by LGC Limited in Abingdon.

November 2013: Detective Superintendent Jeff Riley is appointed senior investigating officer by Sussex Police in the cold case inquiry. The first potential one-billion-to-one DNA match to Bishop is found on the Pinto's inside cuff.

Mid-2015: LGC senior scientific adviser Rosalyn Hammond concludes the DNA on the cuff cannot be relied on, due to the possibilities of inadvertent transfer.

June 2015: New one-billion-to-one DNA evidence is found linking Bishop to matter taken from Karen Hadaway's left arm. This time scientists believe it is beyond dispute.

10 May 2016: Bishop is taken from Frankland Prison and re-arrested for the murders.

12 December 2017: Bishop's acquittal is quashed in the Appeal Court. He is ordered to stand trial for a second time.

15 October 2018: Bishop goes on trial at the Old Bailey.

10 December 2018: Bishop is found guilty of the murders.

11 December 2018: Bishop is sentenced to life imprisonment with a recommended minimum term of 36 years.

APPENDIX II –
THE FAMILIES

THE HADAWAYS

Michelle Hadaway (née Johnson), born 7 January 1957.
Lee Hadaway, born 16 September 1948, died 1998.
Their children:
Darren, born 29 November 1974.
Karen born 21 December 1976, died 9 October 1986.
Lyndsey, born 21 January 1981.
Kimberley, born December 1986.

THE FELLOWS

Susan Fellows (née Streeter), born 19 September 1949.
Married (1) Barrie Fellows, (2) Peter Eisman.
Susan's grandmother, Mabel Prior.
Susan's mother Mabel (Edna) Streeter.
Barrie Fellows, born 21 September 1949. Married (1) Susan
Streeter, (2) Karen Pacitti.

Barrie and Susan's children:

Jonathan (John), born 7 December 1971, died 5 September 2018.

Nicola (Nicky), born 22 February 1977, died 9 October 1986.

Barrie's brothers:

Nigel Heffron, born February 1954. Married (1) Christine Ledbetter, (2) Christine Streeter.

Ian Heffron, born April 1955. His children: Lorna, born April 1979; Gareth, born September 1983, died February 2016; Gavin, born September 1986; Emma, born November 1998; and Dominic, born May 2000.

Kevin Heffron, born November 1958, died January 1996. Married Christine Howell.

Barrie has three other brothers and half-brothers, including Keith Heffron, born 1937, died 1993, and

four other sisters and half-sisters, and has been father to eight children.

ACKNOWLEDGEMENTS

Like many great tales, this one, for me, started in a pub. Just before Christmas 2017, I ran into an old friend, Phil Mills, in the Lord Nelson, in Trafalgar Street, one of Brighton's better boozers.

He mentioned that he had been asked by Nigel Heffron, uncle of one of the Babes in the Wood victims, if he knew somebody who could write a book about the case.

At that time, the new trial had been given the go-ahead but that was still under a press blackout.

I had never met Nigel but the case, then on-running and far from finished, had already been one of the greatest in my career, both as a reporter and as a Brightonian, and I readily agreed.

I had officially retired from the *Evening Standard* after 33 years of commuting to what used to be called Fleet Street and was looking for one last book project before finally hanging up my laptop.

In my naivety, I thought this would be a slam-dunk challenge.

How wrong I was. For a start, I was unaware of the tension that existed then between the two families of the little girls. I would have to tread carefully to try to speak to all sides without upsetting the other side. In the end, I had considerably less involvement with Michelle Hadaway than I had wished.

Then there was the hostility of the police. I had been asked to help them with my notes of Bishop's High Court case in 1994 and had been happy to oblige.

They thanked me for that and then tried to ban me from speaking to any of the Fellows and Hadaway families!

I tried to point out that I have covered over 1,000 trials in my career – mostly high-end murders, rapes, terrorism and fraud – and knew exactly what constituted a contempt of court and how to avoid any threat to the sanctity of the trial. I put their irrational anxiety down to the fear in Sussex Police of the kicking they would get from the media after the failures of the first trial.

I should add that both Detective Superintendent Jeff Riley and press officer Tim Mahoney were both unfailingly polite.

However, the CPS, no doubt fearing similar post-trial criticism over the 1987 fiasco, decided to impose their own ban on the media contacting the families while at the same time giving full access to a TV-documentary team uninterested in the past failings.

Their subsequent filming, in flagrant disregard of normal pre-trials media practice, resulted in the television people having to disclose to Bishop's defence team interviews with both Michelle Hadaway and Susan Fellows, which were then used to cross-examine them on behalf of Bishop in court. So that wasn't very clever.

Then there were the understandable tensions within the families, especially as it got closer and closer to the Old Bailey trial.

But such is the way. Few things in life are meant to be easy, and the fact that you are reading this book shows that everything, in the end, more or less ran smoothly.

This is a story about two families, and I have quoted from my long conversations with each of them, as well as from their court evidence, which I took down first-hand, and also from police and public statements and comments they made at that time.

For context, I have also relied on contemporary newspaper reports and the accounts of those who wrote them. In particular, I have used the archives of the *Evening Argus*, as it was titled in the eighties and nineties, as it acts as a historical record and gives a flavour of how people lived and thought in Brighton at that time.

Back at the time of the murders, the paper had an outstanding group of reporters and sold more than 100,000 copies a night, giving it a total reach in Sussex of more than a quarter of a million readers. In the pre-Internet and satellite-TV era, when newspapers, particularly the local ones, were the first source of information for millions, the *Argus* had a massive influence in and around Brighton. It was also highly respected for the integrity of its reporting. In stark contrast, the reputation of the Red Top tabloid national press of that time, especially the Murdoch stable of the *News of the World* and the *Sun*, could not have been lower.

Sadly, the *Evening Argus*, in common with all newspapers, particularly the local press, is today a shadow of what it once was. Re-branded as *The Argus* when it switched from an evening to a morning publication, it sells barely 10,000 copies a day and has a young and inexperienced staff.

I personally attended many of the events detailed in the book, including all the court hearings, so can give a first-hand account. I have allowed myself some editorialising, but I have done so from my twenty-three years experience as a specialist reporter when I spent every working day in court.

I must offer my grateful thanks to the host of people who have helped with this book, starting with Nigel Heffron. It was his idea, and from the beginning we agreed that it should be a warts-and-all account, sparing nobody's feelings. Some unpalatable truths had to be spelled out in these pages and Nigel and his family never shrank from confronting that.

It was his decision – which I immediately supported – that the proceeds from this book should go to help set up some legacy in the girls' names.

Nigel smoothed and facilitated access to his family and others. As you will read in these pages, he is quite an operator. So, a big thank-you to the families, especially Barrie Fellows, Susan Eisman and Ian Heffron, who were prepared to sit down with me to relive their most harrowing memories.

I also offer thanks to my old friends at the Old Bailey, who have helped me out time and time again, particularly Emily Pennink of the Press Association (PA), Jeremy Britton of the BBC and Scott Wilford and his gang at Central News.

Also invaluable were Cathy Gordon and Jan Colley of the PA at the High Court, Ted Hynds, former *Argus* reporters Phil Mills, Jim Hatley, Shan Lancaster and Martin Palmer, and also Russell Jenkins and Sir Ivan Lawrence.

Thanks are also due to my editor James Hodgkinson, who always had faith in this book, Andy Garth for the historic pictures (taken by Simon Dack, Jon Bond and Jerry Caswell), Kim Curran for devoting her time when my dinosaur-like IT skills failed and the staff of The Keep archive in Brighton, who were very helpful in my research for this book.

For all their help over the years, I also want to pay tribute to the wonderful court reporters Pat Clarke and Shenai Raif of the PA, Sue Clough of the *Daily Telegraph*, and Adrian Shaw, now sadly passed away, who was the best court reporter of us all.

Finally, heartfelt thanks to my wife, Kathryn Spencer, who has put up with my non-retirement. I promise now that I will pack it in!

February 2019